DATE DUE

GAYLORD			PRINTED IN U.S.A.

DNVP

Right-Wing Opposition in the Weimar Republic, 1918-1924

D N V P

Right-Wing Opposition
in the
Weimar Republic, 1918-1924

by

L E W I S   H E R T Z M A N

UNIVERSITY OF NEBRASKA PRESS
LINCOLN • 1963

Publishers on the Plains

UNP

Copyright © 1963 by the University of Nebraska Press
Library of Congress catalog card number 63-15846

Manufactured in the United States of America

Acknowledgments

The present study has grown from an earlier and somewhat more cumbersome version presented as a dissertation to the Department of History, Harvard University, in 1955. It is based mainly on unpublished materials that have come to light since the end of World War II, particularly the papers of Kuno Graf von Westarp.

Thanks go to the staffs of the many libraries and archives where I have worked in the past decade, with special mention of the *Bibliothèque Nationale* and the *Bibliothèque de documentation internationale contemporaine* in Paris, the *Württemberger Landesbibliothek* and *Bibliothek für Zeitgeschichte* in Stuttgart, the *Bundesarchiv* in Coblenz, the National Archives, Washington, D.C., the Harvard College Library, the Princeton University Library, and the Hoover Institution on War, Revolution, and Peace.

The Westarp Papers were made freely available to me by Count Westarp's daughter, Adelgunde Gräfin von Westarp (*obiit* 1960), and his grandson, Dr. Friedrich Freiherr Hiller von Gaertringen of the University of Tübingen. Without their generous cooperation this study would not have been possible.

Grateful acknowledgment is made also of financial support that has come at various times from research and travel funds of Harvard, Princeton, the University of Alberta, and the Canada Council. I should like to thank my friend, Harold J. Gordon, Jr., of the University of Massachusetts, for his valued advice on certain aspects of the manuscript, and the editorial staff of the University of Nebraska Press.

A great debt remains to my teachers at Harvard, H. Stuart Hughes and William L. Langer, who encouraged my

[v]

interest in the problems of modern Europe and introduced me to the discipline of the historian's craft.

LEWIS HERTZMAN

University of Alberta

Contents

Introduction

This book is a study of the origin of the most important right-wing party in the German Republic that emerged from World War I. It does not aim at completeness even as a party history, but is intended as a contribution toward understanding the complexity of party life in modern Germany, and of the nature of the right-wing opposition in the Weimar Republic. In examining the role of the conservative middle class in the new state, I have particularly tried to show something of the play of forces and personalities within the German National People's Party—the DNVP (*Deutschnationale Volkspartei*). The book might well be read in conjunction with the monograph by Werner Liebe, who is more concerned than I with matters of formal organization. [1] If I have paid relatively little attention to other areas of Party life, say the role of the Party in various state and national bodies, the reason is that I have felt the important developments were elsewhere. Wherever possible I have tried to uncover and explain the line of conflict between announced policies and inside pressures, the very forces which gave the Party its peculiar character—that drive which made it so difficult for others to cope with, and which proved to be ultimately suicidal.

I apologize for my free use of the German letter designations for parties, since I know how annoying the proliferation of abbreviations can be to those unfamiliar with them. I have taken to them not as a cultist, but for very practical reasons, and hope the reader will accept them readily as a useful shorthand variant, as I have had to do.

We are close enough in time to the problems of the

[1] Werner Liebe, *Die Deutschnationale Volkspartei 1918-1924* (Düsseldorf, 1956).

1920's for them to raise strong, sometimes prejudicial, emotions. There is still perhaps as much disagreement as agreement on the interpretation of many issues. I am not able, like some observers, to dismiss the experience of the crucial decade after 1918 as an expected and almost predetermined failure of democracy in a basically authoritarian society. Nor by the same token am I able to regard the Weimar interlude as some sort of Periclean age. [2] I do, on the other hand, accept the need to examine this period in its own terms in order to eliminate some of the myths and absurdities that continue to confuse thought on recent German politics.

For the failures of Weimar it is not necessary to look for scapegoats. Nor is it enough simply to place blame on such factors as the supposed authoritarian German character, the vengeful Allies, or the technical imperfections of the Constitution. The severest failures lay in the inability of statesmen in all political camps to see in true dimensions the major problems facing them. They did not, for the most part, understand the real meaning of inflation as an economic, social, and ultimately political menace. Weimar politicians did not fully appreciate, nor know how to deal with, the disloyal opposition, both in and out of Parliament. They (as a third example) took inadequate responsibility for leadership of press and propaganda in an era of mass communication.

Chancellor Joseph Wirth attempted in vain to identify and denounce the "enemy on the right," in 1922, after years of obstruction, putsches, and assassination. At a high point by 1924, the principal political party of the right, the Ger-

[2] Henry M. Pachter, "Freedom and Democracy in Germany," review article in *World Politics* XI, 2 (Jan., 1959), 300-1: ". . . the Weimar Republic was Germany's Periclean Age—not an aftermath of century-old failures, but a significant experience which posed the problem of freedom in its own way and therefore deserves analysis in its own terms."

man National People's Party increased its standing from fourth- to second-ranking party in the Reichstag, and its share of the electorate from 10 to 20 per cent. The Party was important not only because of the size of its popular support, but also because of the influential social and economic elements that it particularly represented. Outside of Germany, too, the fortunes of the Nationalist Party were of more than academic interest since its intransigence threatened more than once to disrupt the process of peaceful reconciliation. The right was so flamboyantly aggressive in its opposition that a politically conscious citizen could hardly remain indifferent to its campaigns.

Yet because of the variety of voices that sounded from the right, it was not always clear what right-wing parties represented or wanted. Actually many electors never accepted the German National People's Party for its own sake, but preferred to see in it rather the successor party of the values they knew and wanted to preserve—the party of the Junkers, of Old Conservatives or Free Conservatives, of Anti-Semites or Christian Socialists, to name the most important. But in fact the experiences of war and revolution were as much a part of the origin of the DNVP as the known interests of its components and exerted an unpredictable influence on the Party's development, as did the complications of the postwar world. That certainly can be seen in the internal tensions within the DNVP over issues of racism, party leadership, and the role of an opposition party. For that reason I have stressed throughout this study the plurality of interests and groups that comprised the political right in Germany, that particularly complicated the tasks of its leadership.

The years 1918-1924 coincide with the leadership in the DNVP of Oskar Hergt, a relatively unknown *Exzellenz* from the royal Prussian civil service. They form as well a convenient unit of study in the Weimar Republic between the November Revolution and the acceptance of the Dawes Plan. In opposition to government and the Republic during Hergt's tenure of office, the Party twice entered government coalitions under his successor, Count Westarp, only to rejoin the ranks of the bitter and disaffected opposition under Hugenberg in 1928. I hope that the present study will help clarify the reasons for the wide range of tactics employed by Nationalist leaders.

I have become convinced that there is need, on a broader scale than I have attempted here, to look carefully at the interpretation by rightist leadership of the idea of responsibility to the Republican state, especially as partners in the day-to-day business of government. In such an examination the other side of the coin would reveal the meaning of the irresponsibility and uncompromising opposition that were characteristic of a significant and increasingly militant rightist minority. Such a broader study will have to await evaluation of the mass of political *Nachlässe* and party documents that have in recent years become available to historians. But first it is important to consider the significance for the health of the Weimar Republic of the configuration of rightist parties accidentally created in the heat of the November days of 1918—and that has been my purpose in studying the DNVP. While it is hardly necessary to argue the desirability for the political health of a nation of consolidating its splinter groups and special interests into broad parties, in the case of the German right in the Weimar period the wrong combinations were made. The right-wing parties had too little to hold them together; their internal struggles unduly sharpened their attitudes on public issues, and in the long run weakened their chances with the voting public. Eventually the accumulated tensions and bitterness shattered the right into small bits, leaving it ineffective and unavailable as an alternative government in the crises of the 1930's.

Aware of these factors, Gustav Stresemann, having found

his own way toward responsibility in the state and acceptance of the Republic, frequently discussed the question of
a loyal opposition. He did not hesitate to castigate his
countrymen for their lack of the common sense to make
their Constitution work despite its technical imperfections.
He cited, by way of contrast, the respected position of the
Opposition as it functioned in Britain and the Dominions,
particularly the Canadian example where the leader of
the Opposition received the same salary as the Prime Minister. "Thus it is assumed that opposition and government
parties alternate, and that the Opposition must be prepared
to demonstrate whether it can carry out in government the
program it has represented out of power. What we in Germany lack is a truly statesmanlike opposition." [3] True to
his belief in parliamentary government Stresemann made
the mistake of fighting to bring the Nationalists into government, in the hope of teaching them there the lessons of
moderation and responsibility. They learned instead their
own lessons on how further to obstruct Stresemann's foreign policy of international reconciliation and fulfillment
of treaty obligations.

Ernst Troeltsch after the November Revolution questioned the political potential of new parties that were not
continuations of the established apparatus. His comments
were based on the belief that, since parties reflected the
fundamental needs of the population at a given time, very
few were needed or could justify their existence. To be
effective the parties should be as large and as few as possible, which was not Germany's experience in the Weimar
years. The needs, as he saw them, were a strong worker's
party, a Catholic party, an aristocratic Conservative party,
and a party of the middle class and intelligentsia [4]—that is,

[3] Gustav Stresemann, *Vermächtnis*. Ed., Henry Bernhard, 3 vols.
(Berlin, 1932-3), II, 379.

[4] Ernst Troeltsch, article of May 2, 1920, in *Spektator-Briefe*
(Tübingen, 1924), p. 114.

parties representing special, largely class, interests, as one might imagine them grouped in a corporative state.

When compared to that ideal type of Troeltsch, the new Nationalist Party appeared indeed to represent a considerable advance over prevailing pre-1918 concepts of political alignment. A party of "progressive" conservative interests had come into existence that rejected, so it claimed, out-dated remnants of thought and prejudices of imperial Germany, and therefore sought to transcend the special interests of its founding groups. Emerging from the chaos of the war and revolution, this was the announced party of all patriotic Germans, irrespective of class and religion, who would preserve the honor of their country and the timeless values of law, order, religion, and social justice. Needless to say, practice did not always coincide with promise.

Veit Valentin would agree: "It belongs to the being of a revolution," he wrote, "that many of the most reactionary are apt to discover that there is a progressive side to their nature; and just as much does it belong to the being of the counter-revolution that many rebels discover a conservative element in themselves. Herein lies one of the charms, but also the limitations of all party history. . . ." [5] His comment is *à propos* in our period of study. Certainly public pronouncements on the election platform, in the press, and in Parliament were more often rhetorical than accurate. Thus Count Kuno von Westarp, representing the point of view of the Old Conservatives, wrote of the founding of the DNVP that "to achieve our goal [of survival] we accepted, in an urgent situation, decisions that other participants [in the discussions] had been moved to urge under pressure of the general excitement and revolutionary impulses of the time." [6]

[5] Veit Valentin, *1848. Chapters of German History* (London, 1940), p. 265.

[6] Kuno Graf von Westarp, "Konservative Politik in der Republik

The first public announcement of the German National People's Party expressed a desire to work with all parties in the interest of law and order. [7] That promise was comparable to the promise of the German army also to collaborate with the Republic. But in this the civilians of the right were perhaps not as reliable as most of their military confrères. The responsibility they felt was less to the nation than to their own outraged emotions in a world they refused to accept.

1918-1932. Erstes Buch: Neue Aufgaben und Ziele. Bis zum 6.6.1920." Unpublished manuscript, Berlin, 1933-42 (hereafter cited as: W MS), chap. 1, p. 20.

[7] *Neue Preussische (Kreuz-) Zeitung* (hereafter cited as *Kzztg.*), Nov. 24, 1918 (A.M.).

I

Prelude to Revolution

The Second Reich, Bismarck's creation, was an authoritarian, yet constitutional and parliamentary, state in which the unpredictability of public opinion and the obstreperousness of political parties greatly complicated public life. Tensions were not eased in the period after the *Daily Telegraph* affair in 1908 when the Emperor withdrew increasingly from active intervention in affairs of state. [1] Although chancellors usually got what they wanted, they were not assured automatic majorities in Parliament. Even less could they count on support of their policies by the press and the voting public. It was, moreover, generally recognized that Germany as a modern industrial state was unavoidably on the road toward the forms of liberal, and perhaps socialist, democracy. All political talent on the right was in the prewar years consequently directed toward analysis of the wave of the future, hoping somehow to find a formula for survival. The specters of subversion and revolution from the left that haunted Prince Bismarck and General Caprivi [2] grew worse for their successors. The shock of the "red" election of 1912, the last election before the war, [3] confirmed the worst fears of right-wing pessimists, yet seemed to fortify their spirit of reaction. It would be hard to exaggerate the bitterness and uncompromising hardness of mind that colored the political controversies of the empire. That

[1] Paul Herre, *Kronprinz Wilhelm* (Munich, 1954), pp. 16-7.

[2] J. Alden Nichols, *Germany after Bismarck*. The Caprivi Era 1890-1894 (Cambridge, Mass., 1958), p. 333.

[3] Friedrich Stampfer, *Die vierzehn Jahre der ersten deutschen Republik*, 3rd ed. (Hamburg, 1947), p. 14.

attitude, compounded by the eccentricities of political bosses, and by the insistent demands of special interests, was the bane of political life in Germany before and after 1918.

Already apparent in the empire were those qualities of the right that poisoned the political atmosphere and undermined the party system—a characteristic lack of generosity in dealing with rivals, an unwillingness to accept timely compromise, and a refusal to lose graciously. Political men whose careers spanned the Imperial and Republican régimes testify to the fact that the controversies under Chancellors Bülow and Bethmann Hollweg were as sharply drawn, as bitterly fought, and as unsatisfactorily concluded as any that they later experienced.[4] Questions of fiscal reform (especially the inheritance tax), Prussian suffrage, and war aims touched the most sensitive vested interests or inflamed feelings of patriotism. They raised problems that allowed little room for negotiation.[5]

The parties of Imperial Germany, as Maurice Baumont has pointed out, "formed solid blocs in victory as in defeat under the discipline of their leaders. Organized almost in military fashion, they enmeshed Germany in a network of associations; formal conferences brought together delegates from all parts of the empire; everywhere there were bulletins, newspapers, emergency funds, and solid bases for action and struggle. The existence of bureaucratic parties gave political life in Germany its special character; a doctrinaire spirit and a pedantic generalizing attitude tried to force concrete realities into a system, and to formulate

---

[4] E.g., Gustav Stresemann to Julie Bassermann, Aug. 4, 1928, Gustav Stresemann, Papers, National Archives, Washington, D.C., microfilm roll 3163, serial 7409, frames 174367-9 (hereafter cited as: SP:3163/7409/174367-9).

[5] Hans Günter Zmarzlik, *Bethmann Hollweg als Reichskanzler 1909-1914* (Düsseldorf, 1957), p. 46; Friedrich Freiherr Hiller von Gaertringen, *Fürst Bülows Denkwürdigkeiten. Untersuchungen zu ihrer Entstehungsgeschichte und ihrer Kritik* (Tübingen, 1956), pp. 245-50.

dogmas which were incessantly repeated in the attempt to clothe politics with philosophic respectability."[6] We may well agree with Professor Baumont as we examine in brief the odd assortment of right-wing groups that ultimately formed the German National People's Party after the November Revolution of 1918. Most prominent of them before the crash was, of course, the German Conservative party (*Deutschkonservative Partei*—DKP).

The Prussian, monarchist, agrarian, and Lutheran character of the German Conservative party was an axiom of political life in the empire. One of the most venerable and respectable of political parties, though limited in outlook and following, the DKP was a descendant of the group founded in 1848 around Ludwig von Gerlach, Julius Stahl, and the *Neue Preussische (Kreuz-) Zeitung*. It was unlikely that a group so essentially a part of the establishment, so much dependent on the spirit and institutions of Hohenzollern-Prussia could survive the monarchy. Perceptive members of the party were well aware of their vulnerable situation in a Reich that was becoming increasingly industrial, subject to popular pressure, and less willing to accept Prussian domination. In partial recognition of the situation, the German Conservative party had been created in 1876 as a national successor of the Prussian Conservative party, following heavy losses in the Prussian election of November, 1873, and in the national election of January, 1874. But the new foundation had little success in obtaining fresh support outside the Lutheran portions of Prussia, except for a scattered following in Saxony and Mecklenburg. The support of the DKP remained mainly rural and, for the most part, restricted to the German Lutheran areas of East and West Prussia, Pomerania, Brandenburg, and

[6] Maurice Baumont, *L'Essor industriel et l'impérialisme colonial 1878-1904* (Paris, 1949), p. 488. A valuable study now available on this theme is Thomas Nipperdey, *Die Organisation der deutschen Parteien vor 1918* (Düsseldorf, 1961).

Silesia. The German Conservatives remained therefore largely an East Elbian party despite attempts to extend their sphere of influence. [7] In an era of vast industrial and commercial expansion, the Conservatives with their restricted agrarian and old-fashioned middle-class policies had no hope of mass support, nor even enough support to hold their own in the Reichstag. From 1887 their position in the Reichstag steadily declined. [8]

The real basis of Conservative influence in the Reich, apart from the social prominence of many of its members, was of course the constitutional predominance of Prussia. Thanks to the three-class Prussian franchise, the DKP had perpetual control of the Landtag. It dominated the Prussian House of Peers and, through prominent members, the Imperial Bundesrat. With these advantages the party continued to exercise unusual influence on German political life in spite of its declining position in national elections.

Still, the Conservatives persistently sought access by one means or another to the lower-middle and working classes. They hoped against hope somehow by such efforts to find a way to counteract the growing strength of working-class socialism and middle-class liberalism. So, for example, they made overtures to the increasingly noisy anti-Semitic movement, and tried to absorb the new ideas of Christian Socialism. By chance they found both of these elements converging in the person of Adolf Stoecker, the clergyman who in 1876 founded the Christian Social Workers' party. When Stoecker accepted a place in the Prussian Landtag in 1879 under the auspices of the Conservatives of Ravensberg, there began a seventeen-year period of personal union of Christian Social and Conservative party groups. Within the DKP, Stoecker had the warm and active support of Wilhelm Freiherr von Hammerstein, editor of the principal

[7] Hans Booms, *Die Deutschkonservative Partei*. Preussischer Charakter, Reichsauffassung, Nationalbegriff (Düsseldorf, 1954), pp. 5-6.
[8] Booms, p. 42.

party organ, the *Kreuzzeitung*. With their following these men formed a core of Christian Conservative pietists who were generally hostile to the policies of Bismarck and the governmental bloc in Parliament. [9]

The high point of Christian Social-Conservative cooperation was reached in December, 1892, when the Hammerstein-Stoecker group dominated the convention that met in the Tivoli Beer Garden in Berlin. The possibility of a popular Christian Conservative party seemed for a brief while in sight. But, to the disappointment of the enthusiasts of that cause, the new organization of the Farmers' League (*Bund der Landwirte—*BdL) loomed as a counter pressure group. The practical agrarians had a tough mind for tariff policies and other matters close to the soil, but little interest in fancy modern talk about social responsibility that would sooner or later lead to costly projects and, presumably, higher taxes. In two or three years the Farmers' League had penetrated the DKP so thoroughly that there was no further possibility of Conservatives' following a Christian Social direction. On top of that, the social-minded wing was hurt by the loss of its leaders in the years 1895-1896; Hammerstein went to jail for financial irregularities on his newspaper, while Stoecker was compromised by an immoderate letter published in the press. In February, 1896, Stoecker was forced to resign from the Conservative Executive and from the party itself. [10]

The Tivoli Program of 1892 remained as a legacy of the Christian Conservatives' attempt to widen the DKP's social and political appeal. There was nothing sacred about its formulations, needless to say. The program was regarded

[9] Karl Buchheim, *Geschichte der christlichen Parteien in Deutschland* (Munich, 1953), pp. 195, 252.

[10] Buchheim, p. 281; Ernst von Heydebrand und der Lasa, "Beiträge zu einer Geschichte der Konservativen Partei in den letzten 30 Jahren (1888 bis 1919)," in *Konservative Monatsschrift* LXXVII, 16-9 (1920), 502-3.

as nothing more than a useful reference, a kind of prerequisite for the modern party. For that reason it was never repealed despite the many deviations of actual policy. But one attitude incorporated into the Conservative platform at that time was not forgotten. That was a formal affirmation of anti-Semitism: "We oppose the aggressive and degenerating Jewish influence on our public life. We demand Christian rule for our Christian people." The wording of the demand, and its place as the first point in the section on religion, left the impression that the Conservative party still intended to fight Judaism only as a pernicious religious influence. But in fact the Conservatives had long since come to interpret the fight in a racist sense, in a manner calculated to appeal to the racist splinter groups. [11] Although racist anti-Semitism was no doubt contrary to the intentions and spirit of the anti-liberal religious anti-Semitism of Stoecker and his circle, biological ideas were in the air. The year 1890 had marked the first electoral appearance of an anti-Semitic party on a national scale. The Anti-Semites obtained sixteen seats at that time in the Reichstag and usually voted with the right wing. Conservatives certainly hoped to win them over by their Tivoli Program, and to find through them another means of breakthrough to the masses. Nothing much came of the attempt, nor indeed of the anti-Semitic movement generally for the time being. "It soon ebbed because it could not produce any really workable program." [12] But the Anti-Semites were far from being passive, docile followers of the Conservative line. They proved to be a self-willed, explosive, and uncontrollable element. [13]

Besides the groups of Christian Socialists and Anti-

[11] Kuno Graf von Westarp, *Konservative Politik im letzten Jahrzehnt des Kaiserreiches.* 2 vols. (Berlin, 1935), I, 298; also W MS, p. 245.

[12] Ludwig Bergsträsser, *Geschichte der politischen Parteien in Deutschland,* 7th ed. (Munich, 1952), p. 152.

[13] Westarp, *Konservative Politik,* I, 21.

Semites whom the Conservatives had hopes of absorbing, the DKP often maintained ties and working arrangements with other elements on the right. For example, to support Bismarck's military policy in 1887, a "cartel" of DKP, Free Conservatives, and National Liberals cooperated in the national election by not competing against each other.[14] Cooperation with these elements was not difficult since the Free Conservatives were a nationalist offspring of the DKP, and the National Liberals, under the direction of Johannes Miquel, from 1884 were following an increasingly right-wing course.[15] Hammerstein and Stoecker, who opposed the cartel policy, did not have much effect on the pro-Bismarck Conservative majority. In the prewar period the basic tactic of Ernst von Heydebrand und der Lasa in the Prussian House was to ally with the National Liberals on most nationality questions, and usually with the Catholic Center on other domestic policy. In the Reichstag such collaboration did not work as well because there the DKP was too weak to play a significant role. On the national plane cooperation was complicated by the more democratic outlook of the Center and National Liberal parties. But Heydebrand skillfully kept in mind their sensibilities in order to keep open always the possibility of working agreements to help win Conservative fights.[16]

Along this line was the revival of cartel politics after the election of January, 1907, with the formation of a Bülow bloc. "National Liberal, Free Conservative, and even Conservative circles expected a lot not only from the revival of the Bismarckian cartel of 1888, but also from the fact that for the first time other Liberals (*Freisinnige*) had

[14] Buchheim, p. 268.

[15] Bergsträsser, pp. 135-6.

[16] Hans von Dallwitz, "Aus dem Nachlass des ehemaligen Kaiserlichen Statthalters von Elsass-Lothringen, früheren Preussischen Ministers des Innern von Dallwitz; herausgegeben von Albert von Mutius," Part 1, in *Preussische Jahrbücher* CCXIV, 1 (Oct., 1928), 18-20.

joined. Evangelical church and liberal Protestant elements also went along." [17] Yet there was a strong feeling in the DKP that too many concessions were being made in Parliament for the sake of the bloc. When a basic Conservative interest was threatened the DKP did not hesitate to go its own way, as in 1909 when it successfully obstructed Bülow's finance reform until the proposed inheritance tax was dropped. [18] The DKP also led the opposition to the next chancellor, Theobald von Bethmann Hollweg, who in 1910 threatened to broaden the Prussian franchise. Later a loose combination of Center, National Liberal, and Conservative parties, together with the composite "German Group" (*Deutsche Fraktion*) of splinter parties, consistently opposed Bethmann's policies from May, 1915, to the end of 1916. [19]

But the reactionary class interest shown by the DKP on the subjects of financial and electoral reform brought the party uncomfortably under the fire of public opinion. Not only did it bear the stigma of reaction, which might not have been so hard to take for a party that professed contempt of popular pressures, but it lost heavily in the "red" election of 1912. With that experience, at last it appeared that something would be done to bring up to date the outmoded party organization and to develop some skill in the use of propaganda. Committees were organized and a Conservative publishing house was founded. But the results of these late efforts were disappointing, as compared, for example, with what the Farmers' League was able to do. The latter, latecomer on the scene, was far more active and influential in its political agitation than the DKP. Part of the Conservatives' trouble was lack of money. Their usual budget was only about 100,000 marks from a fund

[17] Westarp, *Konservative Politik*, I, 80.

[18] *Ibid.*, pp. 77, 81; Hiller, p. 250; Zmarzlik, p. 78.

[19] Dallwitz, p. 16; Westarp, *Konservative Politik*, II, 52; Zmarzlik, pp. 78-9.

and from a few large contributions. More money was available in election years, though mainly from individuals rather than from business or commercial organizations. But no money was transmitted to the DKP from the Farmers' League which drew on the agricultural masses. When, after the unfavorable election of 1912, funds were collected locally for the party in Silesia and East Prussia, still none of this came to the party central. [20]

One could, in the last decade of the empire, scarcely doubt that the future of the German Conservative party was problematical. Its organization was weak; its appeal was limited; it had aroused widespread hostility through the country; its continued strong influence was the result only of a constitutional anachronism whose days were numbered. Conservatives admitted their failure: "An organization and campaign without any prospect of success are surely crippled. For that reason we found ourselves substantially dependent on landowners, middle class, and officialdom in the countryside and in the small towns of the Eastern provinces." [21] Indeed the only hope of the party lay in postponing revision of the three-class franchise as long as possible, in winning allies among the anti-Socialist, anti-Democratic right, and eventually in finding some access to the masses of the voting public.

One of the most vital of Conservative associations was the highly organized, vocal Farmers' League that had come into existence in 1893 as an agrarian tariff lobby. That organization gave the Conservative party a substantial material and moral boost, even as their identities remained distinct. Even Conservatives who were not themselves agrarians felt themselves naturally sympathetic to agri-

[20] Westarp, *Konservative Politik,* I, 397-400; Walther Graef, "Der Werdegang der Deutschnationalen Volkspartei 1918-1928," in Max Weiss, ed., *Der Nationale Wille* (Essen, 1928), pp. 15-6.

[21] Westarp, *Konservative Politik,* I, 403.

cultural interests by most of their social instincts. [22] The league in turn felt bound to support most Conservative principles and causes, as in 1909 it helped greatly to oppose Bülow's finance reform and to bring about his fall. In many cases without collusion agrarian and Conservative interests conveniently coincided.

The effect of the league's modern methods of campaigning was of utmost importance to the political right. "Adopting the methods of their adversaries in the parties of the Left, the new agrarian leaders, by their demagogic agitation and their open criticism of government policies, gave the parties of the Right new strength at a time when their prestige was diminishing." [23] Not only were their methods of importance, but also their potential following: "The agrarian movement revitalized the Conservative party and gave it greater force in the legislative bodies. Under the banner of the League the most diverse elements of the conservative population were brought together: landed aristocrats, small farmers, tenant-farmers, peasants, Anti-Semites, and friends of Bismarck and Bismarck's enemies. All this wrought a change in the Conservative party itself. Economic interests came to the fore and old conservative principles were to some extent forgotten." [24]

The agrarians, then, were a source of strength to the political right because they brought together diverse elements in a common cause, and were skilled both in money-raising and in the use of modern political tactics. At the same time they were an influence for change within the German Conservative party since agrarians strictly speak-

[22] Cf., W MS, p. 278: "Without ever having been a landowner myself, I have become an agrarian politician through personal inclination, through my administrative experience and my political convictions."

[23] Sarah Rebecca Tirrell, *German Agrarian Politics after Bismarck's Fall*. The Formation of the Farmers' League (New York, 1951), p. 331.

[24] Tirrell, pp. 182-3.

ing were far less concerned about the preservation of Prussian values and institutions than about the prosperity of their special sector of the economy. [25] The Conservative party leadership had to plan over-all policy accordingly, if internal friction were to be held at a minimum.

But in the long run the coordination of agrarian and Conservative interests did neither side much good in the national popularity contest. By the end of the war both were equally discredited among large masses of the population—especially urban, North and West German—as ultra-reactionary. "Conservative" and "agrarian" became terms as derogatory as "war-monger," "annexationist," and "war profiteer." [26] I refer of course to the immediate postwar period.

There is less to say about the early political life of the smaller parties that eventually formed the Nationalist Party. In the empire they were small, active, relatively innocuous groups that usually went their own way, yet were not averse to dealing with one another when a suitable occasion arose.

Most respectable of the small parties was the Free Conservative group with a membership of high officials in the civil service, Silesian aristocrats, and other notables. [27] It had come into existence first in Prussia after the War of 1866 as a pro-Bismarck splinter of the Old Conservative party. To the original group was soon added an influx of Old Liberals, so that after the November, 1870, election one-third of the Conservatives in the Prussian House belonged to the new group. In the first Reichstag, where the ratio of Free to Old Conservatives was even more impressive, the Free Conservatives took occasion to stress their

[25] Alexander Gerschenkron, *Bread and Democracy in Germany* (Berkeley, Los Angeles, 1943), p. 102.

[26] W MS, p. 282.

[27] A useful survey is Fredrick Aandahl, "The Rise of German Free Conservatism." Unpublished dissertation, Princeton, 1955.

nationalist principles by operating under the name of
German Reich party. [28] They gave Bismarck strong support
in his fight with the Roman Catholic church and in repres-
sion of minority nationalities, usually working hand in
hand with the National Liberals. Although in most economic and general political attitudes they still tended to
agree with the Old Conservative point of view, they were
antagonized by the DKP's increasing opposition to the Iron
Chancellor and to government policies, and they were
later displeased by Heydebrand's tactical cooperation with
the Center party. Consequently the Free Conservative leadership aimed as much as possible to bring the DKP closer
to the government and to prevent, wherever it could, Con-
servative-Center collaboration. [29]

These nationalist Conservatives tended to speak much
of right-wing solidarity needed to overcome the weakness
of multiple parties. In their program of 1907 they stated,
"The Reich and Free Conservative party is a constitutional
middle party which has always attempted to unite all
patriots in a common front (*Abwehr*) against socialistic,
radical, and reactionary aims." [30] Hoping somehow to be
a uniting influence, the Free Conservatives thought to
serve their cause best by demonstrating that the right was
reasonable as well as patriotic. They tried to avoid the
stigma of reaction that dogged the right, shunned the term
"right" in the program, and sought support under the label
of a "middle party." For all that, they were threatened
with extinction at the polls.

Of the Racist and anti-Semitic party splinters in the
empire little need be said. There were numerous anti-
Semitic groupings, most of which enjoyed brief and at best

[28] Bergsträsser, p. 90; Buchheim, p. 175; Gerhard Stoltenberg, *Der
Deutsche Reichstag 1871-1873* (Düsseldorf, 1955), pp. 29-30.

[29] Dallwitz, p. 21.

[30] Walter H. Kaufmann, *Monarchism in the Weimar Republic*
(New York, 1953), p. 18.

ephemeral existences. Party anti-Semitism did not prosper after its entry into national politics in the 1890's. [31] In 1907, under the name of Reform party, the Racists were still able to muster sixteen seats in the Reichstag. But in the last prewar election, that of 1912, the Racists, this time calling themselves the Economic Union, were almost wiped out. They were able to salvage partial existence in the House only by combining with other similarly threatened elements to obtain the minimum of fifteen deputies required to form a parliamentary group (*Fraktion*). The so-called German Group was formed only as the result of an emergency situation by the Racists, Free Conservatives, Hanoverians, Christian Socialists, and Bavarian Peasants. [32] Although in this case, union did not bring much strength, still, as a measure of self-help, the working alliance did at least enable the badly depleted right-wing splinter elements to retain a slight parliamentary footmold in the following six years.

It is surprising to find how small a mark the Christian Social movement had made before 1918, considering the considerable influence it later had in the DNVP. Nine months after their leader, Adolf Stoecker, broke with the Conservative party in 1896, his Christian Socialists were in turn split by the formation of Friedrich Naumann's National Social Union. The latter was a decidedly more secular, down-to-earth, democratic group. And, when the Republic came, many of the Naumann men, along with their mentor, joined the Democratic party. The main body of Stoecker's adherents in the empire meanwhile had an uncertain existence, seeking allies in the Center on the one hand for their Christian workers' movement, and in the anti-Semitic movement on the other for tactical convenience.

[31] Hans Hilpert, "Meinungen und Kämpfe. Meine politische Erinnerungen." Unpublished MS, n.d., p. 17.
[32] Kaufmann, p. 21; Buchheim, p. 319.

Stoecker had personally found that anti-Semitism was a popular political theme, that by using it he could win a sympathetic hearing, and attract with minimum effort both attention and followers. The only catch was that the Anti-Semites tended to come not from the working class, but from the lower middle class. Perhaps in recognition of this fact the Christian Social Workers' party became in January, 1881, simply the Christian Social party. Essentially it was a small urban middle-class group working in coalition with the Conservatives. In their separate existence the Christian Socialists, known often as the Berlin Movement, pursued a marked anti-Semitic and anti-Liberal campaign. [33] As a result they brought a number of Anti-Semites into the Conservative party, for which service the Christian Socialists were considered valuable allies by many who otherwise had little use for them. But with the waning of Stoecker's influence, the DKP soon lost most of its radical anti-Semitic adherents.

Friction developed in the DKP with the Christian Socialists as a result of the latter's continued interest in workers' organizations, and particularly by their participation in the founding of Christian unions beginning in 1894. The chairman of the Conservative *Fraktion* in the Prussian House, Friedrich Wilhelm Graf zu Limburg-Stirum, attacked Stoecker publicly for these working-class associations in March, 1895. When the Christian Socialists showed interest in extending their organizing activities to agrarian as well as to urban workers, they finally alienated most agrarian Conservatives, who would accept the corporative ideal when applied to urban industry, but would not tolerate any interference with the labor force on their own land. [34] The matter was brought to a crisis when the party's Committee of Eleven issued Stoecker an ultimatum to cease his undesirable activity among unions. The ultimatum re-

[33] Buchheim, pp. 254-6; Kaufmann, p. 20.
[34] Buchheim, p. 286.

sulted in Stoecker's withdrawal from the DKP under unpleasant circumstances. [35]

On their own the Christian Socialists did not have any easier time. In election campaigns they were at a constant disadvantage in competition with Anti-Semites; their brand of anti-Semitism was usually not radical nor racist enough to outbid their rivals. Men like Stoecker, who did not go so far as to campaign against Jewish emancipation, were soon left outside of the party anti-Semitic movement. [36] On the other hand, the Christian Socialists were encouraged by the favor they found among certain government circles, beginning in 1897 with the appointment of Arthur von Posadowsky-Wehner as head of the Imperial and Prussian Ministries of the Interior. With the increase in government favor came also slightly better support in elections. [37] The Christian Social party became firmly rooted among the Calvinist population of Westphalia, Nassau, and the Rhineland. Calvinist mine and factory workers in these regions were mostly Christian Socialists, while the middle class was National Liberal. In those regions until the war the SPD was an insignificant factor. [38] But in spite of all gains, the Stoecker organization at its best never commanded more than 100,000 votes. And many of these votes came from sympathizers of the Center party in areas where no Center candidate was presented. [39] As a political force the Christian Socialists remained, then, of minor importance.

[35] Walter Braun, *Evangelische Parteien in historischer Darstellung und sozialwissenschaftlicher Beleuchtung* (Mannheim, 1939), p. 33.

[36] W. Braun, pp. 27-8; Buchheim, p. 290. With the term "party anti-Semitic movement" I refer to the group of doctrinaire Racists who were impelled to active participation in politics for the prime reason of their hatred of Jews. That is in contrast to the usual, casual anti-Semitism that otherwise colored the attitudes of most men of the political right.

[37] W. Braun, p. 36.

[38] Buchheim, pp. 289-90.

[39] Reinhard Mumm, *Christlich-sozial und Deutschnational* (Berlin,

Trying to get more votes, and also, as they said, to free themselves of undue dependence on Center party voters, the Christian Socialists combined in 1903 at the polls with the Anti-Semites. This of course also helped reduce the competition they had to face. They cooperated again in 1907 by joining the Economic Union *Fraktion,* and in 1912 by joining the German *Fraktion.* These associations, it should be remembered, were only tactical parliamentary arrangements; each party preserved its independent character and reserved its freedom of action. With all that, the Christian Socialists sent only three deputies to the prewar Reichstag. [40]

After Stoecker's death in 1909 the leadership of the Christian Social party and of the allied Free Church Social Conference passed to the old pastor's son-in-law, Reinhard Mumm, also a clergyman. Under his direction the group pursued the task of building up Protestant unions in the nationalist Christian working-class movement. This activity indeed seemed potentially the most fruitful and promising one for the Christian Socialists in the social and political climate of the prewar period. The idea took hold not only among the Westphalian Calvinists, but also elsewhere among such groups as white-collar workers in the great commercial world of Hamburg. [41]

Although there may have been some doubt concerning the real political nature of Christian Socialists originally, when the test came in the war their sympathies were with the "patriotic" right wing. As Pastor Mumm admitted, in the matter of war aims he found himself very close to the

---

n.d.), p. 3.

[40] W. Braun, p. 36; Buchheim, p. 293; Mumm, p. 3.

[41] Paul Rüffer, *Die deutsche Gewerkschaftsbewegung in der Gegenwart* (Berlin, 1927), p. 4; Braun, pp. 37-8; Buchheim, p. 295. For a description of the Hamburg group see: Hermann Schuon, *Der Deutschnationale Handlungsgehilfen-Verband zu Hamburg* (Jena, 1913).

position and outlook represented by the Pan-German League (*Alldeutscher Verband*—ADV). [42]

Most famous of all nationalist organizations was the Pan-German League, founded in 1891 as the General German Union (*Allgemeiner Deutscher Verband*), and taking its definitive name in 1894. Although members of all right-wing parties as individuals assisted in the establishment, most of the founders were National Liberals. The new league did not want to be just another party. Its aim was to become a pioneer movement in the cause of modern German nationalism. "It was the feeling of the need for an intense nationalism at home, in order to further the expansion of the Empire abroad, that led directly to the formation of the Pan-German League. In this we find an organized effort to keep frenzied nationalism at fever heat. It was a truly idealistic, though entirely misguided, movement to awaken public opinion to the past, present, and potential greatness of the German Empire. . . ." [43]

The Pan-Germans did not succeed any better than the other right-wing groups in becoming a mass movement. Their active members came from a small segment of the Nationalist middle class, amounting to 22,000 in 1901, and 17,000 in 1912. The group remained strongest in Western Germany in National Liberal territory, and spread very slowly in the Conservative East. Although under the stimulus of the war the membership doubled in 1917, it is obvious that the chief influence of the ADV was indirect, through popular agitation in the press, and through relations with active political groups and parties. [44]

[42] Buchheim, p. 375, quoting Reinhard Mumm, *Der christlich-soziale Gedanke* (Berlin, 1933), p. 83.

[43] Mildred S. Wertheimer, *The Pan-German League 1890-1914* (New York, 1924), p. 21.

[44] Lothar Werner, *Der Alldeutsche Verband 1890-1918* (Berlin, 1935), pp. 43, 63, 66, 213, 287; Wertheimer, p. 57.

In accordance with its supra-party principles the league tried to avoid direct interference in domestic politics, to concentrate rather on foreign policy questions relating to the colonies, the navy, and the nationalities. Even here the league could not always be sure of consistent support from its adherents in the Reichstag since ". . . almost all of the Reichstag members listed as members of the Pan-German League were good party-men first and Leaguers secondarily. . . ." [45] Perhaps most vocal in their support of the Pan-Germans were the Anti-Semites. [46] The latter recognized the friend they had in Heinrich Class, who held a leading place in the Pan-German movement from 1900, and who became its chairman in 1908. It was he who affirmed racist anti-Semitism as an official policy of the league. Class also nourished the hope of uniting the right-wing parties in a persistent reaffirmation of Bismarckian policies to block and undermine the new course followed by the Iron Chancellor's successors. But it was his experience that the parties resented and resisted the ADV's self-appointed role as their political conscience. [47]

Class wanted very much to reach an understanding with the Conservatives. This seemed essential if the ADV were to extend to Eastern as well as Western Germany. When the league's independent exploration in the East had few results, and failed to get cooperation from local Conservative leaders, Class assumed that DKP headquarters had decided on an obstructionist policy. To try to improve the situation Class sought an interview with Heydebrand in 1910. The Conservative leader was cool in his reception; he hardly saw why the DKP should assist in establishing a potential rival in its own territory. He suggested that if the

[45] Wertheimer, p. 137; Werner, p. 72.

[46] Werner, p. 73.

[47] Heinrich Class, *Wider den Strom. Vom Werden und Wachsen der nationalen Opposition im alten Reich* (Leipzig, 1932), pp. vii, 96, 130, 267.

ADV were seriously interested in Conservative principles it attempt to win new territory for them in the South. Heydebrand seemed little impressed by Class' explanation of the non-party nature of the ADV, or by the fact that some important Conservatives were already closely associated with the league. The interview ended by Heydebrand's declining flatly to assist the establishment of the Pan-Germans in the East. [48]

Relations between Pan-Germans and agrarians on the other hand were more cordial. Class found a reliable friend in Conrad Freiherr von Wangenheim, head of the Farmers' League. Gustav Roesicke cooperated also, if more circumspectly as befitted his Conservative party ties. A conference in 1913 of both leagues brought further expression of good will, though few tangible results, on the subject of right-wing unity. [49]

After the outbreak of the war the Pan-German League tried to get maximum support for a program of far-reaching war aims. On Pan-German initiative, meetings were held in the winter of 1914-1915 of representatives of industry, agriculture, ADV, and DKP. Still, a common agreement proved impossible because of Conservative recalcitrance, for which Class bitterly assailed Heydebrand's shortsightedness and Kuno von Westarp's double-dealing. [50] Westarp, head of the Conservative *Fraktion* in the Reichstag since November, 1913, could not imagine his party's binding itself on such unpredictable matters as postwar frontiers. [51]

Only the war brought the DKP and ADV together in serious negotiations, but even then the Conservatives seemed primarily interested in trying to modify the Pan-German attitude. While the ADV stressed broad national

[48] Class, pp. 267-8.
[49] *Ibid.*, pp. 270-2.
[50] *Ibid.*, pp. 354-5, 361.
[51] Westarp, *Konservative Politik*, II, 44-5.

goals, the DKP limited itself to considerations of military and strategic necessity. Conservatives had no desire to acquire extensive colonial areas or foreign subjects who would alter the nature of the Prussian-German empire. Old Conservatives still had little enthusiasm for the basic Pan-German demands for fleets and colonies. Nor as tradition-minded and rather provincial Prussians did they share the Pan-German irredentist and *grossdeutsch* outlook. As a result of the conferences the DKP agreed to cooperate only in certain war aims propaganda, but acting separately. Formally the DKP committed itself to nothing. [52] Rebuffed by the Conservatives, the ADV sought and obtained cooperation from the National Liberal and Free Conservative parties. [53] Fuller cooperation within the nationalist spectrum was not apparent until later in the war. Then, as the situation was fast deteriorating at home and abroad, the call went out to a broad public for support of still another right-wing organization—the German Fatherland party (*Deutsche Vaterlandspartei*—DVatP).

The German Fatherland party originated as a protest movement intended to combat the signs of war fatigue and pacifism that were evident in 1917. But it was no party in the ordinary sense, any more than was the ADV. It wanted no competition with existent groups; it proposed no candidates for elections; it promised to dissolve at the conclusion of peace. The party was the brain child of Wolfgang Kapp, civil servant, member of Dietrich Schäfer's Independent Committee for a German Peace, and later conspirator against the Weimar Republic. When Kapp learned of the peace resolution in the Reichstag in July, 1917, he felt it was time to organize a protest movement beyond the limits of Schäfer's small group of intellectuals. From headquarters in the East, he hoped his new group would spread across

[52] Booms, pp. 123, 126-7.
[53] Class, pp. 355, 360.

the whole country. [54] If it succeeded, thought the founders, it could overcome the geographical limitations of the ADV and of other right-wing formations.

With that thought in mind the German Fatherland party was jointly created in September, 1917, in Königsberg, by individuals coming from the Conservative, National Liberal, and even Progressive People's parties, with Johann Albrecht, Duke of Mecklenburg, as honorary chairman and the recently retired Admiral Alfred von Tirpitz as chairman. As expected, the DVatP also obtained immediate support from the Pan-Germans and agrarians; both Class and Wangenheim became members of the twelve-man executive. The constitution of the new group stressed its character as a "people's" party aiming for the support of all patriots, whether as individuals or in organizations. At the first convention held the same September it was decided further that the movement would keep an active interest in all phases of national policy. All this was to be in line with the group's *raison d'être*—defense of the Fatherland. [55] Tirpitz somehow seemed to think that the Fatherland party might be in Germany an ersatz for the imaginative, dynamic wartime leadership of the West—a kind of corporate counterpart for the inspirational qualities embodied in Lloyd George and Clemenceau.[56]

Even though the Fatherland party spread rapidly it never did become the galvanizing force that Tirpitz and the others hoped it would be. Within a year it could tally the impressive number of 2,500 local branches organized in thirty-two provincial units, and claim a total membership of about a million and a quarter. [57] But the program had

[54]Karl Wortmann, *Geschichte der Deutschen Vaterlands-Partei 1917-1918* (Halle, 1926), pp. 25-9.

[55] Wortmann, pp. 34, 37, 39, 67; Werner, p. 241.

[56] Gottfried Traub, "Erinnerungen" (Munich, mimeographed, n.d.), p. 122.

[57] Wortmann, p. 72; Westarp, *Konservative Politik*, II, 622.

little to offer besides condemnation of the 1917 peace resolution. If the DVatP had indeed attempted any more direct intervention in public affairs than that, it might well have become a more significant political force. But then it would have risked the danger of immediate splits. Certainly the Conservative party, which took no formal part in founding the DVatP, found itself willing and able to cooperate only as long as the group's non-party character was maintained. As Westarp remarked, "It seemed important to us that the freedom of action of the new party in promoting a powerful war leadership not be encumbered by the contradictions of internal politics in which we were involved. We thoroughly approved of its practical and programmatic abstention from domestic controversies." [58] Yet, once again, in spite of their comparative aloofness and independence vis-à-vis comprehensive movements like the Pan-German League and Fatherland party, the Conservatives were highly conscious of their vulnerable situation in political isolation in the changed atmosphere of the times. Basically the Conservatives had nothing against the idea of cooperation with trustworthy elements, and were prepared even for organic union if need be—but only under Conservative auspices, and only as the result of Conservative initiative, which would satisfy their sense of propriety, and would befit their belief in Prussian superiority.

A few years before the war Hans Delbrück, noting the tensions that were transforming all parties, remarked that the Conservative party was "already not much more than a dependency of the Farmers' League," while the Free Conservative group was "in patent danger of becoming a branch of the Pan-German League." [59] It was true that both groups of Conservatives seemed unlikely to last much longer by themselves. The sense of failure haunted particu-

[58] *Ibid.*, p. 622.

[59] Eugen Schiffer, Papers (hereafter cited as: ESP), *Hauptarchiv,* Berlin-Dahlem, Blatt 5, p. 1360, referring to Hans Delbrück in 1909.

larly the Old Conservatives who, despite their principles of
loyalty to king and country, found themselves in latter
years uncomfortably in opposition to both the king-emperor
and his government. Isolated in a sea of liberalism and
threatened by democracy, they were regularly attacked by
wide segments of the public, the court, the government,
and some colleagues of the right. Thus, considerably before
1918, the right felt pressed for survival. Already its spokesmen struck the accusing note that was their theme after
the war. Only with bitterness did the Conservative party
in 1918 recognize the fact that the war was hastening the
transition of Germany from an aristocratic constitutional
monarchy to a liberal democratic state. The class vote in
Prussia, the last prop of Conservative privileged status, was
about to fall.

The Conservative party decided at long last in the spring
of 1918 to replace the 1892 program by something more
modern. It went so far as to explore the possibility of
close working arrangements, even union, with the right-
wing parties that formed the German *Fraktion* in the
Reichstag. Separate committees of Conservative deputies
of both Imperial and Prussian Houses set to work on the
suggestions, and by the end of October had drawn up a
draft program. Finally in the last days of the empire—on
November 7—the Conservative Inner Executive, the Committee of Twelve, set up a joint committee of deputies and
executive members under the chairmanship of Count
Westarp. An announcement in most accommodating terms
was published next day attempting to establish the new
image of the Conservative position: "The shift in political
conditions resulting from the war impels the Conservative
party to refresh its old and honored traditions with the
new spirit of the time so that it will be in a position to
meet the challenges of present-day life." [60] But the hour

[60] Kuno Graf von Westarp, *Die Regierung des Prinzen Max von
Baden und die Konservative Partei 1918* (Berlin, 1928), p. 114.

was a little late for such promises and manifestos. It was also a little late for organizing a nationalist union in the empire. The special Conservative committee under Westarp never met in a normal session. On November 9 members of Parliament found their entry barred to the Reichstag building. The Revolution had arrived.

II

The New Party:
From Founding to Election
November 1918-January 1919

The political forces that supported the old order in Prussia and Germany at large were caught unprepared by the Revolution of November 9, 1918, but they were not completely disorganized. Like the bureaucratic structure of the state which continued by and large to function, the old party offices remained in existence with their permanent staffs and machinery; bank accounts were available to assist the regrouping and consolidation of only briefly confused elements. In spite of grave handicaps, the scattered members of the right reorganized after the November election with surprising speed. [1]

The public was first made aware of the new Party when a manifesto (*Aufruf*) dated November 22, 1918, appeared as a small advertisement in the Berlin press two days later. The notice was in the form of an appeal for a new party, "for which we suggest the name of German National People's Party. We are ready to cooperate with all parties that share our aim: to heal the wounds inflicted by the war on our sorely tried Fatherland, and to restore law and order." At the same time points were suggested for the Party's eventual program. In these first tentative items the right-wing nationalist tone was set in cautious, though un-

[1] Much of this chapter was published as an article, "The Founding of the German National People's Party (DNVP), November 1918-January 1919," in *Journal of Modern History* XXX, 1 (March, 1958), 24-36. Acknowledgment for its use here is made to the University of Chicago Press.

mistakable, terms. A stand was taken for German *Volkstum* "determined to maintain its unity, freedom and independence against external coercion—a people independent of foreign influence." The demand was made for "a return from the dictatorship of a single class to the parliamentary form of government which alone is possible after recent events." Other items on a long sixteen-point list ranged from support of liberal "freedoms" (person, conscience, speech, property, universal suffrage), through defense of the "Christian" public school system, to concern for the current problems of special groups (intellectuals, government officials, teachers, military men, clerks, pensioners). The appeal was signed by forty-five men and four women identified only by occupation and place of residence, not by previous party affiliation. Some of them had been well known, though far from leading, figures in the public life of the empire. But the proportion of actual founders of the Party among the signers was small, and some important participants in the first formative negotiations did not sign at all. [2]

The Revolution was just two weeks old, the Nationalists had acted rapidly, but even so theirs was the last middle-class Party to enter the political field of the new régime. Few people, least of all the Party's founders, were under any illusions about the new-found unity on the right. The first leader of the Nationalist Party, Oskar Hergt, knew that the founding groups had come together mainly as a result of their overwhelming conviction that alone and divided they had no future in the Republic. [3] Though there

[2] *Kzztg.,* Nov. 24, 1918 (A.M.); also later dates, as *Berliner Lokal-Anzeiger,* Nov. 28, 1918 (A.M.). The list of signers, with an indication of the original party affiliation of each where known, is in the author's dissertation, "The German National People's Party (DNVP), 1918-1924" (Harvard, 1955), p. 34fn.

[3] Oskar Hergt, "Geleitwort zu Walther Graef (Anklam), 'Der Werdegang der Deutschnationalen Volkspartei 1918-1928,' " in Weiss, ed., *Der Nationale Wille* (Essen, 1928), p. 13.

had been some tendency toward a broad party of the right in the empire, only the sudden and immediate question of survival hastened the positive cooperation now of Conservatives, Free Conservatives, Racists, Christian Socialists, Pan-Germans, and other assorted agrarians and "patriots." The resulting political creation was a complex coalition of interests, disparate enough to raise considerable doubts about its effective existence.

Talks for the founding of a new political party on the right started informally, contrary to the expectations and probably the wishes of the Conservative leaders, Heydebrand and Westarp, who were prudently absent from the capital. [4] Yet the talks had some precedent in the work of the Conservative committee that the Revolution disrupted; subsequent events turned it into an informal committee-at-large. When, a few days after the Revolution, the funeral of a prominent Free Conservative provided the first occasion for men of the right to meet in numbers, many stayed behind to discuss the possibilities of a new party and its probable program.[5] While the informal committee that emerged from the impromptu meeting had no fixed membership, its participants were assumed to represent a somehow valid consensus of the leading men in their respective parties. [6]

[4] W MS, pp. 8-10.

[5] Otto Arendt, "Freiherr von Gamp," in Hans v. Arnim and Georg v. Below, eds., *Deutscher Aufstieg. Bilder aus der Vergangenheit und Gegenwart der rechtsstehenden Parteien* (Berlin, 1925), p. 331. Karl Frhr. v. Gamp-Massaunen, Reichstag member for Deutsch-Krone, died Nov. 13, 1918.

[6] Walther Graef, "Der Werdegang der Deutschnationalen Volkspartei 1918-1928," in Weiss, ed. *Der Nationale Wille*, p. 17; W MS. Notable participants were: *Conservatives*—Hermann Dietrich (deputy leader of the Conservative *Reichstagsfraktion*, chairman), Walther Graef-Anklam, Wolfgang v. Kries, Ferdinand v. Bieberstein, Joachim v. Winterfeldt, Martin Schiele, and Karl v. Böhlendorff-Kölpin; *Free Conservatives*—Gustav v. Halem (who in the summer of 1918 had several times suggested to Westarp a coalition of the right), Otto v.

In the initial discussions of that working committee the attitudes of Free Conservatives and Christian Socialists tended to modify old-line Conservative thought on specific points [7]—the most important being the decision to enter the political scene as a completely new party, and not as a bloc of existing parties. Immediately opposed to this idea was a group of Conservative editors and party officials around Bruno Schroeter, the secretary general in charge of DKP headquarters. Sharp conflict threatened to develop when this group pressed for stronger representation of the official Conservative party and presented a counter-appeal of its own. This incipient split was promptly squelched by Chairman Hermann Dietrich, himself a Conservative of rank, who put through a motion allowing only members of the Reichstag or Landtag a vote in the deliberations.[8]

Such had been the progress made when Count Westarp joined the committee on the morning of November 19, following his return to Berlin. He immediately objected that the committee had accepted too much of the democratic revolution, mainly at the cost of basic ideals of the Conservative party. Such capitulation to the masses was not only moral betrayal, he claimed, but tactically wrong. This approach would not influence the left but would undoubtedly add confusion to the ranks of the right.

Westarp's remarks were passionately countered by the policymakers who argued that not a day was to be lost in organizing the political fight against the forces of the Revo-

Dewitz, Max Rewoldt, joined later by Siegfried v. Kardorff; *Christian Socialists*—Franz Behrens, Wilhelm Wallbaum; *Racists*—Ferdinand Werner-Hersfeld, Wilhelm Bruhn.

[7] The draft program was drawn up by Wolfgang v. Kries and Franz Behrens.

[8] The group around Bruno Schroeter included, among others, Georg Foertsch and Otto Hoetzsch of the *Kreuzzeitung*, Paul Baecker of the *Deutsche Tageszeitung*, Ulrich Kahrstedt, Paul Georg Herbert v. Berger, Karl Stackmann, and Salomon Marx. Report by Schroeter, Nov. 24, 1918, W MS.

lution. There was a danger that the initiative in organizing middle-class opposition would be lost to others if immediate steps were not taken. The strong feeling of the committee was that the Nationalist opposition should avoid the handicap of the odium attached to the old parties, particularly the Conservative party. This point of view was given sharpest expression by the Free Conservative Siegfried von Kardorff and the Christian Socialist Franz Behrens. They were supported in their argument by other members of the committee, including Conservatives. Indeed Westarp complained that his Conservative colleagues, Hermann Dietrich and Wolgang von Kries, constantly allowed Conservative influence and thought to be sacrificed to demands of the other participants, especially the Christian Socialists. [9]

Westarp also tried to defeat the plan to issue an appeal for public support of an entirely new party. Such an appeal, he felt, could be only a thin disguise in any case, since the signatures supporting it would clearly reveal previous party connections. For a compromise, he proposed that the four parties sign the appeal as an official notice of the new formation. Apparently Westarp hoped through such a move to reserve (at least formally) the possibility of an independent decision by the Conservative party directorate, for to get Ernst von Heydebrand personally accepted into the discussions was by then an impossibility, even assuming he were available. But Westarp was able to obtain only trivial modifications in the wording of the *Aufruf* and in the supplementary text attached to it. [10]

The choice of a name for the new political group also went against Westarp's wishes. The Count was much upset by the designation of *Volkspartei,* a term in vogue among National Liberals and Centrists and suggested in the present instance by the Christian Socialists. In the term

[9] W MS, pp. 13-4.
[10] W MS, p. 17.

"People's party" he saw a dishonest wooing of the masses. The state, he thought, should have as much notice in the official name as the people, and the name should clearly indicate the Party's contemplated position on the farthest right of the political spectrum. In spite of these objections Dietrich supported the new name. [11] The counter-proposals made by Westarp failed completely as talks continued late into the night of November 20 and 21. So bitter did the controversy become, and so little did he accomplish, that Westarp finally walked out on the committee, announcing his intention not to return. "These were among the most heated discussions I have ever experienced," Westarp wrote, "and ended on November 21, 1918, with my arguing bitterly, in front of the whole assembled committee, with my own party colleagues who had voted almost solidly against me. I finally left the meeting with a statement to the effect that I did not plan to take further part in the negotiations." [12]

The break was a clear danger to the prospective Party. Theoretically it was still not impossible for Westarp to lead a determined Conservative minority against the DNVP, an action feared by the Nationalist committee. The resulting wasteful competition for votes and confusion on the right might lead to the early exhaustion and dissolution of both sides. So it was that, the day after Westarp walked out of the founding committee, he was urgently asked to return. [13] On the twenty-second Westarp, judging discretion

[11] In time Westarp came to accept the final name as a happy one for a Nationalist group. And in a letter of the time even Heydebrand suggested *Konservative Volkspartei*, the name in fact used twelve years later by some of the splinter Nationalists who rejected the leadership of Alfred Hugenberg; W MS, pp. 16-7; Graef, p. 17. Ironically, it remained for the German Democratic party in later years to change its name to *Staatspartei*.

[12] W MS, p. 17.

[13] W MS, p. 18: especially Dietrich, v. Winterfeldt, Schiele; also Albrecht v. Graefe, who approved of the point of view represented by Westarp.

to be the better part of valor, returned to participate further. It was then settled that the new Party would begin life through publication of the agreed manifesto on the twenty-fourth.

Actually there was little else for Westarp to do. Most of the Conservative deputies whom he was able to contact had decided to take part in the venture, and it seemed likely that the majority of individual Conservatives had similar intentions. But in declining to sign the manifesto himself, Westarp still wanted to reserve the official position of the Conservative party. He realized, too, that in any case the Nationalist committee did not want to advertise his signature. Consequently Westarp and Karl Stackmann on their own initiative drew up a separate *Aufruf* for publication, also on November 24, in the name of the committee of the Conservative party, referring sympathetically to the new movement as one similar to earlier Conservative efforts to establish a broader program and to attract adherents from other friendly groups. [14] The next day, in view of the urgent situation, they also sent a circular to heads of Conservative provincial organizations asking them to support the DNVP.

Meanwhile the Nationalist committee recognized the fact that the existing party organizations would have to be the temporary operational bases of the DNVP, which otherwise had no means of creating quickly an effective apparatus of its own. They found themselves in unwelcome dependence on the finances and facilities of the Conservative party bureau. This now gave Westarp a strong bargaining position, despite his initial failure. Among his conditions for cooperation was the dissolution of the original constituent group in favor of a small temporary business committee. This maneuver removed the pro-democratic influence of Siegfried von Kardorff, which Westarp feared. Also it assured the primacy of old-party decisions for the

[14] *Kzztg.*, Nov. 24, 1918 (A.M.).

time being since the business committee was to run not according to majority vote, but by agreement of the participating parties.[15] After the Conservative party directorate on December 3 decided officially to support the DNVP, part of the DKP headquarters was turned over to the Nationalists. The business committee itself was replaced on December 13 by a directorate of twenty-one members, ten of whom were appointed by the DKP.[16]

Response to the Nationalist manifesto meanwhile had been good. Money was beginning to flow into headquarters. Schroeter was asked to form the core of the new Party apparatus, and for that he relied on the strength already available in the Conservative and Free Conservative offices. Still, some difficulty was experienced in building up a complete national Party. In December, despite the formation of several hundred local groups, there were still many geographical gaps to be filled. Moreover the Party, lacking formal articles of association, did not yet possess legal corporate status. Nor did it have an acknowledged leader until the election of Oskar Hergt on December 19.[17]

Hergt, who had been a high official in the Prussian civil service and the last finance minister in the royal Prussian administration, was a compromise candidate about whom little was known.[18] The strongest proponents of a broad

[15] Members were: *Conservatives*—Frhr. v. Falkenhausen (chairman), Kuno Graf v. Westarp, Hermann Dietrich, Walther Graef-Anklam; *Free Conservatives*—Paul Lüdicke, Otto v. Dewitz; *Christian Socialists*—Franz Behrens, Wilhelm Wallbaum; *Racists*—Wilhelm Bruhn, Ferdinand Werner-Hersfeld; W MS, pp. 21-3.

[16] Conservative members of the directorate in December were Dietrich, Graef, Westarp, Gustav Roesicke, Paul Baecker, Paula Müller, Paul Hensel, Ernst Julius Graf v. Seidlitz-Sandreczki, Heinrich Kraut, and Johann Friedrich Winckler; W MS, p. 31.

[17] Graef, p. 18; W MS, p. 23; A. W. Kroschel, *Das Deutschnationale Gewissen* (Berlin, 1920), p. 8.

[18] On behalf of the Prussian government, Hergt had urged the House of Peers in October, 1918, to act on the electoral reform, asking the majority parties to work in this with the Conservatives: Erich

national party had wanted as leader one of the respected notables of the Free Conservative group. The Christian Socialists particularly favored Clemens von Delbrück, and others suggested Siegfried von Kardorff. But Count Westarp would never have accepted men of such democratic tinge, while others rejected them for their past association with the policies of Chancellor Theobald von Bethmann Hollweg. The debate on this matter and on related questions of policy was bitter; old-line Conservatives feared further capitulation to the pressure of the Revolution, and new-party Nationalists feared the domination of reactionaries. The compromise choice for leader, Hergt, absent from Berlin, was summoned in a telegram signed by the four constituent party groups. The committee offered him the chairmanship of a new party that would be a rallying point for the whole political right. Hergt accepted the nomination in that spirit, took over the office that was put at his disposal by the DKP, and began at once to create his own Nationalist organization with the help of Walther Graef-Anklam. [19]

On the day of his election the new leader directed his attention to the position of the Conservative party, still the indeterminate factor in the future of the DNVP. He expected that all local groups of the DKP would merge completely with the DNVP, although the *Hauptverein* might perhaps delay its dissolution for a while. That was expecting somewhat more than the DKP was yet prepared to do. The DKP endorsed the DNVP on December 3, but

---

Koch-Weser, Papers (hereafter cited as: KWP), *Bundesarchiv*, Coblenz, Diary, Oct. 2 and 6, 1918, pp. 35, 43.

[19] "Δ" (Gustav Stresemann) in *Deutsche Stimmen*, Feb. 2, 1919, p. 70; Graef, p. 18; Burgmeister, "Mein Austritt aus der Deutschnationalen Volkspartei," in *Berliner Tageblatt*, May 18, 1920 (P.M.); W MS; my conversation in Göttingen with Ulrich Kahrstedt on Aug. 13, 1952, and with Oskar Hergt, Aug. 14, 1952. Hergt, hitherto "nonpolitical," had been closest to the Free Conservatives: Liebe, p. 14.

only after a stormy meeting of its Committee of Fifty (*Erweiterter Vorstand*) under the chairmanship of Heydebrand. The result was equivocal in some respects. On behalf of the executive Committee of Five, Count Westarp fought any plan for final dissolution of the Conservative party. He proposed rather that the DKP, though abstaining from independent open activity, should continue to exist and offer positive help to the DNVP in the coming election. This would provide Conservatives reinsurance in case the new Party did not represent Conservative interests adequately, or should drift into Christian Socialism. Westarp's point of view was opposed by the majority of those present; he received vocal support only from Ernst Count von Seidlitz-Sandreczki of the Silesian organization. The representatives from Pomerania insisted on disbanding the party immediately; Walther Graef-Anklam introduced a motion calling for a special party convention for the purpose of effecting the dissolution. The motion passed by a large majority. Hermann Dietrich reassured his colleagues that the DNVP never intended to drive Conservative persons and ideas into the background; he hoped Westarp would belong to the *Vorstand* of the new Party and run as a candidate in the election. Westarp replied that if the DKP were dissolved he would retire completely from political life.

That threat, bearing the full weight of Westarp's considerable personal prestige, was sufficient to cause the withdrawal of the offending motion. The final resolution, accepted unanimously, expressed instead the intention of the DKP, while retaining its own identity, to support the DNVP. At the same time an important circular was sent to the heads of provincial organizations informing them of the outcome of the deliberations, and recommending that county (*Kreis*) and town (*Ort*) groups merge with the DNVP wherever possible. In view of the continued separate identity of the *Hauptverein,* however, strong provincial organizations with adequate financial means were asked to retain a similar independent existence for the time being. [20]

At one of the first public campaign meetings of the DNVP in Berlin the principal speaker, Siegfried von Kardorff, took the occasion, to point out that "our new Party, in which friendly right-wing parties have united, has no past and rejects any responsibility for the past. We have a present and, if God will, a good future." Then amid stormy applause came another leitmotiv, this time from the audience: "But without Jews!" That cry correctly added an unwritten element of Nationalist feeling that so far had been ignored in the official *Aufruf* and in the speech. Kardorff continued, upholding the rights and values of monarchy, of agriculture, the middle class, and "living Christianity." He warmly welcomed the adhesion of some National Liberals in a group around Gottfried Traub. Broadening the appeal further, another important speaker on the program, Franz Behrens, called on workers, civil servants, and white-collar workers to rally to the DNVP. [21] The hand was thus stretched out, theoretically at least, to all who would accept it in the fight for "national" values (except, perhaps, Jews, though their exclusion was not an official policy).

Since other parties had begun their bid for public support as early as mid-November, the DNVP felt pressed. Too much valuable time had been lost in the long debates on programs, policies, and leadership. The first circular letter and sample campaign propaganda were not sent to local organizations until December 10. For its first election, at any rate, the DNVP proved unable to manage a centrally directed campaign with much success. Given the chaotic circumstances in parts of the Reich and the difficulty of communications, it is easy to understand why local branches of the Party, with their widely differing origins,

[20] *Kzztg.*, Dec. 4, 1918 (P.M.); W MS, pp. 23-6.

[21] *Berliner Lokal-Anzeiger*, Dec. 16, 1918; *Kzztg.*, Dec. 16, 1918 (A.M.).

acted with almost complete independence. [22]

Those conditions largely explain the wide divergence in official and semi-official utterances by representatives of the DNVP in various parts of the country. Not all that was said reflected authorized Party policy. Yet often the incisive phrasing used in the appeals of many local organizations offers better clues to tendencies within the Party than the clichés turned out at headquarters in Berlin.

The broadest appeal was made by those persons in many areas who hoped for the close collaboration of the three anti-revolutionary, eminently middle-class parties in a black-white-red bloc—a union, that is, of the three new "People's" parties, German (DVP), German National (DNVP), and Christian (CVP, i.e., Catholic Center), under the traditional imperial colors. [23] But the most persistent theme of Nationalist propaganda was the new character of the DNVP. This was usually accompanied, implicitly or explicitly, by an expression of hostility toward the old Conservative party. On December 17 the Nationalist Committee on Higher Education (*Ausschuss für das höhere Schulwesen*) sent a circular to university personnel explaining how certain groups had "united themselves into a large, completely new Party under the leadership of new men, with a new political platform—new particularly in its strong social aspects." [24] Similarly the Party in East Prussia, in announcing its intention of organizing all those who were politically to the right of the Democratic *Berliner Tageblatt*, pointed out, "Such persons may all the more easily come to the DNVP without damaging the honor of

[22] M. Weiss, "Organisation," in Weiss, ed. *Der Nationale Wille*, p. 364.

[23] Political pamphlet material in the *Bibliothek für Zeitgeschichte*, Stuttgart (hereafter cited as: Stuttgart Collection). For example, leaflets signed by *Der Ausschuss zur Bildung des nationalen bürgerlichen Einheits-Blocks* and *DNVP Werbeausschuss für Heer und Marine*.

[24] Dec. 17, 1918 (Stuttgart Collection).

their old party because the Nationalist organization is not, like the DVP, an old party with a new name, but it is a completely new Party. Particularly in East Prussia the Party repudiates most vigorously the taint of any other party's past history. The DNVP is not the old Conservative party. It does not wish to be that, nor can it be." [25] But generously the East Prussian spokesman added elsewhere, "What we would allow Liberals (*Freisinnige*) and National Liberals, we ought not to deny Conservatives. Even if we do see their guilt in a special category, they still should be free to go about their business now without restrictions."[26] Far less gentle was a pamphlet issued by the election committee in the western industrial city of Krefeld, which stated flatly, "We are not a Conservative creation, as is frequently maintained in other circles. But we are a group of right-wing National Liberals and Free Conservatives with whom Conservatives, obeying the dictate of the hour, joined later." [27]

Publicists for the Nationalist Party at the same time were going out of their way to stress the existence of the liberal element in their composition. [28] They much exaggerated the importance of this small group, most of whom were National Liberals who during the war had moved farther to the right in the Fatherland party. These Liberals hoped to exert effective influence on the electorate through their Liberal Middle-Class Division (*Abteilung für das liberale Bürgertum*) within the DNVP.[29] No doubt agitation of

[25] Ewald Beckmann, "Stellung nehmen!" in *Ostpreussische Zeitung*, Dec. 10, 1918.

[26] Beckmann, "Unser Streben," in *Ostpreussische Zeitung*, Dec. 5, 1918.

[27] Signed, "Werbeausschuss, Crefeld, Hansahaus Zimmer 74" (Stuttgart Collection).

[28] See, for example, article by Major v. Olberg in *Berliner Lokal-Anzeiger*, Jan. 18, 1919 (P.M.), and pamphlet, *Ziele der Deutschnationalen Volkspartei* (Berlin, n.d.), pp. 3-4.

[29] Led by Dr. Gottfried Traub, Dr. Karl Emil v. Mangoldt, Dr. Max Maurenbrecher, and Dr. Pfannkuche, with the cooperation of Dr. Georg W. Schiele, as indicated in a leaflet signed by the *Abteilung für*

the Liberals, together with the activity of the Racists, did much to encourage the bitter tone of the campaign that developed, and that almost obliterated the original moderate appeals of Free Conservative and Christian Socialist publicists. In the Berlin electoral district of Gottfried Traub a typical leaflet for the Nationalists read, "No class domination ought to decide the future of our people. All classes must be represented in the National Assembly. No wealthy foreign race should continue to abuse its power behind the scenes. Germany must be governed by us Germans. No Romish intrigues are going to rob us of our heritage of the Reformation. Protestant spirit must remain strong in our Fatherland." [30]

The strongly Protestant character of the membership was thus widely stressed. A Nationalist Committee for the Evangelical Church was one of the first action groups formed in December. In circulars to the clergy the committee played up the "active, healthy, progressive social policies" which the DNVP was dedicated to promote. [31] Frequent in many parts of the country were appeals made directly to the Protestant voter, much like one that read: "Evangelical voters, men and women! . . . Your Catholic fellow Christians are represented by the Center party. Where are you, Evangelical Christians, to turn? Your solution can be only this: German National." [32]

The least restrained aspect of the campaign was conducted by the Racists who, as a result, received considerable attention throughout the Reich, more than their importance warranted. Although most of the component ele-

---

das liberale Bürgertum, DNVP (Stuttgart Collection).

[30] "Neue Kämpfe in Schöneberg," leaflet signed by the *DNVP Schöneberg* (Stuttgart Collection).

[31] Circular with signatures *inter alia* of Behrens, MdR; Lic. Cremer, Pastor; Lic. Doehring, Hofprediger; Dr. Jur. v. Dryander; Kunst, Pfarrer; Moeller, Pastor; D. Mumm, MdR; v. Winterfeldt-Menkin, MdR; Margarete Behm (Stuttgart Collection).

[32] Leaflet signed, "DNVP Geschäftsstelle, Frankfurt/M." (Stuttgart Collection).

ments had a background of anti-Semitism in some degree, the DNVP did not yet profess to be an anti-Semitic party. The Party was quite prepared, however, to accept any advantage it might receive in riding along with the anti-Semitic tide following the war. Yet, on the other hand, moderates on the racial question did not like the pressure being put on them by doctrinaire Anti-Semites. They were sensitive to evidence of unfavorable public reaction to extreme positions on the question.

The full artillery of the Racist wing in the Party was concentrated on the destruction of the German Democratic party which it attempted to discredit as a red-tainted, unpatriotic Jewish creation. [33] The culmination of this campaign was a virulent attack in the widely circulated leaflet headed, "The Jews—Germany's Vampires." [34] The statement represented, to be sure, an extreme in the Nationalist campaign; it bore no indication of official approval. But it is not possible to absolve the central agency of responsibility of the authorship of all material issued locally. The central office attempted to issue leaflets suitable to the taste and needs of the various electoral districts. Anti-Semitic literature was provided them together with other material for specialized appeals. In Silesia and Posen the party organizations actually declined to accept anti-Semitic material and returned it to Berlin; Jews in those areas, particularly in Posen, were valued supporters of the DNVP, needed in the German struggle against Polish claims. [35]

A strong attempt was made in the first election campaign to make the DNVP acceptable to wide segments of urban voters, especially in Berlin and in Western Germany. Nationalist organizers hoped to gain access to the working-class masses through the Christian Social movement, and

[33] *Berliner Tageblatt,* Jan. 30, 1919 (A.M.).

[34] Signed, "Deutscher Volksbund, Berlin-Schöneberg, Vorbergstr. 4" (Stuttgart Collection).

[35] Weiss, *loc. cit.,* p. 370.

also made a strong bid for the new women's vote. But direct appeals were made as well to intellectuals, to occupational and innumerable other interest groups. [36]

The important process of drawing up the list of candidates in each electoral district was essentially in the hands of the local organizations. Formally the list was subject to acceptance by the central executive in Berlin, which also had the right of nominating one candidate in districts which had more than one sure seat in prospect. That meant, of course, that the executive was rarely able to intervene, except by way of suggestion, since scarcely any seat could have been considered assured in those first January elections. The Christian Socialists congratulated themselves on the extent of their penetration into Western provincial organizations, and were certainly pleased with the extent of their representation in the election lists. [37] On the other hand the Conservatives experienced great difficulty in obtaining nomination of their men as candidates. Most conspicuous among failures to obtain a place on the lists were the chief Conservative leaders, Heydebrand and Westarp. For Heydebrand there was scarcely any Nationalist support either in Berlin or in the provinces. More people were willing to accept Westarp, but his candidacy also failed to go through when no district (not even his home district of Posen) could be found to submit his name. The Nationalist leadership exerted itself vigorously on his behalf without result. "The fanatics of the new Party naturally want to have me," observed Westarp drily, "though mainly to prevent a Conservative group from re-

[36] Graef, p. 20.

[37] Emil Hartwig, "Deutschnationale Arbeiterbewegung," in Weiss, ed., *Der Nationale Wille*, p. 220. Cf. also, Dr. Jäger-Bethel cited in *Berliner Tageblatt*, Aug. 16, 1922 (A.M.): In Westphalia-East a formal agreement was signed by the local founders, Christian Socialists and Conservatives, providing for a Christian Socialist as chairman of the organization and as deputy in the coming Constituent Assembly.

maining on the outside." [38] Summing up the situation, Westarp further observed on the day he was put entirely out of the running: "The result for the Conservative cause, at least for the time being, is a very sad one. . . . This failure is not due to the central executive, where the other parties and Hergt did their best to do justice to our requirements, but to the complete refusal of provincial and local organizations to cooperate. . . . Hergt claims that their motivation was not so much lack of confidence in our policies of the past as fear of losing voters in the present situation." [39]

Though unable to find a place for men whose names were closely associated with the Old Conservative position, Westarp did intervene successfully to obtain the nomination of Gustav Roesicke and Alfred Hugenberg, both powers in their own right, in the electoral districts where he personally had been turned down. Roesicke consequently was sent to the National Assembly by West Prussia, Hugenberg by Posen. Both men, closely connected with the Pan-German League, represented important economic interests—Roesicke, agriculture (as head of the *Bund der Landwirte*), [40] Hugenberg, heavy industry. "Through the agency of Hugenberg," noted Westarp, "industry made the granting of considerable sums of money dependent on the placing of several industrial nominees in sure positions. This money was indispensable for mass campaigning and was not obtainable in any other way." [41]

The Nationalist Party did reasonably well in the national and provincial elections. It emerged from the first

[38] W MS, p. 159: Westarp to Heydebrand, Dec. 30, 1918.

[39] W MS, pp. 42-3: Westarp to Heydebrand, Jan. 6, 1919.

[40] An appeal of the BdL called on members to join, and work for, the DNVP: *Kzztg.*, Dec. 13, 1918 (P.M.).

[41] W MS, pp. 40-2. Other industrial candidates running were Jakob Wilhelm Reichert in Magdeburg, Hans v. Raumer in Liegnitz (later DVP, whom Westarp especially supported), Georg Klein in Erfurt, and Dr. Correns in Potsdam.

electoral ordeal as an important, if not overly strong, political factor. After the grave uncertainties of the immediate post-revolution weeks, the leaders of the right recovered some of their self-confidence as they found themselves able to obtain considerable backing from the electorate in the newly democratic state. The German Nationals were surprised to obtain what they did—as many as 44 seats in the National Assembly in the election of January 19,[42] 48 seats in the Prussian Constituent Assembly seven days later,[43] and even a fair showing in other provincial elections. Many National Liberals apparently voted for the DNVP, especially in Baden, Württemberg, and parts of Saxony and Silesia. More important, the Party did well in winning new territory for the right in some northern cities, notably Berlin, Düsseldorf, and suburbs. [44]

The Conservatives were not much pleased by the picture they saw in the new distribution of support. The DNVP lost territory in the Eastern provinces that had for so long belonged to the Conservative party. [45] It was typical of them to blame the Nationalist leadership for the losses rather than their past record or the political climate of the Revolution. General Hans von Seeckt, a sympathizer though not a party man, could for one write his wife: "By

[42] Statistisches Reichsamt, *Vierteljahrshefte zur Statistik des Deutschen Reiches*, XXVIII (1919), election supplement 20. Final strength of the *Fraktion* was forty-two after two members of the three returned in Electoral District 18 [*Regierungsbezirk Arnsberg*] opted for the DVP; the three had run as joint DNVP-DVP candidates.

[43] Preussisches Statistisches Landesamt, *Statistisches Jahrbuch für den Preussischen Staat*, XVI (1920), 424-5. Final strength of the *Fraktion* was fifty after it was joined by two of the four members elected by the DVP in Electoral District 18.

[44] Graef, pp. 22-3; Ernst Marquardt, "Kaempfer fuer Deutschlands Zukunft und Ehre. Umrisszeichnungen aus der Geschichte der deutschnationalen Volkspartei Württembergs." Unpublished MS, dated Stuttgart, 1934, pp. 14-5; "Δ" (Gustav Stresemann) in *Deutsche Stimmen*, Feb. 2, 1919, p. 68.

[45] *Kzztg.*, Feb. 2 (A.M.), Apr. 20 (A.M.), 1919.

pushing out all the old leaders the Party lost East Prussia, and only the fact that Count Kanitz appeared on the East Prussian list saved the few votes that were obtained. This is a warning recognized in wide circles here." [46]

For Oskar Hergt and his supporters, on the other hand, the election results were a vindication of their stated policy of creating a truly national opposition party. They welcomed the freedom the DNVP won from traditional East Elbia. Of course, even with the new situation it was not possible to obliterate the identity of the founding groups. Even in the inner councils of the Party a kind of proportional representation lasted until July, 1919. But after the first Party Congress in that month no further attention was officially paid to previous party affiliations. To encourage an awareness within the Party of its special position and aims, a Political Coordination Committee (*Staatspolitische Arbeitsgemeinschaft*) was formed by young intellectuals grouped around Ulrich von Hassell, son-in-law of Grand Admiral Alfred von Tirpitz. They talked a great deal, made numerous proposals on the Party's immediate and long-term aims, but their influence was slight. [47]

Despite the encouraging results of the January returns, headquarters was well aware of its inadequate control of the election campaign. As a Nationalist official remarked, his sense of order and *Gründlichkeit* disturbed, "The individual organizations that were formed amid chaotic conditions prevailing throughout the Reich operated completely on their own from the beginning. It was particularly difficult to bring them together into an operative whole, and that is probably the main reason for the decentralization of our entire organization." [48] But at least, in the January

[46] Hans v. Seeckt to wife, Königsberg, Feb. 21, 1919, in Hans v. Seeckt, Papers, microfilm, National Archives, Washington, D.C. (hereafter cited as: HvSP), roll 28, p. 48.

[47] Graef, *loc. cit.*, pp. 19-21; W MS, p. 206.

[48] Weiss, *loc. cit.*, p. 364.

elections, the DNVP had reached its immediate goal: self-preservation and the protection of its weak individual components against the republican onslaught.

As one might have expected, all groups in the new Party framework of the DNVP were not equally satisfied with their situation. The direct influence of the doctrinaire Anti-Semites, for example, was not extensive, yet they considered their prospects in the Party good. [49] They had campaigned freely in the election with tacit support from headquarters. Nevertheless their principles, and even more their methods, were deeply offensive to many conservative-minded citizens. Thus General von Seeckt reported in another letter to his wife, "From Frankfurt-on-Oder I hear that some people won't vote for a party that will put a rowdy type of anti-Semite like Bruhn on its lists. They would prefer not to vote at all." [50] Repercussions within the Party were to be expected.

Free Conservatives were influential in the formation of the DNVP. Though their national following was small, the Free Conservatives drew support from intellectuals and members of the professional middle classes in urban areas important to the DNVP. In the first elections, however, Free Conservatives, like old-style Prussian Conservatives, had considerable difficulty in obtaining Nationalist nominations. [51] Eventually the Free Conservatives found themselves on the defensive within the Party, attacked by the increasingly active Conservatives and Racists who resented their relatively democratic point of view and lukewarm feelings on anti-Semitism. Yet there was scarcely any possibility that the Free Conservative group, with its slight national organization, could have survived as an independent party. The question faced at the time by these

[49] E.g., Wilhelm Bruhn and Ferdinand Werner-Hersfeld.

[50] Feb. 21, 1919, HvSP: roll 28, transcript p. 47.

[51] Axel Frhr. v. Freytagh-Loringhoven, *Deutschnationale Volkspartei* (Berlin, 1931), p. 8; W MS, p. 41.

men, as by other men of the right, was not whether independent survival was a possibility but what new political creation offered the most suitable medium for the preservation of their basic values.

Christian Socialists were most pleased by the initial development of the DNVP. The frequent stress of Christian Social themes in the program and election campaign should not be overlooked. The Protestant section of the Christian Social movement, found mainly in Western Germany, came over almost entirely to the DNVP following the advice of about one hundred leaders. By the end of November the Christian Socialists had set up a National Workers' Committee (*Reichsarbeiterausschuss*) within the DNVP under Emil Hartwig, and shortly thereafter expressed their full confidence in the new Party by dissolving their own political organization. Of course, their actual identity as an economic-political group remained in their national trade-union organizations. Meanwhile Christian Social workers managed to obtain influence in the Nationalist organizations of West Germany, and naturally obtained good places on the nomination lists. Four Christian Social deputies were returned for the DNVP to the National Assembly, and two to the Prussian Constituent Assembly. [52] A Christian Social spokesman, though exaggerating the role of his group, was still able in 1926 to recall with satisfaction:

[52] Graef, p. 17; *Kzztg.*, Dec. 5, 1918 (P.M.); Emil Hartwig, in Weiss, ed., *Der Nationale Wille*, p. 220; Hartwig, "Aus der Geschichte der deutschnationalen Arbeiterbewegung," in Walther Lambach, ed., *Politische Praxis 1926* (Hamburg, Berlin, 1926), p. 290; Hartwig to Central Executive, Oct. 29, 1924, in Kuno Graf von Westarp, Papers, private possession, Gärtringen, Württemberg (hereafter cited as: WP); M. Weiss, ed., *Politisches Handwörterbuch (Führer-ABC)* (Berlin, 1928), p. 118. Other prominent Christian Social leaders of the time were Gustav Hülser, Wilhelm Lindner, Richard Martin, Karl Meyer, Paul Rüffer, and Wilhelm Koch. Deputies in the National Assembly were Wilhelm Koch, Friedrich Knollmann, Margarete Behm, and Wilhelm Wallbaum; in the Prussian Assembly, Richard Martin and Franz Dallmer.

"The DNVP grew out of the collapse of the political life that came with the fall of the monarchy. The Christian Social party became its political basis. Whereas the Conservative party had to transform itself, the Christian Social group was faced with a promising future in line with its past political work and with the aims of its whole political program. Party conservatism was just not suited to the fight against militant Marxist socialism." [53]

The few Liberals in the DNVP were among those least willing to compromise with the new republican régime. Through their active propaganda they, like the Racists, had an importance beyond their numbers. With other remnants of the Fatherland party an occasional individual formerly on the political left came to the DNVP, but such recruits from the left were rare. [54] More numerous were persons who had been close to the National Liberal party and the Pan-German movement, mostly individuals in the West with little sympathy for the philosophy of aristocratic East Elbia. [55] These assorted Liberals and patriots, whether Liberals, Pan-Germans, or *Vaterlandsparteiler* had strong hopes that the Stresemann organization of the DVP would prove superfluous and that the DNVP could unite all Liberals who opposed the Revolution. [56] Response from Na-

---

[53] Hartwig, in Lambach, ed., *Politische Praxis 1926*, p. 289. By contrast Westarp refers to the "preponderant influence of Christian Socialists and ill-feeling in Conservative and Racist circles over the matter."

[54] Among them were Kaethe Schirmacher, Max Maurenbrecher, and Gottfried Traub.

[55] Freytagh-Loringhoven, p. 9.

[56] Gottfried Traub, "Erinnerungen," parts 3-5 (Munich, mimeographed, n.d.), p. 134; Gottfried Traub, "Wie ich deutschnational wurde," in Arnim and Below, eds., *Deutscher Aufstieg*, pp. 437-8. See also Traub in Stresemann, Dec. 11, 1918, SP: 3068/6892/133981-4. Kardorff, who described himself as a "left-wing Free Conservative," also tried to bring Stresemann into the DNVP; see Kardorff to Stresemann, Dec. 7, 1918, Stresemann to Kardorff, Dec. 11 and 12, 1918; SP: 3068/6892/133936-7, 134012-3.

tional Liberals was scarcely important apart from Württemberg and certain local areas in the West. The sharp
right in the DNVP was remarkable for the uncompromising stubbornness of its point of view, a view that was
shared by local federations in certain key areas, but that
meanwhile mustered no great following, and was scarcely
reflected in the central leadership.

The venerable and formidable German Conservative
party itself, following the trend already discussed, tended
to split into progressives and reactionaries. The former
went enthusiastically into the DNVP; the latter were perhaps accepted, but kept in their place. The old-line Conservatives certainly had reservations regarding the DNVP.
Westarp expressed the dilemma as he felt it: "In a Republic ruled absolutely by parties with mass following, a
strong party was the prerequisite of any political work.
That bitter recognition made me feel in all its sharpness
the inner conflict of a Nationalist politician forced by duty
to his cause into political activity in a constitutional system
he rejected. Participation in the founding of a party designed to fit into the new and altered conditions was very
difficult for me. I had a mental block in that direction
caused by the pain of abandoning the Conservative party,
the fear of having to accept weak compromises, and violent
dislike of the inescapable methods and consequences of
campaigning for favor of the voting masses. In addition
there was my deep-rooted, objective conviction of the repre-
hensibility of the entire system which constantly put doubt
into my mind as to whether it would not be more correct,
at least for me personally, to remain in hostile isolation
from that system." [57]

So too, Ernst von Heydebrand did not disguise his satisfaction that Westarp had not obtained a nomination. In
an exchange of correspondence he referred somewhat dis-

[57] W MS, p. 397.

dainfully to the Nationalist leadership as "political non-entities," adding that "in the whole lot there is not a single truly solid comrade-in-arms of our caliber." [58] He definitely reserved the final position of the DKP vis-à-vis the DNVP. Determination to maintain the cadre of the DKP was shared by Westarp, perhaps even more strongly after the election campaign. Westarp felt that the DKP had to be prepared to resume active political life if the DNVP should in time seriously contradict the Conservative point of view. [59]

It becomes clear, then, that one cannot correctly describe the DNVP as merely the continuation of the Conservative party under another name, or to characterize it without qualification as a political grouping dominated by Junkers. Yet there are writers who persist in using outworn polemics that make difficult an appreciation of the actual situation. The Nationalist leadership, for example, was never on good terms with representatives of the former Conservative *Herrenhausgruppe*. Indeed the question of the status of the DKP was so far from settled that the problems of determining its relationship to the DNVP and safeguarding its point of view within the new Party were major themes in the coming year. The question continued to occupy the Party in one way or another throughout the first decade of the Weimar Republic.

A postscript is perhaps in order on the founding of allied parties in Württemberg and Bavaria. There, special conditions prevented the automatic establishment of Nationalist groups similar to others in the country. In Württemberg, class appeal was emphasized from the beginning more than elsewhere, perhaps because the initiative for reorganization came from a group of Young Conservatives. They were soon joined by Old Conservatives, members of the former

[58] Heydebrand to Westarp, Jan. 14, 1919, in W MS, p. 162.
[59] Westarp to Heydebrand, Jan. 20, 1919, in W MS, pp. 49-50.

German *Fraktion,* as also happened in Berlin, but also by a Young Liberal group led by Wilhelm Bazille. Many other National Liberals in Württemberg, dissatisfied with Gustav Stresemann's creation of the DVP, followed the Young Liberals' lead. The group had difficulty finding a satisfactory name; only a minority was willing to belong to a *Volkspartei.* The Stuttgart group decided instead on a "Citizens' party (*Bürgerpartei*) in the hope of winning by that emphasis the confidence of all the circles that detested any connection with the more pronounced radicalism of North Germany." [60] The name connoted citizens, burghers, bourgeois—especially men of substance, the middle class. At the same time the group denied any sympathy for Württemberg particularism.

The *Aufruf* of the Württemberg Citizens' party was intended as a program to combine "the good old middle-class virtues" with "a vital Christianity." [61] The Christian outlook alluded to was the Protestant allegiance of the majority of Württemberg citizens. [62] At the same time these National Liberal-Conservative bourgeois, like Nationalists elsewhere, were not above using Racist slurs to discredit the German Democratic party. And, as in Berlin, their *Aufruf* was notably silent on the question of monarchy, stating only that "we are ready to collaborate on the basis of any constitutional form which is able to maintain law and order." [63]

It was not immediately clear that the Württemberg party would join the Nationalist Party; in fact it did in the first year. As late as January 9, Bazille pictured them somewhere to the left of the DNVP, somehow part of a vague unitary

[60] Marquardt, p. 13.

[61] Dec. 7, 1918; *Schwäbischer Merkur* (Stuttgart), Dec. 10, 1918 (A.M.).

[62] My discussions in Stuttgart with Dr. Ernst Schott, May 14, and Dr. Fritz A. Wider, May 15, 1952.

[63] *Schwäbischer Merkur,* Dec. 10, 1918 (A.M.).

movement. Apparently he still hoped the Württemberg party would retain a definite National Liberal character: "The Württemberg Citizens' party will belong to the union of right-wing parties which will no doubt be formed in the National Assembly," he stated. He continued: "There it will try to act as a connecting link between Stresemann's group and the DNVP until the comprehensive National party of the Reich is created. Of late a large number of National Liberals have joined us. As for the other old political friends who have gone to the Democratic party, we are still united with them by ties of friendship and sympathy based on our common feeling of patriotism. I regret if now and then ill-feeling has come between us over differences of interpretation." [64] The development forecast by Bazille of course did not occur; it was too ambitious and unrealistic for a regional party. The state party soon tacked on the name of the Nationalist Party, and eventually dropped its own name for that of *DNVP, Landesverband Württemberg*. [65]

Peculiar in Württemberg nevertheless was the distinct status retained by agrarian interests. Before the war the Farmers' League and the Conservatives had formed a common *Fraktion* in the Württemberg Parliament while otherwise remaining separate organizations. After the Revolution the agrarians did no more than lengthen their name to Württemberg Peasants' and Winegrowers' Union and Farmers' League (*Württemberger Bauern- und Weingärtnerbund und Bund der Landwirte*) and enter the state election campaign on a straight farmers' ticket. [66] It was "a frankly occupational organization, a peculiarity of Württemberg and for many years a dominant part of its

[64] *Ibid.*, Jan. 9, 1919 (A.M.).

[65] Marquardt, p. 13.

[66] Württemberger Bauern- und Weingärtnerbund—Bund der Landwirte in Württemberg. *Wahlhandbuch für das Wahljahr 1928* (Stuttgart, 1928), p. 18.

parliamentary life." [67] For the first electoral campaign under the new régime the agrarians combined their list with the *Bürgerpartei,* but that was the only time that they did not act independently in an election. In the Landtag, where five members were the minimum requirement for a *Fraktion,* they formed after each election a common *Fraktion* with the *Bürgerpartei.* Results of the first election certainly exceeded all expectations; the joint *Fraktion* made up one-sixth of the Württemberg Assembly, with a vigorous House leader in Wilhelm Bazille. Yet through the years, as one member noted, "the urban middle class . . . and the farmers often had to be . . . forcefully reminded of what they had in common. All in all [the *Bürgerpartei*] was a marriage of convenience." [68] Only necessity held them together so long, for alone their influence in the state would have been slight.

The Bavarian party was also founded on local initiative, led by Hans Hilpert as early as November 14, 1918. Formal alliance with the DNVP was delayed in Bavaria, however, until February 28, 1920, for fear of harmful attacks from fiercely particularist citizens. Hilpert himself came from an agrarian, Conservative background, but only now entered active politics. In earlier years his personal sympathies moved from strictly anti-Semitic groups to the DKP proper. He continued to admire the work of the anti-Semitic German Social party of Liebermann von Sonnenberg and the Christian Social party of Stoecker. Basically Hilpert was in agreement with the Conservative principles expressed in the Tivoli Program of 1892, but objected to the party's position on the franchise. Unlike most Conservatives he believed in universal, equal, and direct suffrage. [69] Hilpert's views thus had a strong personal, South German flavor. After the Revolution, he wrote, patriots had at their dis-

[67] Marquardt, pp. 96-7.
[68] *Ibid.,* p. 14.
[69] Hilpert, pp. 1, 3, 17, 21, 26, 31.

posal only the means for action made available by "revolutionary dogmatism," by which he meant "freedoms of conscience, of assembly, of speech, and of the press. Through them arose the new national party." [70]

The components that formed the DNVP in Berlin were not at hand in Bavaria in quite the same proportion. Hilpert considerably depended in the beginning on the well-organized Farmers' League, much as Hergt in Berlin made use of the facilities of the DKP. The Bavarian party established in Nuremberg on November 14 consisted of Bavarian Conservatives, the Farmers' League, the Central Franconian Agrarian Union (*Mittelfränkischer Bauernverein*), Racists (*Völkischer Schutzbund*), Free Conservatives, and a group called the Middle-Class Association of Nuremberg (*Nürnberger Mittelstandsvereinigung*). The national party name was shunned for fear of harmful particularist prejudice. Hilpert would have liked a name like German People's party as a symbol of its broad national (*grossdeutsch*) sympathies, but that designation was pre-empted locally as well as nationally by Stresemann's party. The name actually adopted, Bavarian Middle party (*Bayerische Mittelpartei*), was a disappointment to the party's founder: "I was hardly edified by the name; it did not adequately describe the character of our party as a right-wing organization. But it was accepted by the majority and I had to resign myself." [71] Since no doubt concerning the character of the party was left by its program, and since little confusion did in fact result, Hilpert also came to accept the name until the time was felt right to become openly the DNVP in Bavaria. [72]

The Bavarian party was chiefly a creation of Franconian Protestants in a largely Catholic state. It obtained immediately the adherence of some lesser agrarian groups and of

[70] *Ibid.*, p. 146.
[71] *Ibid.*, p. 175.
[72] *Ibid.*, pp. 160-1, 173-6.

the active Bavarian Middle-Class Association (*Bayerische Mittelstandsvereinigung*). At the same time it rallied an important circle of intellectuals from the Protestant University of Erlangen. Largely through their influence further emphasis was placed on social duties of the party when the final constitution was drawn up on December 10, a trend that Hilpert welcomed. At the same time the term "German Christian People's party" (*Deutsch-christliche Volkspartei*) was appended as a descriptive subtitle to the official designation. In Bavaria, unlike Württemberg, right-wing urban and rural interests did not dare form separate political structures. They were faced with far more turbulent revolutionary events in Munich than in their equivalents in Stuttgart, and felt themselves a weaker minority in the state. Bavarian bourgeois, agrarian, and intellectual middle classes were urgently concerned, like the DNVP in Berlin and elsewhere, with mutual defense—survival. Strongest evidence of that concern was their ability to form a joint *Fraktion* with the German People's party (DVP) of the Bavarian Palatinate. In spite of many difficulties DNVP and DVP remained outwardly friendly in the Bavarian Landtag until 1928, a marked contrast to the frequently poor relations of the parties on the national level. [73]

[73] *Ibid.*, pp. 181, 184, 186-7, 230-1.

III

1919: Year of
Organization and Orientation

Speaking to an American audience (in 1929) a well-known spokesman of the DNVP, Otto Hoetzsch, presented a personal interpretation of the Nationalist attitude that reflected the views of many men of the leadership in the first years of the Party: "I belong to the conservatives. We interpret the word in the true modern sense as the Earl of Beaconsfield did, fifty years ago, when he reconstructed the Tory party in England. It was then that he found the name of Tory Democracy. This is exactly my political ideal and that of my political friends. The platform of my party, worked out in the first weeks of the revolution in December, 1918 (I was myself a member of the committee for our platform), shows the way to a strong conservative party, not a class party, not reactionary but progressive in a good organic and historical sense of the word." [1]

While its ideal may not have been exactly that of Disraeli's Tory Democracy, the Hergt leadership worked from the beginning for clarification of the Party's character, among its own components, in its relationship with other political groups, and with the state. It sought to inspire, and to get things done—both prerequisites of corporate loyalty. But a satisfactory solution was never found. It can be argued that it was impossible to find. The differences of left-wing, right-wing, and intermediate directions in the Nationalist camp were not petty. The November Revolution had provided only enough shock to shake up parties

[1] Otto Hoetzsch, *Germany's Domestic and Foreign Policies* (New Haven, 1929), pp. 28-9.

and groups and to realign them. But the Revolution did not completely alloy resisting elements in the political melting pot.

Class conflict between workers and middle-class elements, among other tensions, caused difficulty in the DNVP almost immediately, difficulty that increased as time went on. It was complicated at the same time by ideological conflict which did not always coincide with class interests. Problems of ideology were perhaps more dominant in the first year of organization and consolidation than later; they were the most immediate that faced the leadership. Yet on many basic factors there was general agreement among National-ists. In the formulation of the Party program they deplored the Revolution and its circumstances, though of course their expression of opposition was circumspect during the Republic's early, most precarious, months. Most National-ists also, realizing the necessity of mass support in a time of universal suffrage, accepted the concept of social policies pressed by the Christian unions. Strong reaction within the Party against them was not felt until gradually it became evident what these policies meant in practice. But mean-while, despite the many areas of basic agreement, there was an important opposition element in the Party, a right wing of the DNVP, that was hardly edified by the middle-of-the-road leadership of Oskar Hergt, a leadership of "governmental" notables, of Prussian officials who in their opinion did not really know the meaning of opposition: "A royal minister was in fact put at the head of the Party, while two other royal ministers undertook the leadership of the Nationalist *Fraktion* in the National Assembly. . . . [Psychologically] these persons were completely unable to fight the new state and the new government with the bitter-ness and ruthlessness which were the only tactics in order here." [2] The question of opposition *à l'outrance* as the func-

---

[2] Freytagh-Loringhoven, p. 18.

tion of a Monarchist-Nationalist party in a republican state was in the long run as much a tactical as an ideological problem. But in this formative period, especially in this first year of the Party's life, ideology and tactics were not easily distinguished.

In trying to build up an independent Party apparatus Oskar Hergt had his most difficult time until the first Party Congress in July, 1919, supported him fully. Until that time votes in committee were still usually cast according to previous party affiliation. Despite Conservative resistance, Hergt's immediate attention had been turned to the building up of a Party structure and bureaucracy through which his influence could be brought to bear. Though as a leader he was very much concerned with problems of organization, he was frequently hampered in his efforts. In the first election campaign the Nationalist bureau could direct activity only to a limited extent, not only because of insufficient preparation and experience, but as much owing to its lack of authority. The independence of local units and their freedom of action, both by-products of revolution conditions, were characteristic of the DNVP through the first decade of its existence with profound effect on its political development.

As his principal collaborator in the work of organization Hergt chose Walther Graef-Anklam to be executive secretary (*Geschäftsführendes Vorstandsmitglied*). Graef was a man with a useful background both as a Conservative and Christian Socialist. A former Conservative deputy in Prussia and head of the Conservative Publishing Office (*Konservative Schriftenvertriebsstelle*), he had originally been an official in the important Christian Social union of white-collar workers centered in Hamburg, the German National Union of Business Clerks (*Deutschnationaler Handlungsgehilfenverband,* often abbreviated as DHV).[3]

---

[3] Westarp, *Konservative Politik*, I, 353.

Now he became the driving force of the Nationalist bureau and its chief exponent of the use of mass media and other modern methods. A complaint against him was the tendency of his lively temperament to attempt more than the Party could afford. His bluntly expressed view won him the particular enmity of the *Herrenhausgruppe,* the Old Conservative nobility of the Prussian House of Peers who for a while kept a semblance of organization and disbursed funds. Nevertheless Graef was an important man during the transition period when offices and money for the DNVP were still being supplied largely by the DKP. [4] The transition from Conservative to Nationalist character in the Party apparatus was a reasonably rapid one, with progress visible from month to month. The Conservative Publishing Office on March 12 became the Nationalist Publishing Office. While Graef remained its head, all personnel were not identical. [5] The bureau was rounded out further in March by the employment of Hans-Erdmann von Lindeiner-Wildau as general secretary (*Hauptgeschäftsführer*) and in January, 1920, by Max Weiss as assistant general secretary—but Westarp heard that the team did not work smoothly.

Tending to confirm Westarp's judgment was an early revelation by a dissident employee, A. W. Kroschel, who was dismissed in the fall of 1919. He claimed that, although there was little coordination in the bureau's work, about three million marks had been spent in the party's first ten months. [6] The money supposedly came mainly from heavy industry and from agricultural interests. Among specific donations Kroschel mentioned one of half a million from

[4] Formal arrangements lasted until April 1, 1919.

[5] Karl Stackmann, a Conservative of the Heydebrand-Westarp persuasion, left. Bruno Schroeter, who remained for a while, reportedly could not get along with Graef.

[6] Although the figures cannot be checked, they are noted here for the record. The mark was, of course, already much inflated.

industry in the fall of 1919 through the agency of Alfred Hugenberg. [7]

Other money coming to the Party came not only from industry and many small donations, but from the Conservative party which helped in other ways. On their own responsibility when the money was needed most Westarp, Stackmann, and Schroeter had transferred 100,000 marks to the DNVP out of the resources of the *Hauptverein* of the DKP, and promised a further 400,000 marks from special funds collected during the war in the name of the Conservative party units of Pomerania and Silesia. In spite of this assistance the Nationalist leadership suspected the Conservative party was holding back large sums. Actually, after payment of the 100,000 marks and of Nationalist office expenses until April, the DKP had to cut back its own staff. Then, also, the Conservatives had to negate their pledge of 400,000 when Pomerania and Silesia refused to make available the sums promised to Nationalist headquarters, claiming they had already used more than the amount involved to finance the DNVP campaign in their areas. In any case, when the Nationalist Party Executive in April proposed a budget for the coming fiscal year of 750,000 marks, it was clear that the savings of the Conservative party were no longer important for active financing of the DNVP. For needs of that dimension other current income would have to be found. [8]

One of the last gasps of the Conservative *Herrenhausgruppe* served again to confirm Oskar Hergt in the attitude

[7] A. W. Kroschel, *Das Deutschnationale Gewissen* (Berlin, 1920), pp. 9, 11; *Berliner Tageblatt*, May 20, 1920 (A.M.). Reference was made in chapter two to Hugenberg's role in the election campaign. Money essential to the Party, about a million marks, was made dependent on the presence on the ballot of several industrial candidates in districts with good prospects: W MS, p. 41.

[8] W MS, pp. 33-6. DKP resources were soon dissipated by large refunds to local groups, and by the inexorable inflation.

he represented as Nationalist leader. In the course of negotiations over finances late in 1919 the *Herrenhausgruppe*
appeared ready to give the DNVP 200,000 marks with the
promise of more big sums later. The *quid pro quo* included
elimination of excessive barriers to the activity of Old
Conservatives, nobility, and big landowners within the
Party, and the replacement of Graef by Karl Steiniger as
executive secretary. But Hergt did not need this money
badly enough, nor was he willing to change his position
on Conservative coexistence. Only reluctantly had he
agreed to the temporary continuance of the DKP in the
form decided by its governing body. Now he hoped to
play off the *Herrenhausgruppe* against the Heydebrand-
Westarp directorate in order to achieve complete dissolution of the DKP. Hergt seemed willing to comply with the
wishes of these Junkers, at least on the matter of Graef.
In the first place he warned Graef he would have to move
permanently to Berlin in order to hold his position. He
then told Leopold von Buch, the representative of the *Herrenhausgruppe,* that the replacement of Graef by Steiniger
would follow the dissolution of the DKP, or at least the
transfer of all Conservative funds to the Nationalist treasury as a sign of confidence in the DNVP. The matter was
ended to the chagrin of all when Westarp pointed out to
Hergt that the *Herrenhausgruppe* was in no position to
usurp decisions that were in the competence only of the
Conservative Executive and the local groups. The Conservative party itself had no interest in Graef's position,
and no intention of compromising its known attitude
toward the DNVP. Hergt's negotiations with the aristocrats
consequently fell through. [9]

After the January election, to be sure, Heydebrand and
Westarp had hoped to work out more clearly the terms of

[9] W MS, pp. 33, 36, 54, 361-2: The *Herrenhausgruppe* decided April
1, 1919, to remain in existence, and was reorganized under the chairmanship of Count Behr.

coexistence for the Conservative and Nationalist parties. But decisions were seriously hampered by the senior Conservative leader's absence from Berlin at a time when communications were slow and uncertain. Feeling left out, insufficiently informed, and resentful of what he considered Westarp's increasing activity in the DNVP, Heydebrand frequently adopted an intransigent attitude in his correspondence, although he and Westarp could usually agree when both were together on the scene. Both felt after the election that revival of the DKP was not practicable in view of the important support obtained by the DNVP and the sustained general hostility to Conservatives, but were unwilling yet to abandon the *Hauptverein*. When, toward the end of January, Westarp indicated to Hergt their intention of holding on to the bureau and executive framework of the DKP, the Nationalist leader was "beside himself" with anger. [10]

At a meeting of the Nationalist Executive on January 31, Hergt without warning called for the immediate dissolution of the entire Conservative party. The continued existence of the DKP represented in his view a want of confidence in the new Party that he as leader could not tolerate; he threatened to resign if the DKP remained. Westarp, caught unawares, defended the situation first on technical grounds, that the DKP could be dissolved definitively only by its Committee of Fifty or by a Party Congress. But, more to the point, he added that Conservatives were dissatisfied with the lack of opportunity for them in the new Party, although he admitted that the fault lay mainly with the local organizations. In view of such conditions, nevertheless, the DKP required time to decide in what way it could in the long run support the DNVP. At that meeting Westarp found himself, as in the first talks on the Party's establishment, attacked on all sides.

[10] Westarp to Heydebrand, Feb. 13, 1919, in W MS, p. 52.

Graef was especially sharp, while other component group
threatened to maintain separate organizations also if th
Conservative party persisted. [11]

One week later, at a meeting of about a hundred part
representatives, Hergt again placed on the agenda th
question of Conservative dissolution. In the course o
debate Westarp was again attacked by Graef, and wa
pressed particularly hard by Ulrich von Hassell. Hergt
emphasizing that existence of an independent Conserva
tive cadre would justify other groups in retaining thei
separate identity, again asked that the Conservatives a
least turn over their remaining funds to the DNVP.[12]

In Silesia meanwhile Heydebrand prepared independ
ently an official pronouncement of a general nature fo
publication in the *Kreuzzeitung*. The editors as a pre
caution passed it on to Westarp who, of course, recognize
the danger of publishing even a general statement at
time when it would be considered provocative by th
DNVP. With difficulty he persuaded Heydebrand to with
draw it. A break with the DNVP, he feared, would follow
if the DKP continued active work, and the Conservative
were in no position to benefit by the rupture just then. [1]
Heydebrand felt that his colleague was going too far i
compromise with the Nationalists, and hinted at the im
minence of his own resignation: "In my opinion the Con
servative party must remain completely independent.
do not believe the Conservative party would either want
to be absorbed by the Nationalists or that it could be, and
it would be utopian to expect the reverse to happen." [14]

Westarp worked on Heydebrand to give up the idea o

[11] W MS, pp. 45-7, 51-4; Freytagh-Loringhoven, p. 10. Only Dietrich
Winckler, and v. Dallwitz stood by Westarp at that time in the Na
tionalist Executive.

[12] Meeting of Feb. 7, 1919.

[13] W MS, pp. 54-7.

[14] Heydebrand to Westarp, Feb. 16, 1919, in W MS, p. 58.

esigning. Not only would an open conflict with the DNVP greatly weaken the Conservatives at that time, but the resignation would make an unfortunate public impression. The old leader agreed to come to Berlin to discuss matters with the Committee of Twelve. The committee meeting in April reflected the desire of some important local groups (e.g., East Prussia, Brandenburg, Pomerania, Silesia, and Saxony) and the Executive to remain in existence. By courtesy, Hergt was informed in advance of their decision to publish a declaration of the official Conservative position. [15] In the declaration Conservatives were called on to support the DNVP in every way, but were notified at the same time that the DKP had not been entirely superseded and would continue its work of promoting the historic values of the royal Prussian state. [16]

The decision to make a public announcement caused great excitement in the Nationalist *Fraktion* at Weimar. And not only there. At sessions of the DNVP Central Executive on April 15 and 16, Hassell in the name of the Political Coordination Committee asked what steps the Executive planned to take to counteract or eliminate the harmful parallel activity of the Conservative party. He asked that the Conservative Committee of Twelve either dissolve the DKP or that a sharp counter-statement be issued by Nationalist headquarters in condemnation of their refusal. In his defense Westarp carefully avoided the use of similarly sharp terms. The resolution, he felt, could not have been properly understood since otherwise it could not possibly have aroused such agitation. The Conservative party planned no separate political activity outside of the framework of the DNVP. But in the ensuing discussion the attacks on the DKP grew increasingly bitter. The criticism

[15] W MS, pp. 59-60; *Kroschels Gewissen* (Berlin, 1920), p. 12; Kroschel, p. 16. Kroschel claimed that Hergt approved the move previously.

[16] *Kzztg.*, April 13, 1919 (A.M.).

of Kardorff and the Christian Social speakers was unusuall
strong, while only two men, both Old Conservatives,
stood by Westarp. At this point Hergt, sensing the immi
nent danger of an irreconcilable split, intervened despit
his previous standpoint to block an impending majorit
resolution along the lines suggested by Hassell. In doing so
Hergt acknowledged the good faith of Westarp's declara
tion and the consistency of the Conservative party's suppor
so far. Next day, the immediate crisis over, Westarp assured
the Nationalist Executive again that the DKP would no
compete with the DNVP in the raising of funds, bu
warned the Nationalists that in winning new political ter
ritory they must not ignore the danger of losing tradition
ally Conservative areas. [18]

The relationship of Conservatives and Nationalists thu
was settled by the middle of April, though to the entir
satisfaction of neither side. Through most of the crisi
Westarp had been the key figure, tempering the obduranc
of Heydebrand on the one hand and, on the other, parry
ing the attacks directed by convinced partisans of the nev
Party, including men who were also Conservatives. [19] Hergt
who had originally been largely responsible for the in
creasing bitterness between Conservatives and Nationalists
now did what he could to bridge the divergent position
when the situation approached a breaking point. He acte
to avert a situation that threatened to become more seriou
for the new Party than the original problem—a split espe
cially undesirable in view of the far-reaching concession
already made by the DKP. The urgency of the situatio
eased. The Conservatives conserved their pride and watch
fulness, and a good measure of identity. Their party wa

[17] Ernst Julius Graf v. Seidlitz-Sandreczki and Freiherr v. Richthofen
Mertschütz.
[18] W MS, pp. 65-75.
[19] The Conservatives included Dietrich, Roesicke, Hoetzsch, an
Schiele.

never dissolved, but remained quiescent and latent. A Conservative Executive, the hard core of the party, along with their newspaper voice, the *Kreuzzeitung*, continued to function through the fifteen years of the Republic. But from the strict Nationalist point of view, the DKP was always regarded as a possible disruptive influence and potential source of unwelcome pressure. [20]

A few people in the DNVP, especially the young men in Hassell's Political Coordination Committee, thought it might be possible to attract into the Party what was left of the National Liberals, or maybe even to absorb Stresemann's German People's party. The initiative came from two leaders of the Fatherland party, Gottfried Traub and Georg Schiele, both men later involved in the Kapp putsch. According to Traub's own account, he managed to get Westarp and Stresemann together at a table in the Hotel Continental and to plead there for the formation of a strong right in the German National People's Party, an organization that would fight for the values of Bismarck's Reich: "Count Westarp was ready; Stresemann refused and went his own way to Hanover—a painful failure for me." [21] Despite Traub's story, Westarp actually was not especially anxious to unite with the Stresemann Liberals. Nor were Liberals much taken with the DNVP, though some few Liberals in the West and South did actually join the DNVP. Stresemann's party, the DVP, sometimes cooperated with the DNVP in the matter of election lists in local areas, but showed little inclination to disappear from the political scene.

[20] W MS, p. 76: "The very confidential talks which the Executive had held concerning the [Conservative] Committee of Twelve were, by the way, reported extensively in the Democratic party press. Unfortunately that sort of thing was to occur frequently after Nationalist conferences. One could never count on the preservation of their confidential nature."

[21] Wortmann, p. 67; Traub, p. 134.

More aggressive than the *Vaterlandsparteiler* in making overtures to the DVP was Albrecht von Graefe, a racist-minded Conservative from Mecklenburg. Of his ideal for the DNVP he wrote, "My ideal for a party like ours, built as it is on a broad foundation, or for one about to be built on those lines, is mainly of one thoroughly organized into sub-groups that could remain autonomous in their special areas. In that way a large party community could be formed. That had also been the idea of the original Liberal Group of the DNVP of Dr. Traub and Dr. Georg Wilhelm Schiele. Through such an organization relations with the DVP would also be easier because the Liberal Group could just as well be a National Liberal Group. In addition to them there would also be a definite Racist Group, and perhaps others too. Though some persons might fear such groups as the nuclei of later secessions or splits in the Party, I would not hesitate on that account. . . . If new obligations face the Party at some later time, then let it split up if need be." [22] Thus Graefe was not so much interested in building up a centralized political body as in assisting the cooperation of a wide federation of patriotic groups. Components would retain their identity and much freedom of action as subgroups, but in the Reichstag as a working community of the right (*Arbeitsgemeinschaft*) they would present a united front in one *Fraktion*. That was the result Graefe wished for his negotiations with the DVP, unlikely as it was that his Nationalist colleagues would have gone along with his scheme. [23]

For the first months of the National Assembly the *Fraktionen* of DNVP and DVP worked together very closely. It was not in fact until June, 1920, that the parties were tactically much differentiated. Heavy industry, for ex-

[22] WP: Albrecht v. Graefe, "Partei und Judenfrage." Unpublished MS, dated Goldebee, Feb. 5, 1920.

[23] v. Graefe to Justizrat Dr. Knebusch, Aug. 26, 1922, in *Kzztg.*, April 30, 1924 (A.M.).

ample, kept close contact with both of them, giving its particular representatives their choice of either party, whichever might find them good places on the election lists. At the beginning of 1919 the hope of complete union of DNVP and DVP was widely expressed in many circles on both sides. An article in the *Berliner Neueste Nachrichten* on January 31 by a National Liberal spokesman of heavy industry received a favorable echo in many segments of the Nationalist press. [24] Representatives of the Farmers' League made clear their similar views. Stresemann, however, contented himself only with the observation that, since the DNVP was not overly strong in the Assembly, and since the danger of extreme rightist reaction seemed past, the DVP might relax its opposition to the Nationalists and allow future relations to be determined by conditions in the National Assembly. [25] Westarp in fact had misgivings from the first; he doubted the desirability of a merger as well as its feasibility: "From time to time Hergt pressed very energetically for complete fusion with the DVP. Naturally Stresemann is not considering that possibility at all, but seems to be waiting for an influx from the left and from the right to help him build up a new middle party. I left Hergt in no doubt that the idea of fusion with the DVP under circumstances could strengthen the inclination in Conservative circles to remain apart on the political right outside of the DNVP. With my full approval the Nationalists did work closely at Weimar with the DVP, which incidentally elected in Heinze as chairman a warm partisan of the fusion policy." [26]

Thus a confusion of voices was calling for absorption of

[24] Paul Fuhrmann, who was excluded by Stresemann from the DVP.

[25] Hans-Erdmann v. Lindeiner-Wildau, *Wir und die Deutsche Volkspartei* (Berlin, 1921), pp. 8, 10; W MS, pp. 543-4; *Berliner Tageblatt*, Feb. 1, 1919 (A.M.); Stresemann, Jan. 29, 1919, in *Deutsche Stimmen*, Feb. 2, 1919.

[26] Westarp to Heydebrand, Feb. 13, 1919, in W MS, pp. 544-5.

the German People's party. The Hergt leadership wanted to build a parliamentary party with mass following, while Graefe and the Pan-German Liberals of the *Vaterlands-partei* wanted rather a supra-parliamentary mass movement. The tariff-minded agrarians of the Farmers' League wanted practical cooperation with big industry, and therefore with the DVP. On the other hand for various reasons Old Conservatives, Christian Socialists, and Racists were opposed to close relations with the DVP; Conservatives like Westarp saw influences there of the left, Christian Socialists disliked excessive big business connections, while Racists found the DVP weak on the subject of anti-Semitism. [27]

The decision on collaboration was actually out of Nationalist hands. The DVP was itself internally divided on the matter of collaboration or union with the Nationalists. Although its newly elected chairman, Rudolf Heinze, emphasized close cooperation with the Nationalists at the first *Parteitag* at Jena in April, as did General Secretary Otto Hugo, other speakers at that time called for overtures to the Democrats instead. But Stresemann, whose influence was already considerable, resisted both trends and denied with particular vigor any suggestion that the DVP was an adjunct of the DNVP, or that the DVP intended to limit in any way its freedom of action.

The first important differences between the parties occurred over policy to be followed in face of the Versailles Treaty. Discussions at the end of May failed to coordinate policy owing to the opposition of Stresemann. Although individuals on both sides continued talks unofficially on the subject of eventual union, Stresemann pointed out that the "national" idea was too big to be the monopoly of a single party, as the DNVP seemed to claim. Many views were to be represented within that concept. The function

[27] Adam Röder, *Der deutsche Konservatismus und die Revolution* (Gotha, 1920), p. 121.

of the DVP was particularly to nourish the viewpoint of liberalism. Yet on practical matters the parties did continue to cooperate, as for example on a statement against the peace treaty jointly issued on June 21. [28]

Hergt, disappointed at the outcome of discussions between DNVP and DVP, made a further gesture of friendship to the DVP at the first Nationalist *Parteitag* in July: "You know," he told delegates, "that after urging from the DVP certain discussions took place on the subject of closer relations. You know also that the various party organs of the DVP have turned down the idea as momentarily impracticable, and that for this reason the gentlemen of the DVP who had initially approached us have not followed up their plan. Now we have never made a secret of our feeling that we must be tied to our neighbors as closely as possible. We have always believed that a great Nationalist middle- and working-class party would have tremendous force and impact. This would perhaps have been the most favorable time to form such a party. But we are not running after anyone."[29] The definitive answer from the DVP —negative—was given on October 19 at its Leipzig *Parteitag*. [30]

The annual *Parteitage* of the DNVP were much more than formal occasions. They were public meetings of what in effect was the General Assembly of the Party, the foundation of organizational power, and the court of appeal in ideological disputes. The first *Parteitag* had been postponed until the nature of the peace with the Allies was known. As a result it met on July 12 and 13 in Berlin in an atmosphere of unusual patriotic protest, and was concerned as much with foreign relations as with internal

---

[28] *Kzztg.*, April 14, 1919 (P.M.); *Deutsche Stimmen*, May 4, June 15, 1919; Lindeiner-Wildau, p. 10.

[29] Oskar Hergt, *Gegenwart und Zukunft der DNVP* (Berlin, 1919), speech at the first Party Congress, Berlin, July 12-3, 1919, p. 9.

[30] W MS, p. 546; *Deutsche Stimmen*, Oct. 19, 1919.

affairs. In this the Nationalists obtained a certain measure of interest and sympathy from an aroused general public.

Rejection of the "disgraceful peace" of Versailles turned out to be the timely central theme of the Nationalist Party Congress. Consequently, among the fifty or more speakers in the two-day period, none was more à *propos* than Count Westarp who had been invited by Hergt (against the advice of many colleagues) to give the report on foreign affairs. Westarp won many friends by naming as "the task of all policy, the goal of every political endeavor" the freeing of Germany from "the slavery of the peace of Versailles." [31]

There is no doubt that Westarp at the *Parteitag* strengthened his personal position in the DNVP and that, proportionate to this increased strength, the prospects for independent Conservative policy declined. Heydebrand, who had disapproved of the prominent position given to Westarp in the *Parteitag,* was aware of the development and expressed his disappointment clearly. The Hergt directorate was trying to use Westarp as a bridge over which to entice recalcitrant Conservatives into the Nationalist camp. [32] Westarp on the other hand felt that the experience of the *Parteitag* showed both the strength of the DNVP and an improvement in the status of Conservatives in the new Party, both developments which he welcomed.

The Berlin *Parteitag* was perhaps most important for its effect of building up the feeling of self-confidence in an organization that was still unsure of itself. The first big meeting of representatives of units from across the country was an experience in self-discovery. But what was not said at the *Parteitag* was in many respects more important for the internal development of the DNVP than those matters that were given public hearing. Thus questions of mon-

[31] W MS, p. 1 (Part III, new pagination); v. d. Planitz to Westarp, July 23, 1919, in W MS, p. 90.
[32] Heydebrand to Westarp, Aug. 19, 1919, in W MS, pp. 90-1.

archy, restoration, or constitutional form were largely avoided. There was no debate on the status of the DKP. But most tricky was the crowding out of the major anti-Semitic talks which Graefe and the Party Racists were anxious to present to the meeting, contrary to the wishes of the leadership. Tension on the part of the Racists was apparent from their frequent interjections during speeches, especially when speakers stated that membership in the DNVP was open to all. [33] The tension increased when the Racists were prevented from having a debate on a set of anti-Semitic resolutions they proposed to the Party. The *Parteitag* threatened to explode in bitter recriminations. With difficulty, outward harmony was preserved, though behind the scenes there remained dangerous symptoms of basic disagreement. [34]

For Hergt and the Nationalist leadership, the *Parteitag* presented this and other problems that might be called growing pains. There was an urgent need, not met at the Berlin meeting, to find a suitable platform and program for the future. No one had satisfactorily faced yet the problem of obstacles to positive work that faced a party fundamentally in opposition to a régime it detested on constitutional and moral grounds. At the *Parteitag*, for the most part, general principles were expressed which were not necessarily helpful to the leadership, nor necessarily acceptable to the general membership. Thus, for example, Clemens von Delbrück might state that "we are bound, first of all, by the principle of monarchy; secondly, by a Christian view of the world; but, above all else, we are ruled by our belief in the necessity of a strong national state." [35] This had the truth in it of all clichés; obviously true, but by no means exciting. For most members of the

---

[33] W MS, pp. 92, 315; Julius Curtius in *Deutsche Stimmen*, Oct. 19, 1919.

[34] Curtius, *loc. cit.*

[35] *Ibid.*

Party their principles were indeed national, monarchist, and Christian, yet a significant minority preferred a social and Christian stress more than monarchist one. And for certain extreme elements—as yet unvocal—obsessed as they were by hatred of the November Republic, no program could possibly persuade them to accept the idea of a Nationalist right working in peaceful cooperation with an illegitimate state. They were oppressed above all else by the question, "Can the Nationalist right, believing deeply in the state as it does, remain essentially in opposition to the representatives of the state's power over a long period of time without finally clashing with the state itself? And conversely, did not cooperation with that state imply a betrayal of nationalism?" [36]

Sooner than expected the Nationalist Party was presented with the hypothetical problem of participation in government in the republican state. In the early morning of June 23 the Nationalist *Fraktion* in Weimar was informed by the government that an ultimatum had been received from the Entente for unconditional acceptance of peace terms. Since the government doubted that a majority could be obtained in the Assembly for such a decision, it asked whether the opposition was ready to form an alternative government in the event of defeat. The Nationalists readily agreed that the Allied terms were utterly unacceptable, and indicated that in principle they were ready to accept the responsibilities of government. [37]

With the majority Count Westarp felt that it was desirable to work for a situation that would permit the DNVP to take part in a coalition government, provided the coalition excluded the Social Democrats. That was his view in face of the occasional tendency of some Conserva-

[36] Freytagh-Loringhoven, pp. 11-2.

[37] Traub, p. 164; Graefe, July 25. 1919, Verfassunggebende Deutsche Nationalversammlung, *Verhandlungen*, vol. 328, p. 1919 (hereafter cited as: Reich Debates).

tives and Nationalists to seek points of contact throughout the whole political spectrum, even as far left as the SPD. "The pressure to shift from opposition to cooperation by service in government," noted Westarp, "was particularly strong in the Prussian *Fraktion*. That group naturally seemed more concerned with the practical tasks of the Prussian government than with questions of national policy." [38]

Hergt, who sat in the Prussian House, seemed out of place there with his broad considerations and experimental thoughts. Moreover in tone and attitude he often seemed the essence of sweet reasonableness. Early in 1919, for example, he appeared willing to cooperate with the Socialist-led Prussian government of Paul Hirsch. On March 27 he reaffirmed an oft-stated theme that the DNVP was prepared for positive work under the parliamentary system. The Party's interests, he suggested, were primarily stability. With that in mind the DNVP might even accept Socialist solutions in specific economic emergencies.[39] Thus it was with some daring that Hergt spoke in the Prussian Legislature as the head of a major national Party, as well as its *Fraktion* leader. He created a considerable stir when on September 26, 1919, he presented the Program for Order, for long to be associated with his name.

Hergt's *Ordnungsprogramm* probably caused more stir within the Nationalist Party than outside of it, possibly because many colleagues feared their leader was making more drastic concessions than he actually intended. Even so, it came as a surprise to members of the Prussian Constituent Assembly to hear on that September day that the leader of the DNVP was attempting to "take an objective viewpoint and to develop such a program for setting affairs in order that an overwhelming number of persons of all parties, including the left, might participate in it without

[38] W MS, p. 536.
[39] *Berliner Tageblatt,* May 2, 1924 (P.M.).

difficulty." [40] What this turned out to be was a theoretical offer of cooperation to restore order and harmony in the state on the basis of the Christian Social aspect of the Party, with considerable de-emphasis of the strictly rightist aspect of the Party outlook. Thus, while the question of monarchy was not mentioned at all, five out of seven points in the special program covered social and economic matters.

In the first place Hergt proposed to regulate working conditions, to revise the administration of unemployment relief, and to supervise the establishment of wage contracts: "I can point out with some satisfaction that there is a way here to bridge the gap between the right and the left. We are convinced that under present conditions [new] wage agreements are necessary to restore tranquillity to the productive branch of the economy." [41] The wage contracts would be drawn up by an impartial agency of the government. In this connection Hergt proposed the reintroduction of the piecework system in industry as an incentive to productivity, and also what he called "protection of those willing to work," by which he seemed to imply protection of strikebreakers—the "right-to-work" legislation of modern American parlance.

The second point of the program, extension of the social part of the constitution (*Ausbau der sozialen Verfassung*), went so far as to include co-determination of workers in the productive process and profit sharing. The latter "demand of the DNVP" was one that elicited calls of "Hear, hear!" from the benches of the left.

Third, Hergt asked for an end of all compulsory (and hence dangerous) socialist and cooperative experiments. Elimination of the residue of the controlled economy of wartime was the fourth item, followed, fifth, by the de-

[40] Germany. Prussia. Verfassunggebende Preussische Landesversammlung, *Sitzungsberichte*, Sept. 26, 1919, vol. 4, col. 4401 (hereafter cited as: Prussian Debates).

[41] *Ibid.*, col. 4402.

mand for a system of financial reform that would protect the propertied and entrepreneurial classes from organized plundering. The final two items were much closer to the normal Nationalist program: strengthening of the executive of the state (with, as a corollary, full employment and restoration to a position of respect of the agencies of the executive, viz., the military, police, and civil service) , and in foreign affairs a policy directed to revision of the ruinous peace. The revision would hopefully be effected by talks with the Entente in the belief that reason would convince the Allies to reduce demands impossible to fulfill, and bring assistance in the form of foreign credits. But Hergt made it clear, finally, that he was speaking only of a hypothetical program to restore order and confidence in Germany. He actually saw no likelihood of its acceptance by the majority parties, nor of success with the Entente in the present state of relations. [42]

The reaction of Nationalists themselves to Hergt's speech was so mixed, but largely unfavorable, that the attitude of others was skeptical. Westarp took Hergt enough at his word to write Heydebrand that he feared Hergt might already have had talks with the Prussian government on the question of collaboration. The local organizations, and especially Pomerania, were for the most part critical of the program. The noises finally reached the state where the Socialist premier of Prussia, Paul Hirsch, on November 15 in the House accused the DNVP as a party of irresponsibility in refusing positive cooperation in the rebuilding of the country; Hergt's alleged desire for positive work had been overruled, he pointed out, by the Party's spirit of opposition. The premier's remarks hurt. As Westarp noted, "The catch phrases about refusing positive cooperation were cleverly calculated to affect a voting population that was inclined to believe the DNVP could gain more successes in Parliament if it gave up the fight against the con-

[42] *Ibid.*, cols. 4402-8.

stitutional system. That attitude was frequently to play a role in the internal quarrels of the Party." [43]

Impelled to answer the wave of criticism that hit him on all sides, Hergt clarified his position in the Prussian Assembly in December by outlining, first of all, four points under which the Nationalists would always be prepared for positive cooperation. Thus the DNVP would always support the government against the external enemy as well as against the internal one, and would help it especially to maintain law and order. It would never cause obstruction for its own sake, but only where needed on matters of vital interest for the nation. The DNVP would cooperate in committees to improve draft laws and budgets. But that was the extent to which it could promise regular cooperation. Otherwise it reserved the right to fulfill its duty as a critical parliamentary opposition. Hergt referred to practical proposals already made by the DNVP, which belied the charge of irresponsibility: a corporative parliament, limited co-determination of workers and profit-sharing, a forced loan (instead of Erzberger's capital levy), and his own *Ordnungsprogramm* which the majority parties had ignored or misconstrued.

At this point Hergt shed some light on his intentions. The program had not represented a bid for entry into the present government: "No, the *Ordnungsprogramm* says something else. It challenges the left to give up the unhappy system of unemployment compensation in its present form. It asks them to abandon extreme emphasis on the factory council system. It asks them to give up socialistic experimentation and schematic regulation of working hours in favor of any system, whether piecework or any other that would allow planning for maximum production within regular working hours, yet also permit overtime. It asks them to waive strikes. It asks for protection of those

[43] W MS, p. 541.

willing to work and for enforcement of the authority of the state. . . . We, for our part, have also had to make sacrifices in our ideas for the sake of this program." [44]

In Hergt's interpretation of his original speech the key word had become *Verzicht*, i.e., of *sine qua non* concessions expected from the Social Democrats. It makes little difference whether that emphasis was Hergt's original intention or the result of three months of pressure inside the Party. When it comes to cases, it is hard to see where any fundamental Nationalist concessions are involved. It just happened that the views of the leadership were somewhat more imaginative than those of many in the rank and file. Hergt, in proposing a movement to bridge social and regional differences, seemed to count on the formation of a Nationalist working class, one that would be free of extreme class consciousness and that rejected ideas of class struggle and internationalism. Such nationally minded workers in all parties could form the basis of a great patriotic bloc with which the DNVP would gladly cooperate in or out of government. In this Hergt appeared in perfect agreement with his Party's Christian Socialists.

His belief in a comprehensive movement also went far in the direction of full democratic suffrage. "The DNVP," he announced, "stands for universal equal, direct and secret suffrage, female suffrage, and proportional representation today, tomorrow, and forever." [45] But in the same December speech Hergt introduced by the back door the subject of monarchy. "There is no talk of reactionary monarchy. We want popular, social-minded monarchy" [46]—another idea close to Christian Socialist hearts. Hergt made clear that such an idea could never win by force. It could be realized only by legal means such as a referendum, and the time for that was not yet ripe. Finally Hergt, despite the

[44] Prussian Debates, Dec. 15, 1919, vol. 7, cols. 8114-5.
[45] *Ibid.,* col. 8118.
[46] *Ibid.,* col. 8119.

presence of some centralizers in the DNVP, reaffirmed the federalist standpoint of the Nationalist Party as a whole.

What did it all mean? What was left of the *Ordnungsprogramm*? Certainly Hergt's speeches were overtures for cooperation with the political center and even left, but only under special conditions that were hardly possible. But, more important, the unrest and confusion in the DNVP that resulted demonstrated the Party's need still to find itself. It still lacked a clear official and extensive platform to serve as an acceptable guide for all shades of Nationalist belief. [47]

The actual work of preparing the Nationalist platform began in September, 1919, and lasted until April following, when the Executive finally adopted the formal principles of the DNVP (*Grundsätze der Deutschnationalen Volkspartei*) that remained basic until the Party dissolved in 1933. In form it was not far different from the appeal used in the first election.

Both platforms began with preambles that outlined an idealistic goal. But while the earlier platform was dominated by the crushing fact of a lost war and internal chaos, and its keynote was defense of society against the Revolution, in the definitive platform of 1920 the preamble was much in the tone of Hergt's speeches. The weakness and misfortune of the empire were alluded to as well as its greatness. Patriotic and Christian ideals were held as standards for the social and economic aims of a productive nation united in a feeling of common responsibility, reconciling labor and capital. Not much change from the Party's first statements was noted under those items that touched the usual subjects of national integrity, social and economic policy. Notable alterations were apparent on the topics of constitutional form and cultural emphasis, changes that reflected not only a relaxation of the uncertainty of the im-

[47] W MS, pp. 133, 136, 141-2.

mediate revolutionary period but a tendency for Conservative and Racist elements gradually to assert their position.

Conservative influence was brought most directly to bear through the person of Count Westarp on the composition of the first twelve points of the platform under the section headed "People and State." Here Westarp was able to get adequate recognition of the idea of the organic state. [48] He pressed also for an item against the Versailles Treaty, which Free Conservatives opposed as dangerous *revanchisme*. [49] Westarp claimed his policy was not motivated by revenge but by the concept of *irredenta*. With that argument he obtained Nationalist acceptance of his draft, except that his reference to "stolen territory" was replaced by "severed German lands." The goal of a policy of liberation, as the Conservative representatives saw it, was eventually the elimination of the Versailles Treaty. But since the DNVP could not ignore obligation under international law to carry out the treaty's provisions as long as it was in force, the Party officially called only for alteration of the treaty. Reference to the "forced Peace of Versailles" became, in the final version, simply the "treaty."

In Westarp's draft there was purposely no mention made of the colonies, these having never aroused the enthusiasm of strict Prussian Conservatives. The suggestion from other circles that the colonies be included he had perforce to accept. Nor was mention made in the Westarp draft of *Anschluss* with Austria. Westarp was no particular friend of *Anschluss,* although on occasion he would recognize it as a popular demand within the Party. The inclusion of *Anschluss* in the program resulted from a motion of Gottfried Traub which Westarp managed to get watered down considerably from the original. [50]

[48] W MS, p. 219.
[49] Especially Kardorff and v. d. Osten.
[50] W MS, pp. 223-7.

The important constitutional question was the Party's attitude toward the monarchy. Though it was taken for granted that some sort of theoretical affirmation of monarchist belief would have to be made, the mood within the Party was opposed to an unambiguous identification with Hohenzollern restoration. The Free Conservatives through Kardorff were not the only ones to recall the ill will left by the emperor, to condemn his flight from the country, and to blame the November collapse at least partly on him. The younger Nationalists wanted only a general affirmation of royalist sympathy, while Hergt and Christian Socialist spokesmen attempted definitions of a "popular" or "social monarchy." These points of view were, of course, abhorrent to the Old Conservatives whom Westarp represented. The latter wanted a constitutional monarchy as existed in the empire, but in no circumstances a democratic parliamentary monarchy on the British or Scandinavian model. They wanted a clear affirmation that "we believe firmly in the German Imperial Crown and in the Prussian monarchy of the Hohenzollerns." For them there was no Germany without Prussia. They had little interest in the restoration of the score of dynasties that had been displaced regionally; but rather than qualify the monarchist question in any way Westarp wholly supported the principle of legitimacy when regional qualifications were discussed in executive sessions. Not successfully, since it was decided that each state should be free to decide its own constitutional form. [51]

Through the procedure of submitting drafts and counterdrafts Westarp originally managed to influence, to a small degree at least, the wording of the Nationalist platform. Even that amount of Prussian Conservative influence was not long in provoking a reaction in the *Hauptvorstand,* partly from Free Conservatives and partly from members representing non-Prussian states. The objections were to

[51] W MS, pp. 227-32.

some extent to the Hohenzollern monarchy itself, but for the most part (as in the case of Kardorff) due to fear of political repercussions should the Party openly call for restoration. Thus the following ambiguous wording was put into the principles: "In the Reich we are striving for a renewal of the monarchy erected by the Hohenzollerns." In practice the supposed lack of clarity did not hurt the Prussian Conservatives and their cause, despite their fears. Only knowledge of the internal debate in the Party would have made the ambiguities apparent to the public. Shades of meaning and stylistic niceties in the platform did not prevent resolute campaigners from expressing the full force of their convictions in public. The Nationalist Party for all its hesitation on the point stood almost alone in its monarchist conviction, and its willingness to speak up on the subject. Stresemann's DVP alluded to the monarchy in vaguer terms, with no mention of either Hohenzollerns or Prussia, and the more the party got involved in government the more the monarchist principle receded for them into the background. [52]

The Free Conservatives found little support in the Party for their views on a strong central government. Westarp's original draft was, contrary to theirs, strictly federalist in nature, but the definitive version was a compromise from the Party Bureau that left a distinctly federalist impression. [53]

Westarp found some solace for his many disappointments in other areas by the extent to which the DNVP defended the integrity of Prussia. The DNVP's position on the question was here determined largely by the vigorous intervention of the *Fraktion* in the Prussian House. Although not included in the 1920 platform, a special Prussian Program of the DNVP was issued for the Prussian elections which

[52] W MS, pp. 233-7.
[53] W MS, p. 238.

[87]

strongly affirmed attachment to the Prussian kingdom and the federal nature of the German state.

The sharpest divergence within the Nationalist Party at the time existed on the question of anti-Semitism. To the Free Conservatives anti-Semitism was as distasteful as for the Racists it was the *sine qua non* of all policy. For such opposite viewpoints there could be no common ground. But most other groups within the DNVP either had a tradition of anti-Semitism or a tolerance in that direction, though not usually to the extent of questioning, as did the extremists, the right of Jews to national citizenship. Thus in Westarp's draft anti-Semitism was implied as a corollary to the protection and furthering of German nationality. Since this turned out to be hardly adequate for the political Racists, Westarp was willing to extend the Conservative position on this matter by attacking the "predominance of Jews in government and public life," and demanding a ban on Jewish immigration from the East. Although the Party turned down the draft of the extreme Racists, the modified wording of the Nationalist program left little doubt about the Party's general anti-Semitic sympathies. Westarp regretted the caution of the DNVP on the subject: "Item nine of the principles originally was a declaration of war without detailed explanation against 'every disruptive un-German spirit, be it of Jewish or any other origin.' That formula was altered more than pleased me and more than was good for the unity of the Party in order to accommodate that element in the DNVP that was pressing for the greatest possible reserve in the Jewish question. The anti-Semitic program in number eleven of the principles also remained essentially defensive in character." [54]

Regarding the platform as a whole, one should not exaggerate its importance over tactics and political realities

[54] W MS, p. 246.

that changed from year to year. It did serve the purpose of helping the Nationalist Party establish its character in its own and in the public mind. It helped the variety of Nationalists overcome even major differences on some controversial subjects. Westarp as a Conservative was reasonably satisfied, Christian Socialists were gratified by frequent mention of their social and economic goals. Least satisfied were Free Conservatives and Racists, both of whom were unable to get adequate recognition for viewpoints on the centralism and anti-Semitism which they respectively regarded as their *raison d'être.*

One cannot learn much about party history from studying the record of parliamentary debates alone. The heart of the DNVP was not its *Fraktion* but its Executive. Hergt in a way snubbed the new constitutional system by taking a seat in the Prussian Assembly rather than in the National Assembly. Actually that was a tactical error since it kept him away from the major scene of daily battle, especially when the National Assembly met at Weimar during the formulation of the Constitution.

In the National Assembly, as a result of the type of candidate offered to the electorate, very few of the Nationalist members had had previous parliamentary experience. Thus out of forty-two deputies eight were formerly Conservative, two Free Conservative, three Christian Social, and three Racist members of the Reichstag; the other twenty-six were newcomers to Parliament, unfamiliar with its procedure, and for the most part silent during the debates. Yet the DNVP benefited by the presence of a number of men who had been high officials in the empire and prominent in public life. Such a personality was the elder statesman, Arthur von Posadowsky-Wehner, who was chosen to be leader for the Party in the National Assembly. [55] Since

---

[55] Dietrich (DKP) and Delbrück (FC) also ran, the latter supported especially by the Christian Socialists.

Posadowsky had been one of the strongest advocates of social measures in the empire, his election was welcomed by the Christian Socialists. A minority questioned whether an elder statesman had the qualities necessary for leadership. For those who believed in the necessity of the sharpest political opposition Posadowsky was both too old and too non-partisan for the job. This party of the sharp opposition was still cautious in the Assembly, but was already apparent in the persons of Albrecht von Graefe, Alfred Hugenberg, Gottfried Traub, and Kaethe Schirmacher, persons from the camps of Racism, National Liberalism, *Vaterlandspartei,* and Pan-German League. [56]

Under the direction of Posadowsky the tone of intransigence was generally reserved for the subject of foreign affairs, whereas a surprisingly moderate character was shown in domestic matters. The moderate tone was sustained by men who spoke frequently like Clemens von Delbrück, Adalbert Düringer, and Reinhard Mumm. Delbrück and Düringer in particular worked actively, honestly, and usually unpolemically in the committee that drafted the democratic republican constitution, presenting their views as an objective parliamentary opposition. [57] The moderation was more apparent than real; differences smouldered behind the scenes in the DNVP that reduced the show of moderation to the level of play-acting. [58]

On more technical questions affecting the economic and social development of the nation there were also inevitable

[56] Schroeter to Heydebrand, in W MS, p. 212; Annelise Schulz, *Die Stellungnahme der deutschnationalen Volkspartei zu den Problemen der Sozialpolitik* (Rostock, 1927), p. 66; Graefe to Westarp, July 6, 1919, in W MS, p. 213; Graef, p. 26; Düringer, quoted in *Deutsche Stimmen,* Aug. 20, 1922.

[57] Reich Debates, *Anlagen,* vol. 336, no. 391, *Bericht des Verfassungsausschusses,* 2nd Session, March 5, 1919, p. 25; cf. also, *National-liberale Correspondenz,* April 24, 1920; *Berliner Tageblatt,* June 3, 1925 (A.M.).

[58] W MS, p. 238.

differences in the Party. The first breach of outer unity came in the vote on a bill to regulate the coal industry which the Nationalist *Fraktion* rejected, except for the Christian Socialist members. The internal struggle within the *Fraktion* still was kept strictly confidential. [59] But many other breaches of unanimity occurred on many levels— tactical, economic, and ideological. An example was the position taken on the matter of military suffrage by Graefe. He believed it would be unjust to deprive the twelve-year volunteers in the newly constituted *Reichswehr* of the right to vote. On the other hand, Posadowsky warned against the danger of a political army: "An army will always indulge in politics if it participates in elections." [60]

On occasion the small sharp opposition wing was allowed to perform a useful function for the *Fraktion* by spearheading an attack on policy. Hugenberg struck the main note of defiance against Matthias Erzberger's financial policies which he denounced as disastrous. Erzberger's work did much to sharpen the opposition of the DNVP in general. There had already been much resentment of his activity in the direction of economic and political democracy and of supposed appeasement of the Entente. Glowering resentment was suddenly raised to the level of furious attack by Erzberger's proposal of a capital levy. Though the Nationalists professed willingness to accept a forced loan, they never forgave him the unheard-of measure of a capital levy which was repugnant to their every belief in the sanctity of private property.

Keith Feiling remarked of British parties that "the size of modern electorates, the power of party machines, and the velocity of their turning wheels multiply all the perennial chances of friction and have weighted still more the

[59] Reich Debates, March 8, 1919, vol. 326, p. 570 (Hugenberg); p. 586 (Wallbaum); March 13, 1919, vol. 327, p. 772 (Wallbaum); *Sozialisierungsgesetz*, March 23, 1919; W MS, p. 408.

[60] Reich Debates, April 22, 1920, vol. 333, pp. 5347-8.

power of personality." [61] The remark is also apt for the politics of modern Germany. In the case of the German National People's Party the "perennial chances of friction" were augmented all the more by the disparity of the interests which a single political structure was supposed to accommodate in harmony. In the first year of its existence no great achievement of leadership was noted. Neither Hergt nor Posadowsky were men who dominated, or who could persuade the components of the DNVP completely to merge. Examination of the Party's year of organization and consolidation has shown how uneasy was the internal balance of the DNVP, and how unsatisfactory was the basis for its future development as a political party, let alone as a mass movement of the right. In the first year the Nationalist Party as concept and reality was far from its ideal.

As Conservative influence increased in the Party councils, the Free Conservative group found itself losing ground on all essential points of policy. The Free Conservative voice in Parliament was prominent to a degree it was unable to retain in the inner Party circles. The Racists were pleased by this development, but uneasy still about the restraint placed on their own role in the Party. The Christian Socialists felt more secure, but were less than satisfied by the lukewarm reception of their social views by the dominant middle-class groups in the Party. Nor were the opposition activists (mainly northwest German National Liberals, Pan-Germans, and *Vaterlandsparteiler*) happy at the soft trend in party tactics, even though they enjoyed considerable freedom of expression on important matters like foreign affairs and economic policy. Still, they could expect their influence to grow at the expense of the moderate Free Conservative elements. The Party had its platform and program; what it would represent in the Republic awaited the test of action and crisis.

[61] Keith Feiling, "British Parties: Some Reflections on Their History," in *University of Toronto Quarterly* XIX (1950), pp. 213-8.

IV
Right Radicalism: The Kapp Putsch

In the first unsettled years after the Revolution the Weimar Republic was assailed internally by armed movements from the left and right to an extent that often locally approached civil war. The initial disturbances from the left were overcome by the government with the cooperation of the army and the help of the Free Corps. Oriented almost exclusively to the right but unhampered by party alliances, the Free Corps as a movement typified the idea of political activism, authoritarian and devoted to ideals of force and élitism, a middle-class but anti-bourgeois movement inspired with utter contempt for parliamentary democracy. [1]

In that atmosphere grew the threat to the Republic of right-radical terrorism, demonstrated in a campaign of assassination that eventually claimed two of the new state's notables, Walther Rathenau and Matthias Erzberger. There seemed ample justification for the cry that arose in Parliament, in the press, and in the streets that "the enemy is on the right! (*Der Feind steht rechts!*) " [2] It became general belief that the DNVP, if not the whole political right, was implicated in a conspiracy against the Constitution.

[1] On Free Corps literature see Robert G. L. Waite, *Vanguard of Nazism* (Cambridge, Mass., 1952) and Harold J. Gordon, Jr., *The Reichswehr and the German Republic* (Princeton, 1957).

[2] Scheidemann in Reich Debates, Oct. 7, 1919, vol. 330, p. 2886. The expression was also used by writers of *Freiheit* during the street fighting of December, 1918, to refer to the Majority Socialists. The current usage of the term was due mainly to Chancellor Wirth.

DNVP

Oskar Hergt's *Ordnungsprogramm,* though it offered to extend cooperation of the DNVP as far left as the Socialists, lapsed almost as soon as it was spoken. Not only was it controversial within the Party, but it was not enough of a compromise to interest the SPD. [3] Nevertheless, talk about cooperation with the left did not quite stop; it continued through the spring of 1920. Like Stresemann and the DVP, Free Conservatives did not rule out the possibility of a coalition with the Socialist party, and the question recurred during the election campaign in June. Those who were shocked by the suggestion, particularly Conservatives, were glad that the SPD for its part showed no desire to cooperate with the right. Westarp blamed Stresemann for introducing the subject gratuitously, and creating thereby a needless subject of dissension. [4]

Racists were also restive in the spring of 1920, as was seen in a leaflet printed in April by the *Deutschvölkischer Arbeitsring* that called for a united front on the Racist issue and complained of the weak position of the DNVP. At the same time the DNVP was recognized as still the only Party that could lead the fight against Jewry successfully from within Parliament. For that reason the organization pressed the Party leadership to place a number of leading Racists on its election lists in favorable positions: "If, contrary to expectation, the Party leadership should not meet these just demands, then it will be impossible, judging by all our observations to date, to keep our numerous colleagues in the Party." [5]

Though the atmosphere of unrest in the state was unmistakable, the initiative in counter-revolution did not

[3] Reich Debates, June 28, 1920, vol. 344, p. 33; *Kzztg.,* Dec. 1, 1921 (P.M.); Westarp in Reich Debates, Oct. 28, 1920, vol. 345, p. 839.

[4] W MS, pp. 543, 550, 556, 557.

[5] WP: note signed by Richard Kunze-Friedenau (editor, *Deutsches Wochenblatt*), Dr. Arnold Ruge-Heidelberg (university lecturer), and Reinhold Wulle-Berlin (a director of the *Deutsche Zeitung*).

come from obviously restive elements like Conservatives and Racists. The major *coup d'état* directed against the Republican government, the Kapp putsch of March, 1920, originated rather in circles close to the former Fatherland party. Yet, as a result, the whole political right seemed involved by guilt of association. The accusations of conspiracy struck heavily on the DNVP and, to a lesser extent, the DVP. They were based on evidence that men of these parties took part in the putsch actively, or passively by not revealing advance knowledge of the plans, and that many others welcomed the Kapp "government" openly, or were ambiguous as they waited to see which way the wind blew. The Nationalist Party seemed wide open to Chancellor Gustav Bauer's accusations made in the fugitive National Assembly in Stuttgart: "The whole people has arisen and placed itself behind the government, calling in one voice for arms in the fight against Nationalist reaction, against the East Elbian Junkers, and against the officer caste who brought us into this difficult situation. . . . Who is behind the putsch? The Pan-Germans, the adherents of the former Fatherland party, a part of the DNVP and its press, Colonel Bauer and General Ludendorff. . . . We shall have to examine in particular the role played by the Pomeranian *Landbund* in the revolt." [6]

New Chancellor Hermann Müller eleven days later amplified the attack with a masterful summary of the situation as it was then apparent. He referred to statements of March 13 in which the DNVP and DVP presumably indicated their official attitude toward the Kapp régime. In them there was not a word of criticism to be found, nor any indication of the unconstitutional character of the violent move. At the same time they accused the legal government itself of unconstitutional procedure in the postponing of elections. The chancellor cited Westarp's article in favor

[6] Reich Debates, March 18, 1920, vol. 332, pp. 4902, 4904.

of the putsch that was printed in the *Kreuzzeitung*. Instigators of the putsch, the chancellor claimed, were mostly
members of the DNVP, including Wolfgang Kapp (a member of the Nationalist Central Executive), Kurt von Kessel
(Nationalist member of the Prussian Assembly), Gottfried
Traub (Nationalist member of the National Assembly),
Traugott von Jagow, Georg Wilhelm Schiele, and Hans
Freiherr von Wangenheim. Only after it had become evident that the Kapp "government" could not establish itself did the DNVP and DVP show signs of returning to
support of the Weimar Constitution. Though some leading
men in both parties did condemn the putschists from the
beginning, even now the DNVP had not officially uttered a
word of blame. Meanwhile the Nationalist press praised the
instigators and called for a general amnesty for them.
Numerous Nationalist local organizations had openly supported Kapp, including the Farmers' League of Schleswig-
Holstein and the DNVP of Central Silesia. "You did not
conjure up the misfortune on our Fatherland openly and
as a Party, but rather in secret and despite your official
condemnation of all violent undertakings. Count von
Posadowsky, who made your declaration, and numerous
others no doubt stand on the ground of that condemnation. The blood guilt of the fatal March weeks strikes that
wing of your Party which formed around the renegade
Traub, that man who organized the putsch even among our
university youth. . . . The blame falls on the demagogues of
Nationalist agitation, creators of the poisonous atmosphere
in which the madness of this putsch could originate." [7]

The parliamentary defense against these attacks was
offered by two honest and respected individuals, both of
them South Germans: Heinrich Kraut of Württemberg
and Adalbert Düringer of Baden. Neither, incidentally, was
particularly influential in inner Party circles. Kraut in fact

[7] *Ibid.*, March 29, 1920, vol. 332, pp. 4935-6.

spoke up in Stuttgart on his own initiative in the absence
of contact with Berlin and the Party leadership, and presumed to dissociate the DNVP completely from the putsch:
"The German National People's Party strives for a change
in our internal relationships, as has been repeatedly and
authoritatively declared in recent days, only by constitutional means."[8] He was no doubt referring to Posadowsky
who had categorically condemned any resort to arms or
violence as "criminal stupidity." Back in Berlin, however,
Düringer provided a more substantial defense by bringing
to light a number of surprising facts. He related, in particular, that on March 8, Hans-Erdmann von Lindeiner-
Wildau, secretary of the Party (*Hauptgeschäftsführer*),
had first heard rumors of unrest in the army. Delegated by
Hergt, he brought his information to the attention of the
chief of Political Police in Prussia (who had also the title
of State Commissioner for Public Order), only to be told
that the authorities were already aware of the situation.
Düringer went on to stress that the instigators of the
putsch had played no role in the DNVP, adding that "Herr
Traub was not one of those who instigated the putsch, but
was rather one of those who jumped on the bandwagon."
Kapp himself had his own paper in Königsberg, *Deutsche
Aufgaben,* which constantly criticized the Nationalist *Fraktion.* Although Kapp had been delegated by the East
Prussian branch of the Party to attend the Central Executive, he never had been at a meeting. As for Traub, the
Party considered him automatically expelled the moment
he participated in the putsch. Düringer finally character-
ized Traub as a Pan-German and a founder of the Fatherland party: "I consider him to be a very fine human being,
though certainly a poor politician."[9]

It was true that the few Nationalists who participated in

[8] *Ibid.,* March 18, 1920, vol. 332, p. 4914.
[9] *Ibid.,* March 30, 1920, vol. 332, p. 4489.

the Kapp putsch were not influential in the Party, and that the DNVP did not approve of what they did, if only for tactical reasons. Gottfried Traub had been perhaps the most prominent of Nationalists in the implicated group, though it should be remembered that his prominence was due to the fact that he was a rare bird both as a Liberal and as a colorful person. In the Kapp "government" he had been at best peripheral as the "Minister of Church and Cultural Affairs."

To understand what had happened to Traub it is necessary to go back to his position in the Fatherland party. He had been present at the official liquidation of the Fatherland party at a special meeting of the National Committee on December 10, 1918. Traub had worked with Kapp in the Fatherland party, and the closeness of their relationship may be judged from the action of the three-man Liquidation Committee on which both men served. After making provision for outstanding obligations, the committee transferred all remaining assets of the Fatherland party to the Liberal Middle-Class Group of the DNVP in Berlin. [10]

Traub, who had been responsible for that group, entered the DNVP well known as a publicist and non-conformist clergyman. In the DNVP he had hoped to continue the reputation built up through the war years by his *Eiserne Blätter*. This small publishing venture had been resumed in July, 1919, with a Nationalist subsidy. [11] His personal relations with Kapp, now also a member of the DNVP, remained very close. They met with a group of political friends regularly for lunch. Traub has provided an account

[10] Wortmann, pp. 64-6.

[11] Traub put up 8,000 marks, and the Party 12,000 (paid February, 1920); Traub, p. 172. Traub mentions the end of May as the date of resumption of publication; a notice in *Deutsches Wollen* ("Mitteilungen der DNVP") I, 2 (June, 1919), p. 5, mentions the *Eiserne Blätter* for July 1, 1919, as a publication appearing "by agreement with the leadership of the DNVP."

of how he learned about the plot against the government
and how he became implicated:

Secretly Count Westarp also belonged to this circle. At the beginning of February, Kapp visited me in my office and asked
me whether I would take part in an undertaking to overthrow
the present government. Difficult as the decision was for me, I
had to decline. As a deputy of the DNVP I could not take part
in a move involving the use of force. (In taking this position I
did not yet know that the chairman of the DNVP, Hergt, as well
as the chairman of the DVP, Heinze, had been friendly to Kapp,
but had clearly turned down the idea of participation in such an
undertaking, both for themselves and for the parties they represented in the National Assembly.) Then he touched on the
question of a future Ministry of Church and Cultural Affairs
(*Kultusministerium*), and remarked that I could very well take
over such a job. Certainly that tempted me, but I informed him
that as Minister of Church Affairs I would be a considerable
liability to him and his whole undertaking. Among Lutherans I
was still, even today, an object of suspicion in right-wing circles,
and the Catholic church would certainly put difficulties in my
way, as would the Center party. . . . Shortly afterward I wrote
Kapp that he could naturally count on me if he should really
need me later on. Except that "I have never learned to shoot." [12]

Despite the apparent qualms, Traub did not hesitate to
make good his promise, and never later regretted the move
that caused him much political and personal hardship. On
the morning of the putsch he met General von Lüttwitz
and other members of the rebel "government." Present also
was Paul Bang of the Pan-German League who later talked
to Traub about the future school system. But he seemed
uneasy about the possible consequences that might arise
for the Kapp "government" as a result of the escape of the
previous government. Traub recorded a further development in the Pan-German attitude: "Unfortunately this
first day ended with a declaration of Bang that he could no

[12] Traub, p. 188.

longer participate in the undertaking because he believed it to be hopeless. I have never been able to figure out why the Pan-Germans, whose representative Bang was, were so unfriendly and even contemptuous in their attitude toward the undertaking." [13] When Düringer referred in Parliament to Traub as a Pan-German, the *Alldeutsche Blätter* hastened with the correction that Traub had never belonged to the ADV.

In contrast to the cautious and finally negative attitude of the Pan-Germans, many Old Conservatives were more openly sympathetic or even helpful in the Kapp undertaking. Conservative members of the former *Herrenhaus* had participated in the committee that drew up the counter-revolutionary program. And while in West Germany the reaction was almost uniformly hostile to Kapp, in the North and East there were at least a few signs of support. [14] Within the DNVP, Westarp was quietly in favor of the putsch, but Traub got nowhere with the Nationalist Executive, as he noted: "Unfortunately I was not able to dissuade the Party leadership from its reserved attitude. I clearly felt that Helfferich was even annoyed by the new developments because they obviously distracted attention from the doubtless great victory which he had won over Erzberger. It was the Party chairman Hergt above all, as I learned, who assumed a negative attitude in the interest of the Party's future and of its parliamentary representation. Fortunately I did not know that, in his monstrous concern for the Party, he had sent the Party secretary Herr von Lindeiner as early as March 9 to State Commissioner von Berger to report formally on rumors concerning the

[13] *Ibid.*, pp. 191, 193-4.

[14] *Ibid.*, p. 194; "From Hanover came Baron v. Wangenheim, the spiritual leader of the Farmers' League, bringing us a greeting from Hindenburg. That encouraged us as powerfully as did the appearance of Ludendorff on Saturday in the Chancellery building."

Ehrhardt Brigade and signs of a *coup d'état*." [15] The intellectual bankruptcy of the DNVP (from Traub's point of view) was further demonstrated by Posadowsky's comment on the same March 9 that any resort to force was "criminal stupidity," a phrase repeated by other Nationalist deputies including the Christian Socialist Mumm.

After Kapp's resignation from the counter-revolutionary movement, Traub prepared to flee: "I then sought out Hugenberg, and found him sick in bed at his house on the *Viktoriastrasse*. He was deeply shocked and remarked that if I had come to him earlier he would have warned me against participation." [16] Hugenberg agreed to look after Traub's family in his absence. And so Traub left the country with no feeling of having had even the moral support of his Party in the Kapp venture.

Traub felt on the whole betrayed by the Party despite isolated vocal support from individuals like Pastor Pfannkuche in the *Deutsche Zeitung* and Count Westarp in the *Kreuzzeitung*, or a resolution of sympathy from a local Nationalist group like the *Volksverein Berlin-Friedenau*. But Traub did receive support outside of the Party that made it possible for his *Eiserne Blätter* (circulation 6,000) to continue to appear even while he was wanted on charges of high treason. The support came from the Old Conservative circles of the *Herrenhaus* that sharply criticized the Nationalist leadership in May, 1920, for the arbitrary way in which it had publicly abandoned Traub. "They had got the Party leadership to agree not only to allow my publication to appear again, but also to allow me to express myself regularly in its columns." [17] Traub now dropped out of the national political scene permanently; when he returned from exile in Austria he worked as a publicist on a Hugenberg paper in Munich.

[15] *Ibid.*, p. 195.
[16] *Ibid.*, p. 200.
[17] *Ibid.*, p. 219.

The story so far tends to confirm the accusations by chancellors Bauer and Müller that the DNVP was implicated, at least indirectly, in the Kapp putsch. Although the Party officially professed the view that the whole was not responsible for the action of a few rowdy individuals, [18] or of some local Party units,[19] it was a difficult matter to refute responsibility for previous knowledge of the counter-revolutionary movement. That previous knowledge and the Party's indirect implication in the plot were much more extensive than the Party could safely admit, and indeed than even many members may have realized.

The official statement of the DNVP on March 14, the day after the putsch, was ambiguous and inconclusive. The Party's position was merely declared to be unchanged: it expected the government to restore constitutional conditions. But that meant also that the government would finally have to agree to hold an election within sixty days under the law of November 30, 1918. "Until that decision comes the DNVP, true to its normal policy, is ready to co-operate with all elements of the German people to assure peace and order, freedom and national honor." [20] As in the first great crisis, the November Revolution, the Party politicians of the right were instinctively concerned with self-preservation. Afraid to adopt the cause of the Kappists for fear of committing political suicide, the Party adopted an ostensibly neutral position for the sake of law and order. It was in this spirit that Hergt proposed that the government parties and the two parties of the right begin negotiations with Kapp and Lüttwitz for the re-establishment of constitutional conditions—surely a most considerate manner of treating with rebels.

[18] *Vorwürfe gegen die Deutschnationale Volkspartei und ihre Widerlegung* (Berlin, 1920), p. 15.

[19] Especially in East Prussia, Pomerania, Silesia; cf., *Berliner Tageblatt*, April 2 (A.M.), 3 (P.M.), and 16 (A.M.), 1919.

[20] *Kzztg.*, March 24, 1920 (A.M.).

When Kapp and Lüttwitz finally withdrew, the DNVP publicly blamed the whole affair on the "incompetent party government" of the Republic, because it had created the atmosphere of crisis in which the putsch was possible. Besides, the government had destroyed all possibility of peaceful negotiation for settlement by its irresponsible use of the Bolshevik weapon of the general strike. The strike particularly brought Nationalist condemnation. The fact that it had been called independently by the union leaders was unknown to most and overlooked by others in the spate of recriminations.

A statement of March 27 was intended to show that the right-wing parties had long warned General von Lüttwitz against the use of military action or a *coup d'état* as the means of obtaining redress of specific grievances in the army. This had supposedly happened repeatedly in a series of interviews following preliminary contact initiated by a high army officer on March 3. Lüttwitz had been assured that the parties of the right were pushing for new elections and eventually hoped to nominate Hindenburg as presidential candidate. After these assurances Lüttwitz appeared willing to negotiate peaceably through channels. "Under these circumstances," wrote the *Kreuzzeitung,* "any communication with the government would naturally have been superfluous because there was nothing illegal to report, nor was there anything to be taken seriously, nor even anything definite. The government was in any case directed and fully informed about the situation, through their liaison man of whom General von Lüttwitz had spoken." [21] The *Fraktionen* of both DNVP and DVP, having meanwhile learned of the threatening situation, threw their weights against any thought of military pressure to force early elections or any other concessions from the government. Then, although the parties knew of an interview

[21] *Kzztg.,* March 28, 1920 (A.M.); cf., Waite, p. 151.

scheduled between Lüttwitz and government representatives, they knew nothing of the outcome and assumed that the tension was eased. Thus the putsch and its consequences caught the parties of the right by surprise as much as the rest of the population. As a matter of fact, Kapp himself was surprised at the speed with which Lüttwitz moved after the unsatisfactory talk he had with President Friedrich Ebert and Defense Minister Gustav Noske on March 10. [22]

Despite such public utterances, it is interesting to note traces of evidence in the Westarp Papers that the leader of the Nationalist Party not only had early knowledge of the counter-revolutionary intentions of Kapp, but also approved of them in principle. The indications do not necessarily go beyond the implication of Traub's memoirs that Hergt and Kapp were friendly, but that Hergt for tactical reasons was against the use of violence. As early as October 27, 1919, Heydebrand mentioned in a letter to Westarp, "I have just had a talk with Hergt that was somewhat extended by its diffuseness. As for the point that concerned you and me recently, in the carriage in the *Tiergarten* [cover word for the impending Kapp undertaking]: in this we reached agreement, just as you and I did." [23] The attitude was one of approval tempered by realistic skepticism. Thus Heydebrand had written on the day of the putsch, "Buch, whom I visited the other night, showed himself, quite spontaneously, to be exactly informed on everything. In the matter itself he apparently shared our judgment, except that he thought momentary success would come easily and certainly." [24] Westarp prudently destroyed all his records relating to the Kapp putsch, and in later years looked on that remark as confirmation of his memory that Ernst von Heydebrand had not rejected the idea of a

[22] *Kzztg.*, March 24 (A.M.), May 29 (P.M.), 1920.
[23] W MS, pp. 99-100: Heydebrand to Westarp, Oct. 27, 1919.
[24] W MS, p. 79.

coup d'état on principle, only that his doubts concerning its success had been greater than Westarp's.

The fact is that Count Westarp had been personally heavily involved in the Kapp-Lüttwitz affair. "My relations," he wrote years later, "to the preparation and execution of the *coup d'état* planned by Kapp were closer than I allowed the public or even authoritative circles of the DNVP to know at that time, and closer than has been believed to date. After the failure of Kapp, I saw no reason to expose myself to the legal and violent attacks that were directed against the Kappists, or to the political persecution that would have excluded my person from further political activity and influence." [25] Certainly Westarp's role, minor though it was, remained a well-kept secret. It did not leak out during his period as leader of the DNVP from 1925 to 1928 when, even at that late date, the information would have seriously compromised him, his friends in public life, and the Nationalist Party. Such activity or even sympathies were still not to be entertained with impunity by men in public life.

Westarp was informed by Kapp in conversations during 1919 of plans to overthrow the government and constitution of the Republic. In January, 1920, he was invited to join an inner group concerned with drawing up a program and legislation for the counter-revolutionary "government." Westarp felt that much of the group's work was futile, and saw here an exaggeration of the German virtue of thoroughness. He was not opposed in principle to the use of force, but he expected a most careful appraisal of the possibility of success. [26]

The final events in the putsch took place without Westarp's knowledge or approval. He had already expressed his doubts on the suitability of the moment as

[25] W MS, p. 74.
[26] W MS, p. 78.

late as March 10. Nor did Westarp have any part in the talks with Hergt in the days before March 13, and knew of them only what Hergt cared to tell the Executive and inner Party circles. Westarp felt that the negative attitude of most of his colleagues was excessive. But, as he was not kept informed of measures being taken, he listened rather than talked at this period. [27]

Westarp had only a small and occasional part in liaison between the DNVP and the Kapp "government." But on March 16 he had a private conversation with General von Lüttwitz who asked him whether he might consider taking over the office of "chancellor" that Kapp had resigned. Westarp mainly confined his remarks to reminding the general of his duty, while he had power, to resist the Bolshevik disturbances that were breaking out in Berlin. He saw no use in becoming head of the revolutionary "government"; his name carried no weight with the parties and trade unions with which Lüttwitz had begun negotiations. The general did not repeat his offer. [28]

When the Kapp "government" collapsed the wave of recriminations began. The DNVP had to defend itself from the furious campaign directed against the political right in the following months. This was done at last by publicly dissociating the Party from the Kapp revolutionaries, and making clear the extent to which the DNVP had attempted to dissuade them. Westarp was almost alone in his public defense of the Kappists, though some others felt with him that the Party was going too far in disowning the counter-revolutionaries.

The aftermath of the Kapp putsch was unfortunate for the DNVP from every angle, whether seen from outside or from inside the Party. As Westarp remarked, "Personalities often had a more lasting effect on Party life than objective differences, and the disavowal of the Kappists long re-

[27] W MS, p. 99.
[28] W MS, p. 109.

mained a germ of dissension within the DNVP." [29] Nationalist tacticians moreover saw in the Kapp putsch an event that brought a serious setback to the progress of their Party toward the legal acquisition of power in the state. [30]

The problem of acquiring power in the state was not unrelated to the continued bad relations between Conservatives and Nationalists. The Conservatives managed to weather the storm of Nationalist attack against them in the spring of 1919, to maintain the identity of their Central Executive, and somewhat to increase their influence in the DNVP through the person of Count Westarp, even in the formulation of the Nationalist program. They were restive, dissatisfied with their repressed role, resentful of their unpopularity, outraged by the failure of the right to identify itself with Prussian values, and frustrated by their own impotence. No notion brought sharper critical reaction in Conservative circles than that of a "popular, social-minded monarchy" presented by Hergt as a corollary to his *Ordnungsprogramm*. But these differences were relegated to the background once the Party program was finally drawn up. [31] The big quarrels centered around more immediate, practical matters such as representation of Conservatives on the election lists and the continued separate identity of the Conservative party.

In the late summer of 1919, Westarp as a realist told Heydebrand that prospects were dim that the Conservatives would be able either to draw up their own lists in the next

[29] W MS, pp. 115, 117.

[30] Graef, p. 28. But cf. also, letter from v. Oldenburg to Kreth, dated at Januschau, Nov. 1, 1920, copy in WP: "The Kapp putsch, whose harm is certainly clear to us, has had the remarkable effect in *Kreis Rosenberg* of bringing a large number of Liberals (*Freisinnige*) into the DNVP. (I am not informed about the situation in other *Kreise*.) They joined with the explanation that Kapp at least had wanted order, as did they, whereas the others had proclaimed a general strike."

[31] W MS, p. 602.

election or, for that matter, increase their representation on the Nationalist lists. Possible allies in the Anti-Semites and Farmers' League seemed to him unreliable and likely to go their own way. The chief stumbling block to increasing Conservative representation on Nationalist lists continued to be the prejudice still present in the provincial organizations which headquarters could not coerce. The suggestion that Heydebrand be a candidate always met with the sharpest opposition. [32] Heydebrand himself privately turned down the idea that he run except in the greatest emergency, [33] but agreed to meet Hergt in October, 1919, at the latter's request.

The interview, the only one the two men ever had, did nothing to reduce the friction in Conservative-Nationalist relations. Hergt, who had hoped to obtain concessions from the DKP, was shocked to hear instead of the possibility of local Conservative groups in the future. He made it clear to Westarp, thereafter, that he could not be expected to support the nomination of Conservatives to places on the Nationalist list as long as there remained any question of a separate Conservative *Gruppenbildung,* that he would not tolerate retrogression to anything like the old German *Fraktion* in the empire. Westarp, who appreciated Hergt's candor, stressed to Heydebrand the importance of Hergt's cooperation in the matter of election lists. [34]

It was only after Westarp was able to assure him that the DKP no longer had the intention of pursuing the formation of local party groups that Hergt reconsidered the question of Conservative candidates on the Nationalist list. Hergt was also ready to discuss the possible candidature of some members of the Old Conservative *Herrenhausgruppe* with its representatitves, Count Behr and

[32] W MS, p. 94: Westarp to Heydebrand, Aug. 30, 1919.
[33] W MS, p. 97: Westarp to Heydebrand, Sept. 3, 1919.
[34] W MS, p. 103: Westarp to Heydebrand, Nov. 10, 1919.

Count Yorck. Their financial support in the coming election was at stake, but the talks ended abruptly with no result when the Independent Socialist newspaper *Freiheit*, by unknown means, got hold of Count Behr's briefcase and proceeded to publish correspondence and documents revealing the whole intention of the negotiations. The revelation apparently torpedoed the project; Hergt would not risk being permanently labeled a "lackey of the Junkers." [35] Hergt remained extremely sensitive to what he considered the harmful publicity caused by charges in the Populist (DVP), Democratic (DDP), and Centrist press that the Old Conservatives were gaining predominance in the DNVP. He leaned backwards to avoid that impression. Always he turned down the mere suggestion that Heydebrand be nominated on the Nationalist election list, even as a gesture. Similarly, despite Westarp's considerable efforts, attempts to get other Conservative nominations were successful only to a limited degree.

Westarp still kept himself relatively free of Nationalist Party entanglements despite all his activity, and declined notably the vice-chairmanship of the Executive that was offered him on October 12, 1919. Hermann Dietrich, who was re-elected instead at Westarp's suggestion, was ready to step aside in favor of Westarp whenever the latter was ready to accept. Both Dietrich and Hergt continued to try to win him to their point of view on specific questions. But Westarp had turned down the position so that he could freely fight for an election list acceptable to Conservatives, and also because of his uncertainty about the future line

[35] W MS, p. 104; *Freiheit*, Dec. 9, 1919 ("Der Junker Wiederkehr"), and Dec. 17, 1919 ("Hergt, der Lakai der Junker"). Cf. also, W MS, p. 362: "After the group failed to place its list of candidates, it chose as its special field of activity that of journalistic propaganda. Chief movers in that plan were Count Yorck and Steiniger. I acted as go-between and adviser in the talks concerning their financial and political participation in the *Eiserne Blätter* and *Tradition*."

[109]

of the DNVP under Hergt. [36] Immediate developments did little to encourage him.

Hergt and the Executive felt that two additional places at most could be made available to Conservatives. But only one of them could be a place with good prospects of election, and even that presupposed more votes than had been obtained in January, 1919. Through private channels Westarp and Heydebrand attempted to pressure the Nationalists in East Prussia to put the Conservative nominee Hermann Kreth in first place, and a nominee of the Farmers' League in second place. They tried also to convince the DKP organization in East Prussia to retain its separate identity, as had the Conservative organizations of Pomerania and Silesia, and to use its financial resources to influence the Nationalist nominations. Their efforts were a loss. The East Prussian Conservative organization used 500,000 marks of its dwindling funds for the *Ostpreussische Zeitung*; the 230,000 marks in its treasury were paid out gradually and unconditionally to the East Prussian branch of the DNVP that was turning down the nominees of the Central DKP. The local Nationalists were backed by Hergt who was anxious to keep Franz Behrens in East Prussia where he was organizing agricultural workers into a Christian Socialist union. [37]

If Westarp did not end up with a sure place in the Republic's second general election, that at least was an improvement over the first election when he had no place. Actually he was second on the list for Potsdam II, below Racist publicist Reinhold Wulle. It is interesting to follow the events that brought him the nomination.

In the autumn of 1919 two electoral districts with which he had earlier connections in his civil service career, Pomerania and Teltow-Beeskow-Charlottenburg (the later Potsdam II), made tentative offers to place him on their elec-

[36] W MS, pp. 99, 106.
[37] W MS, pp. 108-9.

tion lists. "Personally I would have preferred to accept Pomerania," wrote Westarp, "because that Conservative-agrarian electoral district, a fortress of the Old Conservative party, corresponded more to the lines of my political past than did the new territory of Berlin suburbs." [38] The offer from Pomerania however had been made only by a segment of the DNVP consisting of leading Conservatives who hoped thereby to prevent the nomination of the well-known economist, Karl Helfferich, whom they disliked for his connection with the Bethmann government. But Westarp did not wish to assist the opposition to Helfferich, whom he regarded as a brilliant anti-republican Liberal. When difficulties in Pomerania threatened the Helfferich nomination, Westarp deferred by deciding to run in Potsdam II. Hergt, meanwhile, for tactical reasons, was urging that decision on him also. [39]

In Potsdam II a prospective Helfferich nomination was also causing difficulties, not least because the party Anti-Semites distrusted his close connections with big business. Westarp's nomination would serve there to satisfy the needs of the farthest right opposition and also of the Racists. It would admirably complement the candidacy of Gottfried Traub, and, moreover, through another train of circumstances circumvent a feminist problem. The women, strong in the Potsdam II organization, had warned that if Helfferich ran in their district they would demand second place on the list for a woman. Hergt promised to find Westarp another reasonably sure place (either on the Reich list or in another district) as reinsurance. That was his courtesy to a candidate exchanging a sure first place in Pomerania for a questionable second place in Potsdam II, where he might expect opposition to run high against a Conservative nobleman.

But Westarp's situation changed considerably in the

[38] W MS, p. 191.
[39] W MS, p. 196: Hergt to Westarp, Nov. 28, 1919.

next weeks. The Pomeranian alternative, which had been only a minority offer, was withdrawn by the majority. Helfferich solved his own problems; owing to great personal popularity following the Erzberger trial, he suddenly had a wide range of districts to choose from. Traub was, of course, dropped from first place on the list after the Kapp putsch, and replaced by Reinhold Wulle of the *Deutsche Zeitung,* who had the support of the large group of Racists in the district. When Potsdam II officially offered second place to Westarp on April 14, he accepted and ran there, but without the reinsurance that Hergt had promised when he still had the alternative of Pomerania. [40] Westarp had a revealing comment on his own nomination: "I was and am hardheaded enough to assume that they did not attach all that importance to my nomination as a candidate because of my personal qualities—in any case, not for that reason alone. It was apparent that they hoped to tie the Conservatives to the DNVP through my person." [41]

This feeling was pointed up by a renewal of the attack against the Conservative party. It was taken up again within the DNVP after the Kapp putsch suddenly released the pent-up resentment that had been accumulating since the earlier negotiations on the Party program and nominations. The crisis was precipitated immediately after the Kapp putsch by Christian Socialist union leaders from Western Germany who demanded that the Party dissociate itself explicitly from *Landbund* and other non-union organizations. A committee was appointed to consider the demand, and appeared to disappear in limbo. [42] Then, on April 7, tension was renewed in the Inner Executive when Christian Social spokesmen claimed that Conservative-agrarian candidates were gaining too much prominence in

[40] W MS, pp. 196-200.
[41] W MS, p. 205.
[42] W MS, p. 116: Westarp to Heydebrand, March 25, 1920.

the election lists. At that time Westarp was able to retort that Christian Socialists held the edge in nominations over Conservatives by at least six nominees to the latters' four. On the ninth the Christian Socialists presented the Executive a resolution similar to one of the previous year calling for dissolution of all organizations of the original constituent parties of November, 1918. Westarp informed Hergt in answer to his question that, though he could not accept the resolution, he also would not consider it to be a declaration of war against the DKP. The resolution was then passed, but it was simultaneously decided not to publish it. [43]

At the same time the Party definitively denied any right of counter-revolution, and was anxious to make that feeling public for reasons never entirely clear to Westarp. He felt that sincere attachment to the Weimar Constitution was only rarely the case. If the Kapp putsch had succeeded, he would not have expected opposition to it from the Nationalists. "Decisive factors in the attitude of the DNVP," he felt, "were probably tactical considerations. The Party particularly had to defend itself against the election slogan of the opposition that was warning the public of the enemy on the right." [44] The Party felt strongly enough on the question to insist on unanimity; Westarp felt coerced, but went along in the vote, and then explained it away in the *Kreuzzeitung*. [45]

The session on April 9 was further embittered by a resolution of Siegfried von Kardorff, Count Kanitz, and Otto Hoetzsch calling on the Old Conservative elements either to be absorbed by the DNVP or to leave it. Hoetzsch had told Westarp about the resolution in advance, and many times earlier stated that the nobility and other Old Conservatives would have to fit themselves without reservations

[43] W MS, pp. 116-9.
[44] W MS, p. 119.
[45] *Kzztg.*, April 18, 1920; W MS, pp. 124-5.

into the pattern of the new Nationalist Party and the circumstances of the Republic. After the *Kreuzzeitung* defended the Kapp rebels, Hoetzsch strongly protested to the newspaper, and warned that he could no longer work on it unless he could express an opposite view in its columns. He warned also that tension in the Nationalist Executive might soon have to be resolved by the secession from the Party, either of the Conservative group around Westarp, or the larger Christian Socialist group around Behrens. When the attacks came, however, they were made not on the basis of the Kapp putsch, but on the issue of continued separate identity.

Though the atmosphere had been poisoned by the bitterness of the feelings concerning Kapp, the Kardorff-Kanitz-Hoetzsch resolution was concerned primarily with the refusal of the Conservative party to dissolve. Westarp was temporarily able to overcome most objections with a declaration that the DKP would support the DNVP unconditionally and entirely through the coming elections. But for the future he could give no guarantee. Still, he left the meeting with a feeling of optimism. Though the resolution had not been withdrawn, it seemed likely to fail. The next day, in fact, he had reason to exult as he wrote Heydebrand, "The Kardorff-Kanitz-Hoetzsch wing, the one noted for its pressure for participation in a government coalition and its rejection of all Conservatives, has experienced a severe setback according to prevailing opinion. I have just heard that Kardorff has gone over to the DVP." The majority in the Executive seemed for once to be with Westarp, though differences with the unions remained serious. "Thus," he concluded, "the pull toward the right is not completely feeble in the Party. Elements that might be ready to go along with us in spite of all are at hand in considerable numbers." [46]

[46] W MS, p. 120: Westarp to Heydebrand, April 10 and 15, 1920.

The trend to the right had in no small measure been stimulated by the skillful maneuvers of Westarp who possessed a fine sense of compromise in purely internal Party matters. His differences with the Nationalist leadership at times had gone as far as they could without excluding him from the Party. But he decided to remain in the DNVP and to keep it strong for joint Conservative-Nationalist action. This decision drew upon him the displeasure of Heydebrand whose dislike of Hergt and his policies grew steadily, and who felt Westarp was insufficiently critical of the DNVP. Westarp found himself in an uncomfortable crossfire in the period from October, 1919, through June, 1920. While most Nationalists on the one side pressed for dissolution of the DKP, on the other Heydebrand wanted to call the Committee of Fifty to reaffirm Conservative independence.

Fortunately for Westarp, it took a long time to get that committee together. Since most Conservatives in the Berlin area were in favor of dissolving the DKP, the meeting was postponed until travel difficulties for more distant members could be overcome. A meeting scheduled for March 23 was canceled owing to the dislocation of travel and communications caused by the Kapp putsch. When the Committee of Fifty finally did get together on May 11, 1920, on Heydebrand's initiative it passed a basic resolution expressing confidence in the leadership, determination to continue independent existence "as an unconditional political necessity," and explicit support of the DNVP in the coming election. At Westarp's request, in line with Hergt's procedure in the Nationalist Executive, publication was withheld to prevent possible friction and further misunderstanding. Westarp personally communicated the resolution to Hergt, who made no objection. [47]

The Conservatives thus held their own in the controversy

[47] W MS, pp. 130, 133.

that followed the Kapp putsch. Though Hoetzsch was not quite satisfied with Westarp's position, he withdrew the offending resolution in the Nationalist Executive. Similarly Westarp on his part acted to prevent a breach with Hoetzsch, a longtime collaborator on the *Kreuzzeitung*, by preventing the newspaper's board from acting on Heydebrand's request that it cease to employ Hoetzsch. [48]

The fact is that, with the election of Westarp to the Reichstag on June 6, 1920, the possibility that the DKP might re-emerge into active political life was practically ended. The differences that resulted between Heydebrand and Westarp in consequence were not on questions of ultimate goals but, for the most part, on questions of tactics. Westarp realized early that unity within the DNVP could last only while the Party concentrated primarily on its mission as national opposition against the republican system, and that the danger of permanent ruptures would become serious once an opportunity for positive work permitted intrinsic differences of viewpoint and method to emerge in the Party councils. Westarp did not want the minority strength of the right to be dissipated by unnecessary division in the ranks. While some Conservatives still felt that the DNVP was not capable of really fulfilling the tasks of the political right, Westarp himself was growing into the DNVP and came to see in it the instrument for accomplishing National-Conservative ends. [49] The Nationalist leadership for its part made concessions that did not necessarily come easy in encouraging Westarp's integration in the Nationalist Party.

The decision of Hergt to back Westarp implied in effect his choice between the Old Conservative and the Free Conservative element in the DNVP. The crisis brought on by the Kapp putsch led to the Party's first split. Although

---

[48] W MS, p. 131: Heydebrand to Westarp, April 15, 1920: "The man is not one of us."

[49] W MS, pp. 139-40.

the Christian Socialists first resumed the quarrel with the Old Conservatives, it was the Free Conservatives who pushed it to a conclusion. Forced to choose between the Conservatives with their prestige and influence in high circles and the much smaller group of Free Conservatives, the national leadership abandoned the latter. Yet personally Hergt probably regretted Kardorff's decision to leave the Party and to join the DVP, as much as Westarp welcomed it. A principal object of Conservative strategy had been to eliminate Kardorff, the democrat and non-monarchist, from a position of influence in the DNVP. When he left, the air was much clearer for the Conservatives. Hence Westarp's attempt to keep Hoetzsch, who was, after all, a well-known Conservative, from taking the same step as Kardorff to the embarrassment of both DKP and DNVP. As it was, Nationalist Party lines appeared to be hardening on the far right. Count Posadowsky, a highly respected exponent of social and liberal measures, declined to run in the June election because of age. Similarly Clemens von Delbrück was about to drop into the background as no electoral district nominated him; the Party was running him inconspicuously on the Reich list. But the most startling sign in the developing Nationalist character was the defection of Kardorff.

He left the DNVP after his anti-Conservative resolution was eliminated in the Nationalist Executive on April 9. That was, of course, only the last provocation in a series of grievances based on the persistent neglect of Free Conservative wishes and values. Kardorff's move was a shock, but it did not cost the Party much in terms of men. [50] More important than the loss of even a few talented individuals was the fact that Party matters were hauled into open debate, to the discomfort and chagrin of the DNVP. The secessionists in their frank statements aired grievances

[50] Secessionists included notably Arendt and v. Dewitz.

summing up eighteen months of development of the Party. And they were able to foresee, better than most people, its difficulties.

Yet, on the whole, Kardorff and his friends were restrained in their public statements. In the first place they condemned the use of all unconstitutional methods in public life, and went on to outline a positive political program which was remarkably similar to Hergt's *Ordnungsprogramm* of the previous autumn: "We are working for conciliation with all classes of people. That is not to be obtained on the basis of fundamental opposition, but only through cooperation with all parties and classes concerned for reconstruction of our Fatherland. We desire also to make possible cooperation with the Majority Socialists as long as they stick to strictly constitutional methods, and use their position of strength moderately, in the interests of reconciliation among the people. Such a possibility has been called for by Stresemann, but rejected by Westarp in the *Kreuzzeitung*. We do not refuse to acknowledge the considerable service that individual Majority Socialists like Noske have performed for the Fatherland by judiciously restraining the political ambitions of their party." [51] This statement of willingness to cooperate even as far left as the SPD was only a little clearer than Hergt's public remarks some months earlier. Westarp in the *Kreuzzeitung* tried to play down the nature of their differences: work as an opposition was not the most desirable situation, but would continue while necessary; coalition with Socialists was not a subject for practical discussions. [52] But, more than Westarp wanted to expound in the press, the tension between Old and Free Conservatives was caused by principles as well as tactics.

The differences were explicitly spelled out from the Free

---

[51] Letter of resignation printed in *Tägliche Rundschau*, quoted in *Kzztg.*, April 19, 1920 (P.M.).

[52] *Kzztg.*, April 19, 1920 (P.M.).

Conservative side, and explained why the DNVP could no longer contain them: "These were not differences of tactics, but of philosophy (*Weltanschauung*), since the DNVP has been undergoing a one-sided development toward the right under the aegis of Count Westarp, an individual who is not to be moved to any concessions or compromises. A person like me could not remain in this Party because I did not believe the Conservative party to be right even before the war, and during the war considered the Conservative attitude to be disastrous. I am not blind to the dangers that surround our political life. But I cannot go along with the racial and religious anti-Semitism that is professed by the overwhelming majority of Conservatives. Another point of view which has separated me from my friends is this: I have a different explanation for the collapse of our German people and Fatherland. The collapse resulted from the great guilt of all of us. . . . Another reason [for my leaving the Party] is the question of cooperation with the SPD. . . . We should not give up hope that the Socialist party will become a workers' party on a nationalist basis." [53] The questions touched on by Kardorff were of great interest, but familiar except for the reference to Germany's collapse. Kardorff's words were a far cry from the stab-in-the-back excuses that flashed in the oratory of Hergt and all other Nationalists. Differences of this fundamental sort had made it difficult for Kardorff by the second election to find a constituency willing to nominate him. [54] In going over to the DVP, Kardorff and his friends were leaving behind a political atmosphere in which they no longer belonged.

The Free Conservative secession eliminated from the Party only a minor dissident element. Any momentary satisfaction some Nationalists might have had over the seces-

---

[53] Statement of Kardorff to the DVP on his secession from the DNVP, printed in the *Frankfurt/Oder Zeitung*, quoted in *Berliner Tageblatt*, May 16, 1920 (A.M.).

[54] Lindeiner-Wildau, p. 17.

sion was quickly submerged by realization that the DNVP was little nearer in reality to internal peace and stability as a result of the development. This was very clear in a letter sent to Count Westarp three months later from Breslau by Axel von Freytagh-Loringhoven, a professor close to the Pan-German League and at that time a notable monarchist. He presented an activist point of view in expressing his doubts about the Nationalist leadership, criticizing its weakness in the National Assembly, and denouncing especially its faithless attitude toward the Kapp putsch and its participants. Hergt's direction was bound to bring increasing dissension in the DNVP, he felt: "The offer of cooperation with the majority parties was particularly revealing in this respect. At the same time the Party leadership in Berlin has been attempting underhand maneuvers to assure its supporters the leadership of the provincial organizations, insofar as they do not already control them." Freytagh accused the leadership of trying to eliminate Conservative and Racist strongholds in the Party. He was particularly bitter about inspired articles that had recently appeared in the Party press claiming that the Racists had cost the DNVP votes. Freytagh advocated opposition to what he considered to be the weak leadership of Hergt, but not to the point of advising secession. Conservatives, rather than secede, ought to look for occasions to act with other dissatisfied groups in the DNVP: "The opportunities were available in the Racist organizations, the Pan-German League, the *Deutschvölkischer Schutz- und Trutzbund,* the *Deutschbund,* and *Deutscher Herold.* . . . In all substantial questions their aims match those of the Conservative party and their judgment of Nationalist policy agrees with that of the Conservatives."

Freytagh continued his argument by stressing the great political potential of the Racist idea as a campaign weapon. Its appeal to youth was unusually strong and it penetrated even into the working-class population, offering the possibility of mass support. If the Racist groups had had little political influence up to that time, the reason was partly their lack of experience in such matters, inadequate organization, and impractical leadership: "This, in turn, is primarily a result of inadequate finances, to be explained by the fact that the members of Racist organizations are very largely persons of modest means." And so Freytagh argued the interesting idea of cooperation within the DNVP of Conservatives and Racists. Such cooperation was already fact in some local areas. The Conservatives, he was sure, would dominate the alliance because of their superior experience and wealth. He warned against the irreparable loss to the Nationalist cause that would follow any Racist secession, and regretted the present useless dispersal of the energy of Racist organizations. The Conservatives should lead a reform action in the DNVP in collaboration with the Racists. With this idea a committee had been formed in Breslau by four Racist groups; "On behalf of this Committee (*Arbeitsgemeinschaft*) I have already approached the Conservative Executive for Silesia with suggestions along the lines I have explained. Though no formal answer has been given as yet, I have the impression that von Richthofen-Mertschütz and Grützner are inclined to follow my suggestions. Count Seidlitz, on the other hand, appears to have some misgiving concerning them, although he does not act as though he rejects them entirely." [55]

There were other signs that Hergt could not afford to alienate the Old Conservatives further, for fear of a Conservative-Racist coalition that would have put intolerable pressure on the Nationalist leadership for more brutal opposition to the state, and that would have threatened to split the Party wide open. Freytagh-Loringhoven was not without influential support in Racist and some Conservative circles. Among these men was Franz Sontag, editor of

[55] WP: Freytagh-Loringhoven to Westarp, July 20, 1920. From the text it appears that a similar letter was also sent to Heydebrand.

the monarchist publication *Tradition* that was subsidized by the *Herrenhaus* Conservatives. He informed Westarp that *Tradition* was about to publish an article by Freytagh that attacked Hergt, and was designed to stir up argument on the Party's general approach to politics in the Republic. Sontag then discussed his own thoughts on Conservative-Racist collaboration, and welcomed the practical steps taken by Freytagh to make it a reality: "I have always believed that in this question really lies the [most important] national problem of our time, and even of the future. For we ought not to overlook the fact that the majority of our youth is strongly rooted in the Racist philosophy, particularly that portion of our youth in schools of higher learning and in universities." He believed that without superior Conservative direction the valuable force of racism would be dissipated in utopian concepts and remain politically ineffectual. [56]

The unrest among Conservative-Racists was another side effect of the Kapp putsch, but had been in the air before. Although they did not represent most Conservatives or even the Heydebrand-Westarp leadership, they were in a position to put pressure on them and on the DNVP. The disappointments that centered on the Kapp putsch made the possibility of Conservative and Racist collaboration more than a remote threat. The initiative for action came as much from the Racist as from the Conservative side. To understand how this further complicated the internal Party situation it is necessary to look more closely at the Racist problem in the DNVP. That will lead us further into the

[56] WP: Franz Sontag to Westarp, July 19, 1920. The same *Herrenhausgruppe* that supported Sontag and *Tradition* also reportedly subsidized publication of the *Protocols of the Elders of Zion*. The democratic press reproduced a letter from Otto, Prince Salm to the former leader of the group, Count Behr, dated May 24, 1919, calling for a subsidy for that purpose of 100,000 marks, toward which the prince earmarked his usual contribution of 1,000 marks; report in *Freiheit,* quoted in *Berliner Tageblatt,* May 20, 1920 (A.M.).

realm of right radicalism, and into the series of internal crises that plagued the Nationalist Party throughout its existence. Clearly the sharp struggle over anti-Semitism in the period 1919-1920 prepared the way for the major Racist split of 1922.

V
Right Radicalism:
The Racist Crisis

Even before 1918 the term *deutschvölkisch* began to replace the older adjective "anti-Semitic." It was intended to suggest a larger purpose in the Racist campaign than a mere attack on Jews. Still, in practice the terms were synonymous when the parliamentary leaders of the Racists, Ferdinand Werner-Hersfeld and Wilhelm Bruhn, emerging from the German *Fraktion* helped found the Nationalist Party. As it turned out, the weight of the Racist struggle within the new Party did not revolve around these two men, but around a number of other persons at national headquarters and in the local organizations. These were men of varying backgrounds, as often Conservative as not, who accepted with enthusiasm the anti-Semitism that accompanied the period of war, revolution, and civil war in Germany. The anti-Semitic drive aroused particularly the big cities and suburbs that the DNVP wanted to attract to its side. Hence most Nationalists felt it important to make adequate use of Racist ideas, though no more than might be prudent. For them this was just one political factor among many. [1]

There were some men also, mainly of Liberal or Free Conservative backgrounds—usually men of influence and money—who did repudiate anti-Semitism. But they were usually the weaker side in the controversies that came up at Party headquarters and in certain local organizations such as Berlin, Potsdam I, Potsdam II, Hamburg, Hanover,

[1] W MS, p. 314.

[124]

and Leipzig. In the first years of the DNVP, hardly a Party convention or meeting of Party representatives went by without debate on the subject of anti-Semitism. Nevertheless the Party as a whole did not have enough self-confidence as yet to make an open confession of racism.

The scruples of the leadership are not easy to interpret. Their motivation was not exactly good taste, but much more a distrust of the political sense of the violent Racist elements. In 1919 the chief controversy was the exclusion of Jews from membership. The Nationalist leadership opposed any such constitutional exclusion for the time being. Karl Helfferich, for example, pointed out the unnecessary odium the DNVP would have to bear both at home and abroad if it took such a step. And Count Westarp, though far from unsympathetic to the Racist point of view, had interesting practical considerations for not wanting a statutory exclusion of Jews. His point was the difficulty of defining and determining who was to be considered Jewish. Since to the Racist not baptism but blood was the important consideration, an apparatus would be needed to investigate the ancestry of the membership—a procedure bound to have hateful repercussions within the Party. He and others felt it was "possible to prevent penetration by Jews without any formal stipulation, and to defend the Party from danger of harmful influence from the few exceptions [of Jews among the membership]." [2]

Even some strong Racists for a while were willing to put up with a measure of restraint on the subject. Albrecht von Graefe, the Conservative who was rapidly becoming the leading Racist spokesman, had his own reasons for postponing the question of Jewish exclusion: "It seems to me that a resolution to exclude Jews, etc., from the whole Party on grounds of principle is not in keeping with the nature of a political party, at least not under our civil

[2] W MS, pp. 317-8.

constitution. This viewpoint of mine does not mitigate my open fight with the Jews in the slightest."[3] It is well to remember that for a while Racists like Graefe frequently cooperated with the Nationalist leadership. In Graefe's case the restraint was part of his favorite idea during the formation of the DNVP to establish, not merely a new political party, but a parliamentary community of as many subsidiary political groups as possible from right through center.[4]

But, as the DVP showed little inclination to cooperate with the Nationalists, the atmosphere became more tense through the spring electoral campaign of 1920. Yet the Racist tone of some of the material used in the first election campaign was about as sharp as could be imagined. Nationalist leaflets issued locally described Jews as the "vampires of Germany," or carried a banner heading reading "Germanism—not Judaism! Not religion but race!" Still others printed on bright red paper proclaimed that "the party of Jewry is the German Democratic party."[5] Presumably the authors of these extravagant sentiments were also exerting pressure within the Party for official recognition of the Racist point of view. After the first Party convention in July, 1919, the Hergt leadership began to show much less reluctance in meeting Racist demands. Hergt was reported to have told the Pomeranian *Landesparteitag* that the wave of anti-Semitic feeling should prove to be a decidedly valuable ally in the coming electoral campaign.[6] At the same time Hergt encouraged the convention of the Silesian organization in Breslau to accept the following resolution on

[3] Graefe to Justizrat Dr. Knebusch, Feb. 5, 1920, quoted in *Kzztg.*, Apr. 30, 1924 (A.M.). Similar wording in a memorandum, WP: "Partei und Judenfrage," signed by A. v. Graefe, Goldebee, Feb. 5, 1920.

[4] Graefe to Justizrat Dr. Knebusch, Aug. 26, 1922, quoted in *Kzztg.*, April 30, 1924 (A.M.).

[5] Stuttgart Collection; *Berliner Tageblatt*, Jan. 17, 1919 (P.M.).

[6] Roland von Bremen, *Die neue Heilsbotschaft* (Bremen, 1924), p. 23; meeting of Sept. 27, 1919.

the Jewish question: "The DNVP stands on the ground of German cultural values, and believes it to be its right and duty to speak up for them in the strongest manner. It therefore opposes every un-German degenerative influence, particularly the disrupting influence of Jewry which has been making itself more and more strongly felt in recent decades to the detriment of our people. The Party objects to the fact that foreign elements are grabbing leadership and are leading the state to its downfall. Anyone is welcome in our Party who wants to collaborate honestly in the restoration of Germany. But the prerequisite of such collaboration is acceptance of the German way of thinking and German feeling." [7] This became the official Nationalist position when the following month a similar resolution was passed at DNVP headquarters. [8] These were also the same general sentiments that were eventually incorporated into the Party program early in 1920.

One incident may illustrate the development of feeling among leading men in the DNVP. When the Party was being formed there was some question of making Salomon Marx, a banker and Conservative of Jewish origin, a member of the Executive and possibly Party treasurer. Since his sponsors were from the hard core of the DKP, his chances in the DNVP were not particularly good in any case. Westarp narrated further developments: "In the negotiations which Stackmann, Schroeter and I consequently had with him I thought it only fair to point out to him that anti-Semitic sentiments had gained currency in the DNVP. He thereupon withdrew, stating that in that case he would not be able to raise much money in his circles. . . . Graef, Dietrich, and Bruhn who opposed taking him into the Executive represented the view that his admission should

[7] Meeting of Sept. 23, reported in *Berliner Tageblatt*, Sept. 26, 1919 (A.M.).

[8] *Korrespondenz der DNVP*, p. 237, Oct. 14, 1919; also *Vorwürfe gegen die DNVP*, p. 9.

not follow until he had handed over an advance payment of several hundred thousand marks. Thus the negotiation with him collapsed without my having intervened with the energy that was expected of me by Marx and Stackmann."[9]

Just a few months later the atmosphere was enough changed that it was inconceivable for such a negotiation even to have started. When Marx complained in a letter to Hergt of anti-Semitism in the DNVP, the Nationalist leader sent a reply that earned him a measure of notoriety in the Liberal press, but also considerable scorn from the doctrinaire Racists. In his letter Hergt professed opposition to Jewish prominence on principle, although he was tolerant of the work of individual Jews even in the Party, provided they knew their place and earned this tolerance by their model behavior and self-sacrifice in the Nationalist cause. [10] After the incident Hergt had constantly to ward off the reproach of having accepted money from Jews. Although this was regularly denied, the rumors persisted about the negotiations with Marx, and of heavy cash contributions to the first election campaign from moneyed Jewish interests. Even worse, a Jewish industrialist, Richard Friedländer, had been Nationalist candidate in Oppeln (Upper Silesia) for the National Assembly in 1919, and for the Municipal Council as late as 1921. [11]

The leadership of the DNVP was from all appearances in an embarrassing predicament. Part of its hyper-sensitivity was to be explained by the extent to which anti-Semitism was still felt by the public to be a cultural disgrace. Hergt tried to dissociate the Party in particular from the stigma of "rowdy" or "pogrom anti-Semitism" and to discourage malicious personal attacks on individuals. On the other

[9] W MS, p. 35.

[10] *Vorwürfe gegen die DNVP*, p. 9.

[11] *Berliner Tageblatt*, July 8, 1921 (P.M.); also a leaflet, *Die deutsch-nationale Doppelseele* (n.d., anti-DNVP, no indication of origin), Stuttgart Collection; *Kroschels Gewissen*, p. 11.

hand, as the feeling of anti-Semitism gained momentum after the war the initial sensitivity passed away, and the leadership felt more concerned with denying any softness in its attitude toward the supposed Semitic peril. Hence, official sanction was given to general resolutions attacking Jewish influence and activity in public and cultural life, and the Executive allowed the *Fraktionen* to oppose openly the immigration of Jews from Eastern Europe, for here was an immediate practical aim of the anti-Semitic movement which most people felt inclined to support. Public excitement followed reports and evidence of immigration, natural xenophobia being heightened by increasing economic distress. To politicians alert to the phenomenon this feeling was to be a useful, almost essential, object for the campaign oratory. "From my experience," wrote Westarp, "the cry of 'Jew' would come from the audience at almost all political meetings when criticism was expressed of political circumstances. Besides, I was often able to notice that a sleepy meeting would wake up and the house applaud as soon as I started on the subject of the Jews. Not infrequently I personally felt a more important and more timely theme for discussion would have been the liberation of Germany or the fight against the republican system. But for the success of the meeting the Jewish question could not be omitted. It had to be hashed over again at the expense of valuable speaking time." [12]

Anti-Semitism was not the weapon for a political party to use lightly. Illogical thinkers in the DNVP unaware of the fire with which they were playing were not, for example, prepared for the unpleasant Gierke incident in the spring of 1920. Here was precisely the type of development that the party leadership hoped to avoid by forestalling any Jewish exclusion clause in the statutes. But the leaders underestimated the determination of the Racists. Now, after a campaign of slander from the Racists, Otto von

[12] W MS, p. 333.

Gierke, the famed jurist who had a Jewish wife, and his daughter, Anna, left the DNVP. Because of anti-Semitic pressure Miss Gierke, a member of the National Assembly, had been dropped from the slate of candidates for the coming election by her home constituency of Potsdam II. [13] The withdrawal was bad publicity for the Nationalist cause because of the prestige of the elder Gierke as a scholar and because of the position of Anna von Gierke in her own right as first president of the Party's Women's Committee. She was well known as a social worker and feminist, and the Women's Committee formed immediately after the Revolution was valued highly as a means of attracting the important new female vote in postwar Germany. The work of the committee was badly disturbed by the circumstances that brought the exit of the Gierkes. [14]

Few voices protesting against anti-Semitism were heard within the DNVP. Protests on grounds of tactics were tolerated more than protests on principle. Those who rejected anti-Semitism *in toto* were isolated, and eventually either resigned or moved to another party. For practical reasons only tactical criticism carried any weight in the Party. The hoped-for collaboration with the DVP in the spring of 1920 did not materialize. For the June election the two parties of the right agreed only to direct their attacks against the left rather than each other; the DVP would go no further than that in its cooperation. [15] Peeved by this, the Nationalist leadership saw less reason to check the Racists. Adalbert Düringer, who went over to the DVP himself, remarked that, as the original influence of men like Posadowsky and Delbrück was being displaced by that of Hergt and Westarp, "one sought and found in the toleration and encouragement of anti-Semitism a distinctive policy for the

[13] W MS, p. 321.

[14] *Berliner Tageblatt,* May 23 (A.M.), May 25 (A.M.), June 4 (P.M.), 1920.

[15] Lindeiner-Wildau, p. 20.

Party to distinguish it from all the others, particularly from the DVP, and one expected great political successes from it." [16] But in this respect the June election was to prove a great disappointment. For although the Nationalists did increase their popular vote by almost 5 per cent of votes cast—from 3,121,500, or 10.26 per cent, to 4,249,100, or 15.1 per cent—the relative increase of the DVP was much greater. It now grew from 1,345,600, or 4.42 per cent, to 3,919,400, or 13.9 per cent. [17] The disproportionate increase of their nearest rival's popular strength was a deeply disturbing sign to serious Party strategists in the DNVP.

In addition, the displeasure in responsible circles deepened as they bore the brunt of further attacks from the most ardent Racists. Ironically, Racist attacks were turning increasingly to internal affairs of the DNVP, tending to undermine confidence in its leadership. To face the situation an important article was placed by Walther Graef-Anklam in the party organ, *Unsere Partei*. Graef, a member of the Prussian Assembly and Hergt's close associate in the bureaucracy, directly condemned the use of exaggerated anti-Semitism as a tactical failure. Very few areas had responded to the approach, he pointed out. Even in the traditionally anti-Semitic stronghold of Hesse-Nassau, the DVP with a Jewish candidate, Jacob Riesser, easily elected three members while a Nationalist barely got in at all, and then only with the help of residue votes from Hesse-Darmstadt. In Greater Berlin the DNVP elected four men with the greatest difficulty; the DVP captured five seats there. And whereas the educated middle class of the capital's western suburbs had voted Nationalist in 1919, this time they streamed over to the DVP; in these areas the DNVP showed a new loss over the previous election returns. The post mortem began. "Reasons? Not only the Kardorff and

[16] Quoted from *Tag* in *Deutsche Stimmen*, Aug. 20, 1922.

[17] Germany. Statistisches Reichsamt. *Statistisches Jahrbuch für das Deutsche Reich*, vol. 46, 1927 (Berlin, 1927), p. 497.

Gierke cases, but doubtless the not always happy campaign methods of the Anti-Semites. There is a weak spot in anti-Semitism: the lack of possible practical solutions. . . . As far as laws go there is very little to be done. . . . [except in the matter of Eastern Jewish immigration]. The people understand this quite well, and for that reason the resounding success of anti-Semitic meetings has no lasting effect. Particularly harmful is the frequently committed error of one-sidedness which would ascribe all political and social ills to the Jews. . . . No one is thinking of eliminating the anti-Semitic note from our program or of changing in any way the wording of our Party program on the Jewish question. But we must not allow the impression to arise that we are only an anti-Semitic Party and have not many other demands in our platform that are just as important as the fight against Jewish predominance. Our Party should not become a conventicle for a single idea which, however important in itself, does not exhaust all others." [18]

The difficulties caused the Nationalist Party by the Kapp putsch have already been discussed. The repercussions were also severe on the DNVP from the assassination of Matthias Erzberger in the summer of 1921 and of Walther Rathenau ten months later. Outwardly the Party was assailed by the public outcry against the right-wing associations of the assassins, and by the application of severe new laws that tended to restrict political activity on the right. The Nationalists felt themselves severely injured by the Defense of the Republic Act, by tightening of the criminal code and civil service regulations, and by amendments to amnesty regulations. To their great annoyance local branches of the DNVP might occasionally find their meetings forbidden, or find themselves under investigation for suspected treasonous activity.

In the case of Erzberger, the DNVP was seriously em-

[18] A Nationalist analyst quoted in *Nationalliberale Correspondenz*, p. 178, Aug. 13, 1920.

barrassed because Karl Helfferich was riding the crest of triumph in his vendetta against the Center party politician when he was murdered. [19] Then, before the German public recovered from that shock, came the further shock of the Rathenau murder—Rathenau who as a Jew had been the butt of vicious Racist lampoons, and most recently also of a bitter parliamentary attack by the same Helfferich. Thus the DNVP, though no doubt opposed to the principle of political murder, [20] found itself engulfed in the wave of moral indignation that followed acts of right radical terrorism.

In view of the increasingly tense atmosphere in German public life, the DNVP morally and tactically could not ignore the demands for rigorous clarification of its own position. The demand came frequently from within the Party, similar to the comment that appeared in the Nationalist press: "The Nationalist movement will be shattered if the political left is able to get away much longer with claiming the existence of Nationalist murder centers. . . . How much longer will the DNVP burden itself with forces that inwardly and outwardly do not belong to the Party at all? Among these, according to their own admission are the Racist and right radical circles which seek the salvation of the state through force." [21]

The criticism was correct. The position of responsible opposition was not compatible with the cult of violence. After the Kapp putsch this truism was quite apparent to the adherents of both attitudes, whether politicians of prudence or counter-revolutionary activists. Individually many Nationalists may have been associated with Free Corps, for example, or with other right radical groups. Yet intrinsically there was little in common between the aims

[19] See relevant chapters of Klaus Epstein, *Matthias Erzberger and the Dilemma of German Democracy* (Princeton, 1959).

[20] With some exceptions, as with Kurt Eisner: Hilpert, p. 242.

[21] From *Tag*, quoted in *Berliner Tageblatt*, June 27, 1922 (P.M.).

of the DNVP and of the radical para-military organizations. As Graef later commented, in agreement with similar views often voiced in Nationalist publications, "The Nationalist movement would long ago have reached a much different power position than it has in post-revolutionary Germany had we had no Kapp putsch, no murder of Erzberger and Rathenau, and no November putsch in Munich." [22] The leadership looked with a jaundiced eye on the extreme Racists in their midst, while the latter chafed in frustration.

One could regularly expect the Racist question to recur as an issue in the Party whenever some right radical violence stirred up the country. Tension rose steadily from one annual Party Congress to the next. In October, 1920, at the second Congress in Hanover, Racist agitators were with difficulty checked by Hergt on the Jewish exclusion question. [23] Yet by the time of the Munich Convention the following year, Hergt was himself speaking of the Party's desire to find practical measures to take in the Jewish problem, and even proposed to set up a special study committee. Though the leadership may have felt it was doing a great deal to keep peace in the Party, and going a long way to affirming an anti-Semitic *Weltanschauung*, [24] the Racist activists were not to be silenced by words alone or by the work of a study committee. At the fourth Congress

[22] Graef, p. 29.

[23] Cf., WP: Mimeographed draft resolution of the Potsdam II lobby stated, "Disturbed by the attacks of Dr. Kahrstedt and of Party Secretary Graef-Anklam against the Racist concept in the Party, we believe it to be an urgent necessity for a completely unambiguous position to be taken at last on the Racist question. We therefore renew the motion that a resolution be passed, and made part of the regulations, to the effect that persons of Jewish origin shall not belong to the Party, and that persons of Jewish origin shall hold no party office." See also report of session of Oct. 26, *Kzztg.*, Oct. 27, 1920 (A.M.).

[24] Graef, *Kzztg.*, March 4, 1924 (P.M.).

in Görlitz in 1922 serious talk of secession was again definitely in the air.

If the Racists appear to be getting more attention than
they deserve, the reason is that they were the most volatile
and impetuous group in the Nationalist Party, the most
sensitive, and, while they were still members, its most
persistent troublemakers. Take an incident reported in the
press toward the end of December, 1920, involving Albrecht
von Graefe. It was expected he would leave the Nationalist
Fraktion after the deputy Speaker of the House, his Party
colleague Hermann Dietrich, reproved him for a facetious
remark made in the Reichstag about the chancellor. There
was talk at the same time of other apparent differences with
his Party—his special brand of anti-Semitism, and his vote
with ten other dissidents against a disarmament bill supported by the Nationalist *Fraktion*.[25] Though a month
later it was announced Graefe would remain in the *Fraktion*,[26] he had meanwhile let off considerable steam. He demanded satisfaction from them in the following terms,
which indicated how deeply the grievances went behind
an apparently trifling incident:

(1) The *Fraktion* regretted that von Graefe had not been given
an opportunity to speak on a matter of importance to him on
December 18, 1920, and it recognized in this failure a cause
for bitterness on his part;
(2) the DNVP could never consider entering a government without a fundamental change in the constitutional system, and
that
(3) this principle could be the only basis of negotiation with other
parties; consequently, Nationalist opposition must be more
direct and consistent than heretofore, particularly in parliamentary tactics;
(4) "the *Fraktion* therefore accepts the suggestion that, in the

[25] *Berliner Tageblatt,* Dec. 21, 1920 (P.M.).
[26] *Ibid.,* Jan. 26, 1921 (A.M.).

future, representatives of the so-called sharp opposition (*schärferen Tonart*) be delegated to meetings of the Council of Elders (*Ältestenrat*) ;

(5) "finally the *Fraktion* asks the chairman of the Party and his representatives to keep the members of the *Fraktion* constantly informed by regular reports on all events which affect the course of policy in the Party, particularly any negotiations that may take place and any agreements that may be arranged with other parties or prominent persons. It asks for the same information on the possibility of any special relationships with the financial giants of the big business world." [27]

Graefe, in other words, saw fit on this occasion to raise basic questions of Party policy and leadership, early evidence of serious incompatibility of the aims of Racists and the majority in the DNVP.

Graefe's frustration in his fundamental policy may ac-

[27] WP: paper signed by "Der Antragsteller, A. v. Graefe," with the heading, "Vorschläge für Beschlüsse der Fraktion in der zum 20.1.21. anberaumten Sitzung." Note also another document originating with Graefe, to be found among the Westarp Papers: "Zur Begründung meines Austritts aus der Fraktion" (n.d.). The document relates in detail the occasion on which he was slighted by the leadership and by the Party whips, and placed in an embarrassing position in the House. Hergt, Schiele, Dietrich, Schultz-Bromberg, and Roesicke are bitterly assailed for their behavior. Graefe ascribes the incident to a corridor conspiracy designed to silence the sharp oppositionists in the Party. Concerning his personal position he adds: "Although I am one of the oldest, in fact almost the oldest Member of Parliament in the Party, no use is made of me in the work of the Party, of the *Fraktion* Executive, of the Council of Seniors (*Seniorkonvent*), etc. In this Reichstag the thought has never occurred to anyone to suggest me as a speaker for once in matters where a sharper tone might perhaps be preferable to the diplomatic wisdom of enlightened theorists. . . . The heart of the matter is this: The corridor politicians of the Party for a long time now have not really taken our more determined group seriously, or me as a result, because we upset their political smugness." Graefe consequently refused to allow himself to be used further by the leadership merely as a useful speaker for its campaigns, yet excluded from policy decisions.

count for his joining with other Racists in some views that he did not originally share, especially the constitutional exclusion of Jews from the Party. The Jewish exclusion clause was at least an issue that could easily rally Racists in the country. In the form in which it was presented by Reinhold Wulle to the special study committee set up by the Munich Convention, a Jew for the purposes of exclusion was an individual who himself was not baptized on January 18, 1871, or who had a relative similarly unbaptized. At the same time the committee [28] was faced with Graefe's request for permission to form a separate Racist organization within the DNVP entitled to collect its own funds, though a portion would be assigned to party headquarters. The situation was serious enough for Wulle to feel that the unity of the DNVP was at stake in the negotiations, and that the losers of either side in the struggle would leave the Party rather than accept defeat. [29]

Because of their crucial nature the final decisions were left to the Party leadership. In November, 1921, as expected, discussions of representatives at headquarters ended with defeat of the Racist motions. A resolution by Karl Helfferich rejecting the need to change the Party statutes

[28] Members included Westarp, Helfferich, Wulle, v. Graefe, Lambach, and Henning.

[29] WP: Col. Brauer (of the DKP bureau), report to Heydebrand, Nov. 4, 1921. Also in WP: an account by Wulle, "Die Vorgänge in der Deutschnationalen Volkspartei" (n.d.), which blamed the Racist failure in the special committee on Hergt, Helfferich, Hugenberg, and Schultz-Bromberg, who threatened to leave the Party if their view was not upheld: "The policy of these men is one of a broad, people's party. Yet for this they need the Racists, because without them they cannot obtain the support of youth." Also in WP: Henning, "Darstellung des Abgeordneten Henning über die Ereignisse, die zu seinem Ausschluss aus der Fraktion geführt haben" (n.d.), claimed the threat of secession was first made at that time by the leadership, specifically by Hergt, Helfferich, and Schultz-Bromberg. He said that the Racists lost the first vote in the special post-Munich committee by only one vote.

was passed 103-81, with the support of the entire Executive except Westarp. Provincial organizations were in the future not to exclude Jews constitutionally, although two or three *Landesverbände* (e.g., Pomerania) had already done so. But, at the same time, an even larger majority was found for a resolution released for publication asserting that the DNVP was a Racist Party. [30]

The decision of the leadership was consistent with its general stand up to that time on the subject of separate political formations within the Party. After its long struggle with the Conservatives on their special status, it was unlikely the leadership would accept the formation of a potentially hostile Racist unit. The Racists for their part were not willing to accept further rebuffs, as Wulle indicated. Rumors were immediately current that they planned to go ahead with an informal organization throughout the Reich using trusted members in the Party, and hoped in that way to force more consideration for Racist nominees on the Nationalist ticket in the next election. [31] In view of their attitude few persons could doubt any more the possibility of a major split.

In the office of the *Hauptverein der Deutschkonservativen* Colonel Brauer, one of the leading functionaries of the Old Conservatives, saw in the development a favorable opportunity for their organization. A Racist himself and a believer in "Christian German" activity, he hoped the DKP would support the Racist group of the DNVP in case of a split, and tried to influence Heydebrand in that direction. [32] He did not feel a break was desirable at the time, but suggested the DKP assume the role of mediator without appearing anti-Racist. Brauer mentioned that Racists had widely criticized Westarp for his outspoken opposition to their resolutions in the recent executive meetings. He asked

[30] *Kzztg.*, Nov. 28, 1921 (P.M.).
[31] WP: Brauer to Heydebrand, Dec. 1, 1921.
[32] *Ibid.*, Nov. 4, 1921.

Heydebrand to prevent alienation of the Racists by taking a public stand on the *völkisch* question in the *Kreuzzeitung* on behalf of the DKP. [33] The Conservative leader was apparently receptive to the suggestion. In ten days the *Kreuzzeitung* published an article by Heydebrand that recalled to the DNVP its debt to the Conservatives for their continued support both nationally and locally, support that had not always been properly recognized by the Nationalists, or even welcomed, because of their exaggerated desire to avoid Conservative influence. In the present controversy over anti-Semitism in the DNVP, Conservatives agreed that the basic Racist concept was sound, although the Racists might not always be justified in their emphasis on methods. Close cooperation of *völkisch* elements in the Conservative and Nationalist parties ought not to be hindered, Heydebrand added, "whether that is agreeable to the Party leaders or not." [34]

Though many people paid attention to any statement made by Heydebrand, few persons saw the full significance of the intrusion of a veterans' organization, the Federation of Nationalist Soldiers (*Verband nationalgesinnter Soldaten*—VNS) into the controversy. But in the intrusion can be detected early the characteristic note of bitterness, personal intrigue, and right radical overtones that so complicated the Racist debacle. The first sign was only a resolution of criticism such as the leadership had presumably received many times previously from Racist groups. But this resolution was passed at a special national meeting of VNS representatives just two days after the publication of the executive decision on the petition of Graefe and Wulle. It expressed anger at the ambiguous position taken by the DNVP, and demanded immediate clarification. At stake was the continued support of the VNS. Spe-

[33] *Ibid.*, Dec. 1, 1921.

[34] *Kzztg.*, Dec. 11, 1921 (A.M.); also *Berliner Tageblatt*, Dec. 12, 1921 (P.M.).

cifically mentioned in press reports as present at the meeting was the group's second-in-command, Wilhelm Henning, a Nationalist member of the Reichstag, and well-known activist of the extreme Racist *Schutz- und Trutzbund.* [35]

From the sidelines in the DKP, Colonel Brauer was more aware of the growing crisis than many people closer to the action. He wrote Heydebrand in January, 1922: "Count Westarp sees less danger for the DNVP in the Racist movement than in the policy of the Christian Socialist trade union secretaries. I believe he underestimates the Racist threat. The *Deutschvölkische Arbeitsgemeinschaft* which is now spreading over the whole Reich is going to give the Party leadership many a hard nut to crack yet. And if Hergt, Helfferich, and Hugenberg persist in considering the matter as a power question above all else, then I predict a gloomy future for the DNVP. Particularly since the Federation of Nationalist Soldiers (VNS), according to last reports, is going to demand adequate consideration of its fast growing strength at nominations for the next elections. The federation is strictly Racist in its orientation and has now for months taken over the job of keeping order at Nationalist meetings with tremendous success." [36]

Henning himself denied that he had been present at the meeting of the VNS in the late fall of 1921 when it took its stand on the Racist question, and claimed he had had nothing to do with the decision. He claimed also that this fact was made clear to Hergt at the time in a letter. The letter, however, apparently disappeared from the Party records in the ensuing controversy. [37] The exact nature of

[35] Meeting of Nov. 27, 1921, reported in *Deutsche Stimmen,* Dec. 4, 1921, p. 814. Wilhelm Henning (b. 1879) was one of the youngest members of the Nationalist *Fraktion.* A former major on the General Staff, he was returned in the 1920 election as Reichstag deputy for Weser-Ems; Cuno Horkenbach, *Das Deutsche Reich von 1918 bis heute* (Berlin, 1930), p. 679; *Kzztg.,* July 20, 1922 (A.M.).

[36] WP: Brauer to Heydebrand, Jan. 16, 1922.

[37] WP: "Darstellung des Abgeordneten Henning über die Ereignisse,

the controversy as it involved Henning has remained obscure in many of its aspects. Because of its importance in illustrating the nature of the Racist struggle within the DNVP, I should like to examine it in some detail.

Wilhelm Henning's troubles began after he became second officer in command of the VNS. The troubles were within the organization itself and in his relations with the DNVP. Within the VNS apparently had been elements of the notorious right radical *Organisation Consul* of Hermann Ehrhardt. After a bitter struggle they were finally excluded from the federation, and then apparently out of spite they denounced the VNS to the police as a group planning a putsch. Nothing came of the incident, especially as the denouncers were themselves under suspicion of terrorist conspiracy.

Because of these dubious associations, however, Henning on frequent occasions was to feel the displeasure of influential members of the Nationalist Party Executive. Lindeiner even went as far as to try to prevent his renomination on the Nationalist ticket. On December 9, 1921, occurred an unpleasant personal incident at a café involving Graef-Anklam, Henning, and some of his friends from the VNS who happened to be together. Graef shocked the latter by saying that Jews were not to blame for Germany's defeat in the war, but high staff officers including Hindenburg were. Henning took credit for persuading his colleagues not to report the argument to the newspapers; instead they turned an account of the incident over to Hergt, and asked for satisfaction. Hergt who showed no enthusiasm in the matter did eventually call a hearing, badly conducted according to the standards of the VNS. Hergt finally felt compelled to intervene personally, and Graef apologized.

But from that time on, Henning felt himself to be the

---

die zu seinem Ausschluss aus der Fraktion geführt haben" (n.d.).

object of a whispering campaign directed with consistent hatred by Graef. It became serious enough for Henning to ask Hergt in the spring of 1922 to appoint a committee to look into the rumors being spread about his activities. Hergt agreed immediately since he had been about to suggest such a committee in any case. A committee of eight *Fraktion* members met eight weeks before the murder of Rathenau, and disbanded six weeks before the murder, without having found Henning guilty of misconduct. [38]

From the imprecise language of recrimination and personal enmity that veiled much of the actuality of the case, at least one important impression came through clearly. Through Henning the Racist movement had become linked with right radicalism, however unsubstantial and tenuous actual proof of the matter might have been. When Rathenau was murdered, demands from outsiders like Stresemann that the DNVP break with all elements tainted with right radicalism were almost superfluous. The same demands were being insistently made in the inner Nationalist circles, and in segments of the Nationalist press (including, for example, the *Tag* and the *Deutsche Tageszeitung*). On the day of the Rathenau assassination the Nationalist *Fraktion* had again to defend Helfferich against a storm of abuse, as it had after the Erzberger murder. But

[38] WP: Henning report. But cf., M. Weiss, ed., *Politisches Handwörterbuch*, p. 978: "A committee, set up at Henning's own request, had established that Henning had too often left the impression in the course of his public appearances that secret plans were lurking behind his words and actions. . . . The Committee had affirmed that Henning had not conformed to the principle in the Party program which stated that any change in the constitution was to be brought about only through means the constitution itself provided. The elimination of Henning from the DNVP was requested in particularly sharp words in a letter from Herr Kube—the same Herr Kube who later went over to the German Racist Freedom party (*Deutschvölkische Freiheitspartei*), became a colleague of the Racists again, and even the principal secretary of the new party."

when in following days parliamentary and public opinion denounced the Racists, the latter found little moral support in the *Fraktion*.

Another bitter blow for the Racists came in the Foreign Affairs Committee of the House when Chancellor Wirth read extracts from an article by Henning that had appeared in the June issue of the *Konservative Monatsschrift*. The article, entitled "The True Face of the Rapallo Treaty," was an anti-Semitic denunciation of Rathenau. Wirth stated he could no longer believe the DNVP guiltless in the murder of Rathenau if that Party did not sever connections with Henning and his supporters. At this, Hergt and Hoetzsch immediately declared their disapproval of the article, Hergt adding that he could not be responsible for activities of the Racists behind his back. [39]

Hergt meanwhile asked Wulle to prepare a report on the groups with which Henning had been associated. He looked on Wulle apparently as a man one might deal with, unlike the Racist hotheads Henning and Graefe. The report was to be presented to a joint meeting of the *Fraktionen* of the Reichstag and Prussian Landtag. A rumor was current on the day of the meeting that the Landtag *Fraktion* was going to ask for the expulsion of Graefe, Wulle, and Henning. Perhaps as a result of Wulle's report the motion was not made. But Wulle recorded that several individuals (he specifically named Count Kanitz) asked him to resign his seat in the House. An investigating committee was formed to continue hearings on Henning. Its business was essentially to establish facts, not to pass final judgments. [40]

[39] WP: Brauer to Heydebrand, July 8 and 18, 1922; and Wulle report. Wulle added that Hergt and Hoetzsch indicated their disapproval in the committee even before they had read the article in its entirety for themselves.

[40] WP: Wulle and Henning reports.

The fact-finding committee had, in particular, to consider four points of complaint with respect to Henning: (1) his questionable article in the *Konservative Monatsschrift*; (2) charges of unreasonable empire-building in the VNS through the expulsion of members of the moderate Escherich militia and other persons connected with patriotic organizations; (3) charges of direct connections with secret terrorist organizations, shown by solicitation of funds to finance the Erzberger murder plan; (4) Henning's alleged intention of forming a separate military party. According to Wulle, no grave fault could be found in the Henning case by the committee; there was nothing exceptionable found in the article as a whole; it was established that Henning had resisted the radical Ehrhardt elements in the VNS, and had rejected especially their suggestions of forming a separate military party; he had rather combatted than approved illegal secret organizations.

Henning was satisfied with the first day of discussion in the committee under the chairmanship of Max Wallraf. The next day, with Adolf Wermuth in the chair, was another story. The floor was open to an airing of stories of right radical activity by Henning; Henning felt he was not allowed time to refute them. The most damaging vaguely hinted at some connection with the assassination of Rathenau. The committee at the end of the second day censured Henning in a public statement that he considered libelous.

The Racists were particularly bitter that the fact-finding committee had turned itself into a court (at Hergt's behest they claimed) even though no incorrect action by Henning had been proved; the judgment passed on him by a vote of 5-2 was based on the grossest hearsay. [41] Henning in retaliation also issued a public statement. Though that action

[41] Graefe and Laverrenz both voted in favor of Henning; WP: Brauer to Heydebrand, July 18, 1922.

might have been his only defense against a vocal party machine, the effect only aggravated an already tense situation.

In the Henning affair not only the man, but the whole Racist position in the DNVP was, of course, being re-examined. This soon became apparent when six prominent members of the *Fraktion* called for elimination of extreme Racist elements from the Party, failing which they threatened themselves to leave either the *Fraktion* or the Party. The question was put in this way not only by Düringer and Hoetzsch whose feeling had been clear earlier, but now also by three influential agrarian leaders, Count Kanitz, Friedrich Edler von Braun, and Gustav Roesicke, as well as the Pan-German spokesman of big business, Alfred Hugenberg. [42] Hergt's main concern, as Henning recorded immediately in his notes, was that the Party could not become *koalitionsfähig* without suppressing the violent Racist direction of activity. Thus (according to Henning still), "not daring to attack Graefe and Wulle directly," the attack on the Racists was being made obliquely through the "insignificant" Henning. [43] The fact is, however, despite Henning, that Wulle and Graefe were by July also being included in the attacks. [44] Particularly direct comment came from the Christian Socialists in specific reference to the Henning-Wulle-Graefe trio: "The exclusion or voluntary departure

[42] Statement of Graefe in *Mecklenburger Warte,* reported in *Deutsche Stimmen,* Aug. 20, 1922, and in *Berliner Tageblatt,* Aug. 16, 1922 (A.M.). Also WP: Brauer to Heydebrand, July 8, 1922; Henning's report mentioned only Düringer by name, but alluded to two other members who joined him in asking for the exclusion of all Racists. One of these men claimed that Henning had asked Ehrhardt for 1,000 men to help establish a Seeckt dictatorship.

[43] WP: Henning's report. A similar view of Nationalist *Koalitionsfähigkeit* was expressed by the DVP in *Deutsche Stimmen,* Aug. 20, 1922, p. 537.

[44] WP: Wulle's report. Graefe, quoted in *Deutsche Stimmen,* Aug. 20, 1922, p. 534. Kanitz and v. Braun were both outspoken.

(as the case may be) of right radical leaders from the DNVP is to be regarded as an important political fact. By this split the DNVP and its policy will be freed of the ballast of reactionary political elements." [45]

Yet for the time being the leadership did not want necessarily to lose the entire Racist wing, lest the DNVP too much resemble the DVP. But hoping to control the Racists, the leadership joined with the six protesting *Fraktion* members to bring about the exclusion of Henning on purely disciplinary grounds. In this they were also supported by about thirty members of the Prussian *Landtagsfraktion*. When Henning refused to leave the Party voluntarily, he was formally expelled from the *Fraktion* by vote of the Central Executive on July 18. [46] The public was informed only that Henning had left for personal reasons. Düringer's individual withdrawal at almost the same time can be interpreted as his protest that the Executive had not made its action and its underlying reasons more obvious, and that it had limited its action merely to a disciplinary measure. [47]

---

[45] *Evangelisch-soziale Stimmen*, V-VI (May-June, 1922), p. 4 (publisher: Pastor D. Jäger, Bethel; editor: Hartwig). Cf., *Berliner Tageblatt*, Aug. 16, 1922 (A.M.): by Aug. 8, Jäger was demanding (in *Aufwärts*) an independent Christian Social party if the DNVP did not eliminate the anti-Christian, anti-social Racist elements.

[46] WP: Brauer to Heydebrand, July 18 and 20, 1922. Members of the Executive who opposed the action were Wulle, v. Graefe, Westarp, v. Gallwitz, Hensel-Johannisburg, and Frau Paula Müller-Otfried. Cf., *Kzztg.*, July 20, 1922 (A.M.).

[47] *Berliner Lokal-Anzeiger*, July 21, 1922 (A.M.); *Kzztg.*, July 20, 1922 (P.M.). Düringer was apparently not even present at the July 18 session of the Executive when Henning was excluded, probably having issued his ultimatum in the *Fraktion* in much stronger terms than the other five members. A rumor was circulating at the same time of Hoetzsch's plan to follow him. The *Kreuzzeitung*, Oct. 7, 1922 (A.M.), spoke of Düringer as a respected "expert" who did not really belong in any political party by temperament. It was recalled how he had embarrassed the DNVP on numerous occasions, as when

The Party did indeed try to localize the issue in the public mind by denying strongly that the incident was in any way an expression of Nationalist hostility toward anti-Semitism or the Racist movement. As Graef put it, "The actual cause of separation was their notion [i.e., of Graefe, Henning, and Wulle] . . . of converting the DNVP to the political methods of fascism which the majority of the Party rejected as not applicable in Germany." [48]

The Racists, grievously insulted by these latest developments, naturally were not willing to localize the issue as the Nationalist leadership wanted. Henning had powerful friends in Graefe and Wulle who resigned from the *Fraktion* (though not the Party) the day he was expelled. Wulle had at his disposal the *Deutsches Abendblatt* for the purpose of a last-ditch campaign which they planned to fight largely in the open. And it soon became apparent that their attack was aimed directly at Hergt and the Party line that had been formulated under him. They attacked the Nationalist leadership for its mania of "positive cooperation" and related longing for ministerial portfolios. Wulle denied he was leading a movement to break up the DNVP. He recalled that, on every occasion in the past when he had brought a Racist proposal before the Party, he had been confronted with governmentalist considerations ("the cabinet question"). He had been faced also with threats of resignation from the Party by Hergt, his right-hand man Helfferich, Party whip Georg Schultz-Bromberg, and Hugenberg. Until now the Racists had always submitted to their coercion for the sake of unity. Now Wulle felt that conscience required them to leave a non-

---

he spoke favorably of the foreign policy of Prince Max of Baden, and used terms in speaking of Traub after the Kapp putsch that left very bad feelings in many quarters. As an elder statesman (former *Reichsgerichtsrat* and Justice Minister of Baden) he had a place in the DNVP more of respect than of influence.

[48] Graef, p. 41.

Racist party whose action was definitely heading in the direction of anti-racism. [49] In denouncing Hergt to his friends, Wulle implied that only a radical shift in leadership and policy could prevent the impending split. Though pessimistic, he still wanted to continue working within the DNVP, but a solution would have to come within the next few weeks. Brauer in the DKP estimated that Hergt would have to resign his office by September 1 or the Party would begin to disintegrate. [50]

But the Hergt leadership of course had no intention of meeting the Racist opposition on its own terms. It sought and received support from the *Fraktionen* of the Reichstag and Prussian Assembly. [51] It was also at pains to win a following in the Party at large, and numerous meetings were held at the local level to explain the leadership's position. As the Racists also appealed to the Party at large, it was for a while by no means clear who was going to win the upper hand. Forty persons attended a meeting of provincial organizations called by Wulle on the last day of July. It included representatives of twelve organizations that presumably favored the Racist cause: Potsdam I, Potsdam II, Berlin, Pomerania, Weser-Ems, Silesia, Thuringia, Mecklenburg, West Saxony, Dresden, Grenzmark Posen-West Prussia, and Schleswig-Holstein. Of interest was the presence of Count Westarp in the committee set up by that Racist meeting to study the questions at issue in the DNVP. [52]

Westarp was in fact becoming rapidly a key figure for the possible resolution of the crisis. He was perhaps the

[49] *Berliner Lokal-Anzeiger,* July 21, 1922 (A.M.); *Kzztg.,* July 21 (A.M.), July 27 (A.M.), 1922.

[50] WP: Brauer to Heydebrand, July 18, 1922.

[51] *Kzztg.,* July 21 (A.M.), July 27 (A.M.), 1922.

[52] WP: "Protokoll der Sitzung vom 31. Juli 1922," other members included Thomas-Pommern, Laverrenz, Kube (secretary), Gandig, v. Feldmann-Thüringen, Steiniger; Brauer to Heydebrand, July 31, 1922.

best placed person to mediate among Racists, Conservatives, and other Nationalists. By the dissidents he was most frequently named as the desirable successor to Hergt, and even as the only man who could still hold the DNVP together. [53]

Old Conservatives tended to stand by the Racists in the controversy, perhaps because a number had been Conservatives before the war. Some Old Conservatives feared also that the attack by the Hergt leadership on the Racists was only a prelude to a renewal of the previous struggle for complete dissolution of the DKP. Lindeiner was reported to have told a meeting, untactfully, that the DNVP planned no action against the Conservatives. By the very mention of the subject he gave the opposite impression. [54]

Aware of these suspicions, Wulle hoped to bring Racists and Conservatives together, and proposed to talk over the subject with Heydebrand. He was encouraged by Brauer and others in the Conservative bureau to do so. Meanwhile Brauer was writing his absentee leader, "In my opinion the hour for us Conservatives has now struck, and we are faced with the question of whether or not to turn to practical measures." He added the caution, "Unfortunately one must reckon with the personal ambition of individual leaders, especially so among the Racists." [55] The measure of feeling among some loyal Old Conservatives can be

---

[53] Cf., WP: Memorandum (signature illegible), July 25, 1922: "Wulle expressly mentioned that the only sure possibility he could imagine of still holding together the Party was acceptance of the stopgap leadership of Count Westarp." In similar vein was the resolution of confidence in Westarp and Wulle passed by Potsdam II Inner Executive, mentioned by Brauer to Heydebrand, July 31, 1922, who continued: "According to my information, Count Westarp is being given primary consideration as Hergt's successor."

[54] WP: Brauer to Heydebrand, July 8, 1922; impression relayed to Brauer by Könnecke, secretary of Potsdam II.

[55] WP: Brauer to Heydebrand, July 20, 1922.

judged from the fervor of a letter sent to Westarp by Friedrich Everling: "If a new party is to come, then it must be the Old Conservative party. Its platform: Racist, Prussian, monarchist, federalist, Christian, and corporate-social (*ständisch-sozial*). . . . It is necessary (not only desirable, but necessary) that the leader of the Old Conservative party finally become leader of the renewed DNVP! There is only one person [i.e., Westarp] who has the confidence of the Racists, although he is not a Racist in the narrow sense, and who at the same time has the confidence of Old Conservative circles, although at the moment he is numbered among the Nationalists. The time is ripe not only for a new party but for a new leader. If you can use me, I am at your disposition as aide, the only honorific position to which I aspire. If it would do any good, I can intrigue as well as Lindeiner. Then something like real policy might be formulated and carried out . . . in contrast to Hergt and his half-way measures, Düringer and his democratic sympathies, Graef and his bravado." [56] The *Kreuzzeitung,* on the other hand, tried to avoid sharpening the current struggle, and made as little reference to the difficulties as possible. Such guarded language as editor Georg Foertsch was willing to hazard merely regretted the Henning incident and hoped for reconciliation between Racists and Nationalists. [57]

Count Westarp was also noticeably restrained. Though he had voted against the exclusion of Henning from the *Fraktion* and tried to mediate the situation with Graefe, he refused to enter into public discussion of the situation. He thought the Racist idea could fit well into the general Conservative framework when it avoided extremism. [58] Privately he expressed his deep disappointment with the

[56] WP: (copy) Everling to Westarp, July 25, 1922.
[57] *Kzztg.,* July 23, 27, and 30, 1922 (all A.M.).
[58] *Kzztg.,* Aug. 20, 1922 (A.M.).

action of the leadership, but showed no personal or political ambition beyond the role of mediator and reconciler. "It was a misfortune," he wrote in August, "that we were practically crippled at this very time by the inner struggle over Henning. I hold those persons and groups responsible who brought up the subject of Henning and who wanted to separate him from the Party even before the murder of Rathenau, and who forced a decision after the Rathenau murder by introducing the cabinet question." [59]

As reports continued to come in of restiveness among Old Conservatives in the country, Westarp joined forces with his leader, Heydebrand, and Count Seidlitz, the head of the Silesian Conservatives, to prevent the split occasioned by Graefe and Wulle from spreading, and to help bridge the gap, if that were still possible. They definitely turned down the idea of taking advantage of the DNVP's difficulties to set up an active new DKP. [60] As the crisis gained further momentum, the Conservative Executive openly deplored the separatist action of Racist elements and called for cooperation of Conservatives and Racists within the DNVP. [61]

In line with that policy Westarp continued to work for the Racists in the DNVP. Prior to the 1922 *Parteitag* an impasse had been reached, as was clearly seen in a preliminary conference of party representatives on September 14 and 15. Three-quarters of the votes backed Hergt on the Racist issue, leaving Westarp as the leader of a small Conservative-Racist opposition. When Schleswig-Holstein proposed to censure Graefe and Wulle, Westarp entered a counter-resolution signed by nine provincial organizations. To avoid the head-on collision the meeting was suspended

[59] WP: Westarp to Count Stillfried, Aug. 15, 1922.

[60] WP: Westarp to v. Kleist, Aug. 21, 1922.

[61] Meeting of *Engerer Vorstand* of the DKP, Heydebrand presiding, Sept. 12, reported in *Berliner Lokal-Anzeiger,* Sept. 13, 1922 (P.M.).

for three hours, and each side was persuaded to withdraw its motion. The issue was by-passed, not settled. [62]

Tension mounted in the following weeks as Hergt took steps to have Henning finally expelled by his local organization, Weser-Ems, on the pretext of a dispute between him and Hoetzsch. [63] The Racists nevertheless went ahead with their plans for a Racist Cooperative Group (*Deutschvölkische Arbeitsgemeinschaft*—DVAG) within the DNVP that was to be not merely a central committee, but was to have branches on the local level. It appeared in every way to be the party-within-a-party that Hergt feared, and Westarp declined to join, though he promised cooperation from Conservative Nationalists.

But with the definite formation of a Racist party-within-the-party, the quarrel was advanced into open ground where personal grievances were less pertinent. The Nationalist Executive called on Graefe and Wulle to justify their latest action, and deemed unsatisfactory their replies. The Executive ruled further that the existence of a Racist organization with local branches throughout the country was not consistent with the best interests of the DNVP. Not only did the arrangement disturb the unity of the Party, but also gave the false impression that the Racist idea was not otherwise respected. As a confidential circular from the leadership saw the situation, "The Racist standpoint of the Party remains firm. Different points of view concerning tactics can be resolved only within the framework of regular party organs. In conformity with paragraph 12 of party regulations, a Racist committee is to be formed and attached to the Party Executive in order to work out thoroughly, and deepen, the potentialities of Racist thought."[64]

The Executive, in denying that racism was an issue,

[62] WP: Brauer to Heydebrand, Aug. 19, 1922.

[63] WP: Hergt, mimeographed circular to members of the Executive, Sept. 18, 1922.

[64] WP: Copy of the resolution.

stuck to matters of discipline and organization. Avoiding publicity as much as possible, the leadership kept informed only members of the *Fraktionen,* and the heads and chief officials of branch units. [65] Westarp meanwhile assured the public that the DVAG was no split, but represented a widening of the opportunities for conscious Racist, anti-Semitic activity among Nationalists. [66] Privately he felt that the situation had deteriorated alarmingly, and even remarked that Conservatives would eventually have to leave the DNVP since the Party would doubtless follow an increasingly left-oriented policy after the Racist split. [67] Although he retained his self-appointed role of mediator, by early October, Westarp was pessimistic concerning results: "Meanwhile it seems to me that the establishment of the Racist Cooperative Group has progressed so far that Graefe and Wulle could back out only with difficulty now. I believe that under certain conditions it would still be possible for the Party to come to terms with that development. But there is little prospect of the Executive's doing that." [68]

It is of interest to note that the Bavarian *Mittelpartei* was meanwhile fighting its own Racist struggle, complicated by local issues, with Colonel Rudolf von Xylander, the head of the Munich branch. The splintering that took place in Munich almost wiped out the party there. It took years to recover some of its strength, but it was never as strong again in the Bavarian capital. [69]

On the national scene the situation also continued to deteriorate. When the Executive forbade the work of the

[65] WP: Registered circular described the meeting of Sept. 28-9, signed Dr. Weiss ("Protokollführer"), dated Berlin, Oct. 2, 1922, marked "Confidential, not for publication," directed to prescribed categories of Party members.

[66] *Kzztg.,* Oct. 1, 1922 (A.M.).

[67] WP: Brauer to Heydebrand, Oct. 3, 1922.

[68] WP: Brauer to v. Feldmann, Oct. 6, 1922.

[69] My dissertation, pp. 260-2.

Racist Cooperative Group within the Party, Graefe and Wulle acquiesced on the assumption that their work would continue outside the Party, like the Pan-German League or Farmers' League, with no incompatibility of membership. On October 17, however, Helfferich introduced a resolution in the Executive to eliminate the separate Racist operations entirely by requiring total submission of Racist leaders to the Executive's directives. [70] In the *Fraktion,* Graefe found he could muster only thirteen votes as against the Party leadership's thirty-six. [71]

Under such circumstances Westarp saw little hope of settlement at the Party Congress in Görlitz. Obviously Graefe would not yield any further and the Nationalist leadership remained intransigent. Westarp's only hope was that he might yet persuade the DVAG to dissolve and to begin its work on another basis. [72] Westarp received indirect assurance from the leadership that he need not fear the wrath of the Racists in his home constituency of Potsdam II. The Party would guarantee him a good place, come what may, on the national list. The promise came from Graef-Anklam who feared the Racists might succeed in pulling Westarp to their side. He feared also the re-emergence of some Old Conservatives, including Heydebrand, into active political life. [73]

With good reason the leadership was unsure of the reaction in Conservative circles when the chips were down on the Racist issue. With Conservatives on this were also a number of persons of the bitter opposition Fatherland

[70] WP: Printed confidential sheet of the DVAG; mimeographed copy of the Helfferich resolution, Oct. 16, 1922.

[71] WP: Brauer to Heydebrand, Oct. 18, 1922. He noted also: "The instigators of the fight are supposed to have been the Christian Socialists, but Helfferich is also one of the anti-Racist ringleaders."

[72] WP: Brauer to Heydebrand, Oct. 25, 1922.

[73] WP: Behr to Westarp, Oct. 25, 1922, reported talk with Graef-Anklam on Oct. 22, following the meeting of the DNVP *Vertretertag* for Pomerania.

party group. [74] The Pan-German elements remained ambiguous, except for Hugenberg who for once sided with the leadership. Thus, before the Görlitz *Parteitag*, the Party leadership of Hergt and Helfferich could be reasonably sure of the support only of the main economic pressure groups, i.e., commerce and industry, agriculture, and Christian workers, all of them (except Hugenberg) anxious to obtain power legally in the state through participation in government as soon as possible. Of the groups, the Christian Socialist workers were now particularly vocal in their opposition to the doctrinaire Racists, and even threatened leaving a party that retained them. [75] Their reason was that the Racists harbored reactionary and anti-labor sentiments.

That was the background of the annual Congress of the DNVP that met in Görlitz, October 26 to 28. For informed persons the decisions at Görlitz were a foregone conclusion. If there was a test involved, it was not really one of Party leadership against doctrinaire Racists, but rather a show of the actual measure of strength the leadership possessed in the DNVP as a whole. Hergt was completely vindicated in the voting; the DVAG was condemned, and an official Party Racist committee was set up.

The Görlitz Congress did not expell Graefe, Wulle, or Henning from the Party. Technically they remained, as individuals, members of local branches of the DNVP. But they had no intention of giving up their work outside of the DNVP though they knew this would inevitably lead to an independent party organization. On the last day of the Congress a handbill appeared to announce reorganization of the DVAG, not to fight the DNVP as such, but rather to oppose the "system" of the Hergt-Helfferich lead-

[74] Cf., WP: Pfarrer Dr. Pfannkuche (alternate chairman of *Bezirksverband Osnabrück*) to Westarp, Aug. 14, 1922, strongly pro-Henning.

[75] Pastor D. Jäger-Bethel, *Aufwärts,* Aug. 8, 1922, quoted in *Berliner Tageblatt,* Aug. 16, 1922 (A.M.).

ership. The DVAG proposed to circumvent the leadership without splitting the Party. It therefore invited sympathetic Nationalist elements to name representatives who were beyond the discipline of the Central Executive to cooperate with the reorganized DVAG. It also demanded a boycott of the Executive's own national Racist committee, but recommended thorough infiltration of the new study committees to be set up by the DNVP on the local level. [76]

Westarp thought there was some chance of peaceful coexistence with the DVAG. He did not think the Party could prevent members from belonging to a non-parliamentary organization of this kind. [77] But he turned to the Racists to explain his own position, and to warn them of extreme action. He explained privately to Graefe why he had finally expressed his confidence in Hergt and accepted the situation at Görlitz. Although he knew this would harm his position with the Racists, he felt that Conservative interests were not to be served at that time by splintering the DNVP into its components. From the beginning of the active phase of the controversy in July, Westarp had made it clear that he would not help any action to remove Hergt as leader. He resented rumors circulated by the Racists that the issue had arisen because high circles in the DNVP were corrupted by the interests of "Jewry, capitalism, and the needs of coalition respectability." Hergt and Helfferich had only pressed the matter at Görlitz on what they considered to be a breach of discipline, Westarp now insisted. To this he added a note of admonition: "The Party does not, and cannot, tolerate the sending of non-confidential circulars, whether by you, Wulle, Henning, Reventlow, or others, that raise accusations of conscious and unconscious subservience to Jewish interests." [78]

It was apparent that serious differences were arising be-

[76] WP: Printed handbill.
[77] *Kzztg.*, Oct. 31, 1922 (P.M.).
[78] WP: Westarp to Graefe, Nov. 2, 1922.

tween Westarp and Graefe because of the latter's attacks
on Hergt and Helfferich in the *Mecklenburger Warte* and
elsewhere in the press. Graefe was reported to be completely wild after the Görlitz experience and determined to
carry on the fight against Hergt at all costs. He hoped to
form a broad Racist party to include, besides his own
Deutschvölkische, members of the Nazi party and of other
anti-Semitic groups. Westarp, realizing regretfully and
somewhat belatedly the dangerous extent of Graefe's ambitions and their disruptive effect on the whole Nationalist movement, decided to ask his friends in Potsdam II to
abandon any thought of keeping up relations with the
DVAG. [79]

Graefe was very angry at Westarp's acceptance of the
decisions of the Görlitz Congress. Westarp by defending
Hergt, said Graefe, had betrayed his Racist friends and
made a Conservative-Racist alliance impossible: "I only
wish to make you understand what doubly grieves me in
the position you finally took; in the first place, you in
effect abandoned us Racists for the Pyrrhic victors of
Görlitz; in the second place, I firmly believe your action
has greatly weakened the position you held as a check on
the H^4 coalition (Hergt-Helfferich-Hoetzsch-Hugenberg) ." [80]
Graefe's list of enemies was thus broadened from the Hergt-
Helfferich leadership to include particularly Hoetzsch, who
might be described as a progressive-conservative intellectual, and Hugenberg, the Pan-German industrialist spokesman. In a later letter he also named Gustav Roesicke, the
chief agrarian representative, as well as prominent Christian Socialist leaders, and other Party bureaucrats. [81]

With this preparation, there was no reason for surprise
when Graefe, Wulle, Henning, and their friends, mostly
secessionists from the DNVP, founded their own party, the

[79] WP: Brauer to Heydebrand, Nov. 10, 1922.
[80] WP: Graefe to Westarp, Nov. 4, 1922.
[81] WP: Graefe to Westarp, Nov. 10, 1922.

German Racist Freedom party (*Deutschvölkische Freiheits-partei*–DVFP) in Berlin on December 17. [82] Though Westarp hoped the Nationalist and Racist parties would still be able to work together, he must have had some doubts after Henning casually expressed doubt on the value of monarchy in a Racist state. [83]

Nevertheless most Conservatives wanted to minimize differences. Heydebrand in particular threw his weight and that of the DKP into an attempt to bridge the gap. By trying to eliminate the polemic that was further damaging relations, he hoped to create an atmosphere favorable for peace talks. [84] But it was a little late for the Conservative party to intervene as honest brokers. In any case the decisions lay elsewhere. Bitterly disappointed were the people in the DKP who had most strongly advocated a Racist-Conservative union as their answer to the challenge of republican democracy. [85] But Heydebrand, Westarp, and other Conservatives were soon alienated by the evidences of "vanity, demagoguery, even of pathological megalomania" in the Racist leadership as it drifted into nazism. Such behavior, it was remarked, had more in common with revolutionary manners than with the correct, straightforward and loyal military manner expected in the Nationalist and Conservative political community. [86]

The relations of Racists and the Pan-German League followed a rather similar development of love and hate, com-

[82] *Kzztg.*, Dec. 24, 1922 (A.M.).

[83] Statement of Henning in Halle, Dec. 21, to the effect that the form of government, monarchical or republican, was a secondary consideration in a Racist state, quoted in *Berliner Tageblatt*, Dec. 28, 1922 (P.M.).

[84] Public announcement of the Inner Executive of the DKP, meeting Mar. 8, in *Kzztg.*, Mar. 8, 1923 (A.M.).

[85] WP: Franz Sontag to Heydebrand, Nov. 21, 1922.

[86] WP: Düsterberg [DNVP *Landesverband Merseburg*] to Westarp, Dec. 21, 1922, referred especially to the intrigues of Henning in the Halle area.

plicated by a web of personal animosities. As in their attitude toward the Kapp putsch, the Pan-Germans were jealous of rivals and intolerant of failure. When the Racists failed to make good their bid for prominence in the DNVP, the ADV, which had at least tolerated them, definitely turned on them.

We have so far seen in some detail how the DNVP lost various segments of its membership in the course of unpleasant and painful controversies. In turn, *Vaterlandsparteiler*, Free Conservatives, and Racists left the Party while the fortunes of the remaining groups shifted. What was left, we might ask, in this Nationalist Party after four years? What remained of this catch-all of the right and its ambition to be a truly national Party? Was this still a movement (even by its own standards) to lead Germany back to middle-class standards of political sanity, justice, social stability, and economic freedom?

Oskar Hergt stubbornly remained on the scene, supported by the majority of Nationalist Party members who refused to allow a leadership crisis to be forced on them. The support came especially from the economic interests of business, agriculture, and Christian Socialist labor. Also, more closely associated with Hergt than ever, was the economist and National Liberal publicist, Karl Helfferich, who, after the fight with the Racists, felt he had cleared himself of the charge of right radical sympathies. The Hergt-Helfferich leadership had emerged from the difficult internal crisis with complete victory. It had risked much in order to discipline the Party and to restore a measure of tranquility in its public life. Yet it must be said that it had operated on unclear principles, often in a most awkward and roundabout manner that left a residue of mistrust. That was true particularly of Pan-Germans and Conservatives who went along with the majority in the DNVP in the absence of an acceptable alternative.

In the reduced DNVP, Pan-Germans and Conservatives

were to have more importance than they had had before. That was true not just because they were relatively much stronger in the DNVP, but because they were overcoming inhibitions on public expression of their feelings, and were infinitely more vocal and self-confident in the internal and external struggles of the Party. From this time Pan-Germans became a recognizable force in the DNVP, just as from the beginning the Conservatives had been a real, if mainly negative, force in the Party's existence. Though Conservatives found little satisfaction in the Racist crisis, no doubt Westarp's personal stature in the DVNP was enhanced as a result of his attempted mediation between Racists and leadership, as well as his judicious acceptance of the final decisions in the controversy.

In those days Westarp also did much to hold the DNVP together after the Racist secession and ironically, considering his past, came to represent the cause of unity in the shaken Nationalist circle. However, defections appear to have been far less numerous than expected, even in traditionally Racist strongholds. Where many local Nationalist organizations had still backed the embattled Racists after Görlitz, this largely ceased to be the case after the DVFP emerged as a reality. The leadership meanwhile pressed Wulle, Graefe, and Henning to give up their seats in the Reichstag—a request of course ignored. The applicable procedure was just a gentleman's agreement and the understanding in German politics that a parliamentary seat was at the disposal of parties, not individuals. [87] But this was a minor annoyance. Elections were not immediately in

[87] WP: Resolution of *Landesverband Mecklenburg-Strelitz,* Nov. 19, 1922, asked v. Graefe to retain his seat in Parliament, though he was excluded from the *Fraktion;* DNVP *Landesverband Mecklenburg-Schwerin* to Westarp, Jan. 8, 1923, reported that by a vote of 33-6 it asked v. Graefe to give up his seat; *Kzztg.,* Feb. 7, 1923 (P.M.), statement on Wulle.

sight, and three seats fewer or more in the House did not make much difference to the Nationalists.

The Racist controversy had only one slight repercussion on the physical make-up of the Executive—the resignation of Walther Graef-Anklam from the important post of executive secretary. Though Graef had been one of the staunchest exponents of the Hergt viewpoint, there had been friction between him and the Party leader on the subject of organization. The Party was also embarrassed by Graef's excessive drinking which was getting him into personal difficulties. [88] His removal was a further step in the consolidation of the Hergt-Helfferich team.

It is not necessary to provide a full sequel here on subsequent Nationalist-Racist relations. Nationalists and doctrinaire Racists went henceforth different ways and were never reconciled. When the Racists were discredited by implication in the Nazi Munich putsch of November, 1923, they seemed for a time eliminated as effective rivals of the DNVP. The Nationalist Party could afford to be magnanimous by championing the cause of civil liberty when the DVFP was banned along with the NSDAP. The DNVP was pleased for once to be spared the odium of responsibility for right radical madness.

The new Nationalist Racist committee formed by the leadership at the Görlitz Congress was on the way to rendering harmless, in an atmosphere of academic discussion, the explosive material placed in its hands. It might very well have remained content to while away the time in plotting mild agitation—sponsoring annual Racist weeks, planning anti-Semitic articles in the press, and passing resolutions—had there not been other matters to complicate its life. The fact was that it became a convenient vehicle for the promotion of Pan-German ambitions in the

[88] W MS, pp. 209-12; WP: Brauer to Heydebrand, Feb. 9, 1923.

DNVP. In later years Axel von Freytagh-Loringhoven gained control to turn it into a strong counter-force against the party policy of the day.

Meanwhile under the Hergt-Helfferich régime, the Racist committee was stirred to life by the unexpected victory of the DVFP in provincial elections in Mecklenburg and Thuringia early in 1924. It seemed a gloomy omen for the DNVP in the approaching national elections. There was a sudden fear of Racist competition that brought a more drastic statement of policy in the press than had perhaps ever been ventured officially. [89] Behind the scenes however it appeared that the statement was inspired by the Pan-German representative, Leopold von Vietinghoff-Scheel, whose efforts the committee did not receive with the enthusiasm that press reports suggested. Many in the committee found the views "unclear and hazy" (*unklar und verschwommen*) and proposed to revise them.

Hergt himself expressed Racist views in the committee meeting on February 17, 1924, with surprising vigor, ". . . which would cause one to marvel," wrote Brauer of the DKP, "were the explanation not to be seen all too clearly in the latest Racist election victories and in Hergt's fear of the ruinous results of the anti-Racist policy pursued by him. Graef-Thüringen, the chairman of that committee,

---

[89] Statement issued by the Racist committee of the DNVP, meeting Feb. 17, 1924, quoted in *Berliner Tageblatt*, Feb. 19, 1924 (P.M.): "1. Germany is to be ruled by persons of German blood! Public administration in the Reich, the States and Municipalities should be run on German lines. 2. The German family must be protected from foreign intruders. 3. German culture must be purged of the influence of foreign races; law, science, literature, press, and art are to be rigorously purified. 4. German economy must be based on the principle of free development of the individual. Domination by Jewish international capitalism, and the remnants of Marxist economy, are to be eliminated and replaced by a social and economic system that corresponds to the character of the German people—a reform that will allow the German worker to share in the fruits of his labor."

has stated that at the coming Party Congress in Hamburg
(April 1, 1924) the paragraph to exclude Jews from the
Party will be adopted without opposition." Ruefully,
Brauer added that even half of this willingness to meet
Racist wishes earlier would have prevented the split. [90]
Westarp could have said, "I told you so," but contented
himself with keeping open the door to reconciliation and
doing what he could to hold the DNVP together. In this
vein he wrote, "The victories of the Racists in Mecklenburg and Thuringia show among other things how wrong
it was to allow the separation to take place that I opposed.
. . . I keep close contact here with various agencies of the
Patriotic Organizations (*Vaterländische Verbände*) in order
to keep their following in the DNVP. But naturally it is
not going to work unless the Party assumes an objective
Racist position and unless personal concessions are made.
. . ." [91] In those observations are seen again the canniness
of Westarp. As a politician he was astute, judicious, tough,
and stubborn. He was also influential in many circles, and
well on his way to the achievement of a leader's prominence in the DNVP, as much because of his personal
qualities as his key connections.

This study has so far been mainly concerned with crises
in the development of the Nationalist Party: its founding,
the first elections, the Kapp putsch, the Free Conservative
and Racist secessions. Though observation of crises helps
one penetrate realities of character usually half-hidden in
the ambiguities of routine life, nevertheless, to understand
the role of the DNVP as the principal opposition of German political life in the 1920's, it is necessary to turn to
less dramatic reality and consider factors of personality,
leadership, and class interest among the countless complexi-

[90] WP: Brauer to Heydebrand, Feb. 19, 1924, reported an unnamed
informant, member of the *Völkischer Reichsausschuss der DNVP*.
[91] WP: Westarp to Count Seidlitz, March 22, 1924.

ties of the Party. Most important, we must consider again the basic question: the fundamental outlook of an opposition party in a state it regarded constitutionally and ideologically unacceptable. The next chapter will approach these problems by trying to show what the Nationalist Party was under the leadership of Hergt in its positive program of action.

VI

The Will to Power

The Dawes Plan of 1924 appeared to bring with it a few years of tranquility for the Weimar Republic. At least it coincided with a period of relative political stability and comparative economic buoyancy. This was also a time when the Nationalist Party was strong in Parliament and on two occasions joined the government coalition. But it should be remembered that the DNVP grew to its height at the polls in the Republic's time of troubles; it emerged after the elections of 1924 as the strongest non-Socialist party. The triumph was never repeated. After the good years, the Party in the 1928 election entered a slump from which it never recovered.

The depressed and unstable early years of the Republic were for the DNVP its years of growth. The mid-twenties were the pleasant bachelor days of the Party when it could still indulge the luxury of opposition without responsibility. That, at least, was the extravagance of which it was accused by its detractors, and which its leadership was always quick to deny. The leadership stressed the theme of responsibility to a degree that extremists of the Kapp, Racist, and Pan-German schools resented, and rather soon they were raising questions about Hergt's fitness in office. But it was not until the controversy over the Dawes Plan that the Party was inescapably faced with a leadership crisis serious enough to end with the retirement of Oskar Hergt.

The Hergt régime was not the same at the end of its term as it was at the beginning. It had always been a hyphenated leadership; that is, it began virtually as a Hergt—Free-Conservative coalition, and changed in the course of the 1920 into a Hergt-Helfferich duumvirate. Hergt, through all, was a common denominator as Party organizer, and representative somehow of the Nationalist general will. But, the formative influence on policy seemed to come less from him, than from collaborators whom he admitted to tacit partnership in his office. These were, in the first year or so, mainly the Free Conservatives Kardorff and Delbrück, and the independent Posadowsky—men who believed in compromise and the desirability of a broad comprehensive party. Yet, though they were the original voices of right-wing Nationalism in the National Assembly at Weimar, gradually but definitely they were displaced by a more strident polyphony of Old Conservatives and Racists in Reichstag debates. In the brief Free Conservative era of Nationalism the leader of the DNVP still made conciliatory gestures toward Socialists and still recognized some restraints on anti-Semitism. Tension that existed within the Party was then due mainly to differences with Old Conservatives, and less with Racists or *Vaterlandsparteiler*. But the character of the Party was altered after the Kapp putsch when *Vaterlandsparteiler* and Free Conservatives lost their influence in the DNVP. At the same time, Karl Helfferich won himself a seat in the inner councils of the Party through his vendetta against Erzberger, and by election to the Reichstag in the June, 1920, election. With his arrival, the Hergt leadership took on new color, and, by the time the major Racist crisis was resolved late in 1922, one could speak fairly of a Hergt-Helfferich leadership.

A recent study has misleadingly referred to "the influential Helfferich-Hergt wing of the DNVP, which represented financial and business interests. . . ."[1] Hergt, though he was once head of the Prussian Finance Ministry, was never a representative of business interests. His outlook was

[1] Walter Kaufmann, *Monarchism in the Weimar Republic* (New York, 1953), pp. 110-1.

basically Free Conservative, but he was not bound by party limitations before he entered the DNVP. He stressed constantly his wish to bring into the Party the mass of "little people" who had never before been politically organized or even politically conscious—including women, small tradesmen, and unorganized labor. [2] Hergt's concern for the petty bourgeoisie and his friendly collaboration with Christian Socialists did not exactly endear him to the world of business and finance.

Karl Helfferich, once considered for appointment as the head of the *Reichsbank,* was on the other hand much closer to that world. He had had a notable managerial career in such enterprises as the Berlin-to-Baghdad Railway and the *Deutsche Bank.* Before entering the cabinet ranks during the war, he had also acquired a respectable reputation as an economist and expert on money and banking. An industrialist friend of Alfred Hugenberg, the channel for funds from big business to the DNVP, believed that Hugenberg was happy to work on the sidelines as long as Helfferich handled economic policy for the DNVP. [3] Yet, while Hugenberg remained quiet, he had serious misgivings regarding the wisdom of the party leadership, especially on the question of positive participation in the state. Both Hugenberg and Helfferich however were strong men

[2] My interview with Hergt, Göttingen, Aug. 14, 1952. Cf. also, letter of Hergt to me, Feb. 13, 1952. He regretted that he no longer possessed documentary material; "I particularly regret being unable to help you in the manner you expected. I would have desired very much to have seen clearly brought to light the special approach of the Nationalist Party (especialy in the first period of its existence) toward the subject of social grouping, as it concerned the cooperation of workers, both men and women, and particularly as it referred to the so-called 'little people.' "

[3] Quaatz, p. 244: "As long as Helfferich was active in the Reichstag, Hugenberg remained in the background. This was a conscious and intended retirement based on a close relationship with his colleague." Also, Otto Kriegk, *Hugenberg* (Leipzig, 1932), p. 62.

in their own right, and not merely agents of a class. Just as they often differed on questions of method and policy, they also could on occasion hold views unpopular with business. This was true, for example, in their uncompromising opposition to the Dawes Plan which most financial interests in Germany supported. In talking about either man, one should look as much to his real political character as to his economic background.

Hergt was proud of his part in bringing Helfferich into the DNVP, and was pleased to have helped him find a place in the 1920 election. In a conversation with me a few years ago, Hergt recalled with satisfaction the days when he and Helfferich together managed the Party. This was a partnership in which Hergt attended to problems of internal organization and Helfferich worked on public relations and propaganda. [4] As a politician Helfferich combined energy with skillful oratory. [5] Even so, in entering Nationalist politics, he had to overcome the taint of past association with the Bethmann Hollweg government. He actually could find no district to run him as a candidate for Parliament until he had engineered the Erzberger controversy and directed it relentlessly in the public eye for almost a year. [6]

In its very essence the Nationalist Party was obsessed by hate—of the Weimar system, of the Weimar coalition, of the foreign enemies of the late war. This had been the real meaning of the Party's fierce persecution of Matthias Erzberger, who to them was the embodiment of "the national constitution itself, the alliance of democracy and socialism, and the foreign policy of fulfillment of the Versailles Treaty." [7] Yet, many Nationalists who pictured

[4] My interview with Hergt, Göttingen, Aug. 14, 1952.

[5] Helfferich's power as a speaker was attested by Graef, p. 29; Westarp in his introduction to *Helfferichs Reichstagsreden 1922-1924* (Berlin, 1925), p. 10; Weiss, *loc. cit.*, p. 376.

[6] On the Erzberger trial see Epstein, chap. 14.

[7] Troeltsch, Sept. 12, 1921, p. 209. Cf., W MS (part II, new pagina-

themselves as the custodians of a tradition of national honor and patriotism, were much distressed at the prospect of their complete and permanent separation from responsibility in the state, the shrine of their devotion. Economic interests were also alarmed lest the apparatus of the state fall permanently into the hands of unfriendly and reckless leftists. Thus practical reasons and sentiment combined to make the Nationalists leadership consider the question of how it might best obtain power in the state even if that meant coming to terms temporarily with the republican constitution.

The Free Conservatives, while they were still in the DNVP, particularly pressed the question. Under their influence Hergt had made the gesture of the *Ordnungsprogramm*. In this spirit also, Otto Hoetzsch explained to a foreign audience that "no one in Germany, least of all my own Party, entertains any idea of changing by force the present Constitution. We work in this state on the basis of the Republic and we endeavor to achieve the Conservative program by peaceful constitutional and legal cooperation in the Republic." [8] As a matter of fact, the Nationalist *Fraktion* in the National Assembly at Weimar

---

tion), pp. 1-2: "For me personally from the very beginning of the postwar period, and since, the guiding light of my political activity was, and has always remained, the slogan of the 'fight against the System,' together with that of the 'fight against foreign domination.' . . . As a weapon of mass propaganda in the struggle for political power, more effective was the theme of resistance against the representatives of the System."

[8] Hoetzsch, *op. cit.*, p. 29; cf. also, v. Delbrück, Reich Debates, July 2, 1919, vol. 327, p. 1216: "We know that this Republic is an unavoidable fact, and we are decided to cooperate politically on the basis of political facts for the good of our Fatherland. For our part we have decided to follow a line of activity that will prepare the way to power for us." Also, Düringer, Reich Debates, July 30, 1919, vol. 328, p. 2092: "We shall . . . endeavor to cooperate positively with the young Republic, as indeed we have done for the past half-year."

was surprisingly ready for cooperation, even to the point of considering the possibility of participation in a cabinet. [9] Until the Party was considerably stronger such talk was, of course, purely speculative. Nevertheless it provided clues to future action.

After the June, 1920, election, positive participation was at least within the realm of possibility in view of the enhanced strength of middle-class parties in the Reichstag. Posadowsky, no longer leader of the *Fraktion,* made clear from the sidelines at least that he approved the entry of the DVP into the Fehrenbach government. He called the move a sacrifice made in the national interest, and hoped the DNVP would act similarly if it had the opportunity, even if that involved working with the left: "It is improbable in the foreseeable future that the DNVP, either alone or with the DVP, could form a parliamentary majority. Therefore, if it is to enter government, the Party will have to look for allies on the left. Such action will naturally be harder for a certain segment of the Nationalist Party to take than for members of the DVP. But the sacrifice must be made. . . . Benevolent neutrality is not sufficient here. On the contrary, as a formation of the right the Party has the fundamental obligation in the nature of things of supporting actively the middle-class element in government, thereby helping it toward the political strength of a majority party." [10]

In 1920, Hergt still expressed views similar to Posadowsky's. He was disappointed at the result of negotiations for a new government that followed the June election. The

[9] Graefe, Reich Debates, July 25, 1919, vol. 328, p. 1919: "The Nationalist Parliamentary Group has officially indicated in a resolution that it would be prepared in principle to participate in the formation of a cabinet (although at the moment there appears hardly a possibility for such an eventuality), provided a working majority stood behind such a cabinet."

[10] Posadowsky in *Tag,* quoted in *Nationalliberale Correspondenz,* p. 146, July 5, 1920.

technical possibility of a government of the right (since
the right had doubled in size) had been effectively blocked
in the course of three dreary weeks of talks with Democrats, Socialists, and Populists (DVP). Hergt resented especially the objections raised by the Democrats to the monarchist sympathies of the DNVP, and retorted in the
Reichstag: "No one surely could believe that the question
of monarchy could have any immediate relevance at the
moment or in the near future for the tasks now facing
Germany. The parties of the right have declared clearly
enough that they would completely desist from all efforts
to alter the Constitution during any period in which they
might be called on to share in a coalition." The objection
to the monarchism of the DNVP, he felt, also seemed
particularly ridiculous coming from the Social Democrats,
in view of their attempt to draw the "Communist" Independent Socialists into a coalition. Hergt berated the SPD
for this attempt to ally themselves with a revolutionary
party that did not accept the Constitution in any sense.
The Socialists should rather have accepted the judgment
of the voters by seeking a working agreement with the
right. Although the DNVP and SPD differed sharply in
their respective economic and foreign policies, the DNVP
would cooperate with workers of the left in a common
patriotic program if the workers would only demonstrate
their patriotic sentiment: "In our *Ordnungsprogramm,*
which was made public a while ago in the Prussian House,
we pleaded for the idea of a national bloc, and similarly in
later statements we have called for a united front. We have
constantly spelled out our feelings on this. With that in
mind we entered the election campaign. Even in recent
weeks in various statements we have expressed our readiness
to cooperate with a reformed political Left, naturally ourselves accepting the consequences of terms agreed on even
though this would mean heavy political and organizational
sacrifices."

[171]

The reference to the *Ordnungsprogram* as late as June, 1920, was only a rhetorical device. Hergt continued his Reichstag speech by blaming the negative attitude of the SPD for the lack of political unity in Germany. Since the SPD would not cooperate, the DNVP called for an all-bourgeois coalition as the only feasible solution to the cabinet question. Bitterly he pursued his attack against the obstructionists in the middle-class parties—Democrats, Centrists, Populists—for their false objections to the Nationalists. Not only its monarchism had been wrongfully held against the DNVP, but also allegations of racial hatred that the Party denied. ("Racial hatred does not exist in the DNVP. We approve of it as little as do others. Nevertheless we will not allow anyone to undermine the principles of our platform designed to protect the German race.") The Democrats were called the principal obstructionists, but the DVP too had failed to insist on cooperation with the Nationalists despite their formerly close relations.[11]

In fact the DNVP was on generally bad terms with the other parties in the Republic, and even Hergt could not speak of his *Ordnungsprogramm* with much spirit. Soon the press was pointing out that the program had really gone by the board, and that other more right-wing influences were apparent in upper echelons of the DNVP. [12] Among these other influences was Helfferich. He too spoke of the necessity of positive work in the state to protect public tranquillity. He justified Nationalist cooperation with the Republic on grounds of expediency and patriotism, but he never suggested that partnership with the left could serve a useful purpose. [13] The DNVP he regarded as an opposition party with its own social and political ideals to promote. [14] Yet, this was not opposition for its own sake, but

[11] Reich Debates, June 28, 1920, vol. 344, pp. 30-5.
[12] *Berliner Tageblatt,* Jan. 25, 1921 (P.M.).
[13] Reich Debates, July 2, 1920, vol. 344, pp. 131-2.
[14] *Ibid.,* March 16, 1922, vol. 353, p. 6309.

opposition with an end in view. The goal was to obtain power in government and to carry out a positive, creative program: "The only guarantee which a party can provide itself for the carrying out of its principles consists in my opinion of going into the government and there seeing to its adequate influence." [15]

Another spokesman of the far right, Count Westarp, was also heard in the DNVP with increasing frequency. His view of the role of an opposition party coincided closely with that of Helfferich. Indeed their attitudes reinforced each other on the question, and tended to overshadow the party leader. Westarp also did what he could to banish any remaining traces of Hergt's *Ordnungsprogramm*. The opposition attitude of the DNVP, Westarp told the Reichstag, was heightened by the fact that the present minority government was attempting to bridge the gap with the left while excluding the powerful right from practical work in the state: "There may have been differences of opinion among us [Nationalists] on whether one could expect the Majority Socialists to reform their party in any way that might make it possible for us to work with them. May I remind you that our chairman, Herr Hergt, mentioned in his speech last July that there were pessimists among us on the possibility, though not so many strong pessimists? But [now] there is not the slightest difference of opinion on the fact that these Social Democrats have not fulfilled the conditions required of them, and that an unbridgeable gulf separates us from them." [16]

If prominent members of the Party were discussing the possibilities of abandoning the status of opposition for a more positive role in the state, the outcome would depend on the attitude of other Nationalists as well as other parties.

Among Nationalists, the Christian Socialists were per-

[15] *Ibid.*, March 20, 1922, vol. 353, pp. 6381-2.
[16] *Ibid.*, Oct. 28, 1920, vol. 345, p. 839.

haps the most eager to participate in government. The economic, social, and political goals of the working class they represented could not be realized without the cooperation of government. For this purpose they were willing to work with a republican régime. In a similar spirit of compromise these Protestant Nationalists had long been associated in the Christian trade-union movement with Catholic Germany, and so indirectly with the Center party. They frequently referred to these connections as valuable potential for a political alliance, much to be preferred to one with the party of big business, the DVP. [17] They did not even rule out agreements with the Marxist left, and were probably more willing to move in that direction than middle-of-the-road Hergt. [18] Consequently they bitterly resented the prejudices of the republican parties that blocked the way of monarchists to positive participation in government. As Emil Hartwig mused, "All that is not favor-

[17] Cf., Behrens, Reich Debates, Jan. 22, 1925, vol. 384, p. 182; also W. Lambach, "Um die Führung im Reiche," in Lambach, ed., *Politische Praxis* (Hamburg, Berlin, 1927), pp. 50-1, quoting his article from the *Politische Wochenschrift*, Jan. 1, 1926: "A National government of workers and farmers, extending from the Center party to the Nationalists, is the solution for our internal political problems. . . . But, contrary to accepted opinion, the way from the Nationalists to the Center party does not pass through the DVP, which sits between them in the Reichstag. Rather, contact should be sought directly by Nationalist and Centrist politicians who are interested in social, economic and cultural matters."

[18] Behm, Reich Debates, Oct. 20, 1919, vol. 330, p. 3278: "I feel quite comfortable [in the DNVP] although, as I have said, [*to the Social Democrats:*] I have found myself in your company in many demands for reform. You see that there are still bridges in Germany today between right and left, and the longing of my heart is that we may build these bridges more and more solidly." Cf. also, Hartwig, Reich Debates, Nov. 10, 1921, vol. 351, p. 4921: "In the last three years the policy of the millions-strong Nationalist Christian workers' organizations has not been as actively directed against the negative forces of social democracy as hundreds of thousands of their followers would have liked."

able for realizing the social policy of our working people." [19]

In a general way the program of the Christian Socialists was a kind of corporate state where class consciousness would be eliminated by cooperative participation in the productive process. As Nationalist workers heard in 1920 from one of their leaders, "We Christian Socialists know that all depends on the socializing of capitalism, that is, extracting the poisonous fangs of profit. . . . The monopoly of capitalism must be broken and cooperative work raised to equal status." Specifically, profits were to be regulated in mining, heavy industry, and other basic sectors of the economy. "In place of the capitalistic profit motive we put the interest of the community." [20] Workers were to share more actively and directly in the economics of production under the watchwords of "Christianity, race empire!"[21]

These sentiments were expressed at the third Congress of Nationalist workers. This meeting in Hanover in October, 1920, was intended to publicize the organizations of Nationalist workers. The idea of cooperation of capital and labor remained a constant in Christian Socialist thought, and was many times echoed in the Reichstag. [22] And at the Party Congress in Königsberg in 1927 a labor leader reaffirmed the 1920 statements: "Walther Lambach's cry of 1920 in Hanover must find a much stronger echo today, 'Down with the one-sided dominion of capitalism; we must achieve a society of cooperative production!' " [23] Walther

[19] E. Hartwig, "Aus der Geschichte der deutschnationalen Arbeiterbewegung," in Lambach, ed., *Politische Praxis 1926*, p. 292.

[20] Speech by Rüffer, reported in anonymous pamphlet, *Deutschnationale Arbeitertagung in Hannover am Dienstag, den 26. Oktober 1920* (n.p., n.d.), pp. 17-21; meeting held in connection with DNVP convention, with 200 workers' representatives present.

[21] Same speech, reported in *Kzztg.*, Oct. 27, 1920 (P.M.) .

[22] Cf., Lambach, Reich Debates, Feb. 25, 1921, vol. 347, p. 2496; Feb. 1, 1922, vol. 352, pp. 5710-1.

[23] Union Secretary Dudey-Duisberg, Sept. 22, 1922, in *Kzztg.*, Sept. 22, 1922, (P.M.) .

Lambach, who headed the white-collar workers' union, one of the most influential and vocal Christian Socialists in the DNVP, was described by a Party colleague as "always one of the strongest advocates of association with trade unionists in the other *Fraktionen,* a tireless champion for the improvement and extension of social legislation, and a believer in positive cooperation and participation in government at any price." [24]

The views of the Christian Socialists were influential in the Nationalist Party, particularly in the early years. What little support the DNVP mustered in the West was mainly due to the Christian Socialists. They also provided a not inconsiderable following in northern urban centers. This support was valued beyond its numerical importance by the eager Nationalists in the leadership who wanted to prove how much more the DNVP represented than prewar parties like the DKP ever could. This added significance of their presence was an asset used by union representatives in council meetings, often to good effect. The Christian Socialist leaders indeed felt for some years after the Revolution that their movement had made a profitable alliance by merging with the DNVP. [25]

The Party leader took every opportunity to stress the importance of the membership of workers in the strongest middle-class party. But when he "preached" (as he termed it) the Christian-National-Social idea at the third Party Congress at Hanover in 1920, it was a thoroughly middle-class notion: "We must draw the workers into our social order. Yes, we must give this section of the population its

[24] Freytagh-Loringhoven, p. 53. (Freytagh-Loringhoven was no friend of Lambach's.)

[25] Gustav Hülser, *Der Deutsche,* Feb. 8, 1929, quoted in Walter Braun, p. 38: "For a while after the Revolution it seemed as though Christian Social thought would effect a brilliant recovery through the DNVP which it co-founded." Cf. also, Annelise Schulz, p. 66.

due. We must fit the workers into our economic order because only then can we expect of them their best work,
their highest productivity so necessary for reconstruction." [26] In its propaganda the DNVP stressed the com-
patibility of working and middle classes, as seen in the
Christian Socialist-Nationalist alliance; the irreconcilable
difference was not between classes, but between nationalist
and internationalist parties. [27] Until 1920 the Hergt leadership continued to make overtures to the whole working
class. After that the leadership no longer admitted even
rhetorically the possibility of cooperation with the SPD,
though of course the Socialists were blamed for the impasse. [28]

The Christian Socialists led by energetic men like Emil
Hartwig, Paul Rüffer, Wilhelm Lindner, and Walther
Lambach had formed a workers' committee in the DNVP
almost as soon as the Party was itself formed. The committee's work penetrated the regional organizations so
thoroughly that by the time of the fourth Party Congress
at Munich in October, 1921, they could obtain for the so-
called *Arbeiterbund* a special position beyond the normal
cadre of the DNVP. [29] Yet, though the Christian Socialists
were often able to get what they wanted, it should not be
assumed that all was going well for them. Their friends,
the Free Conservatives, did not remain in the Party very
long. Many, really most, other groups among the Nationalists resented the prominence often allowed to the workers'
viewpoint and disliked the special consideration the Christian Socialists appeared to enjoy with the leadership. Resentment was found not only in the ultra-oppositionist

[26] Spoken Oct. 25, 1920, in *Kzztg.*, Oct. 25, 1920 (P.M.).

[27] Friedrich Everling, in *Kzztg.*, July 4, 1920 (A.M.).

[28] Hergt at meeting of *Landesverband Braunschweig*, Sept. 18, 1921,
reported in *Berliner Lokal-Anzeiger*, Sept. 19, 1921 (P.M.).

[29] W MS, p. 266.

sector of the Party (the so-called "sharp direction" of Pan-Germans, National Liberals, and Fatherland party men), but also by the non-labor economic interest groups.

Internal party differences with the Christian Socialists were not merely questions of tactics, or of participation in government. More significant differences of material interest and ideology lurked behind the political framework. The stresses and strains in the Party were so considerable that sometimes the basic necessity of presenting a united front against the friends of the Republic was barely realized. The Party was obviously to have even greater troubles when it acquired strength to exercise more definite influence on policy and legislation in the state. That time came perhaps more quickly than most Nationalists expected. The Nationalist middle-class leaders were concerned with the problem of getting agreement with their working-class colleagues on their aims in the state and the nature of their possible positive work.[30] Few outside of the Party leadership were optimistic about prospects of easy or close collaboration. The extreme right remained reluctant to face the situation, and was even openly hostile to the Christian Socialist wing.

The Conservatives had suffered under strong attacks from the Christian Socialists in the early days of the Party. Westarp had been involved in debates with them, and made no secret of his feeling that the Nationalist workers had acquired status in the DNVP that far outstripped their actual importance.[31] He did not get on well with Hartwig, whom he considered to be largely responsible for pressing Christian Socialist claims for a special place in the Party and on election lists. Yet Westarp claimed that he, like the Party leadership, always valued the Nationalist workers movement as an essential weapon for use against social democracy and communism, to combat the idea of class

[30] W MS, p. 313.
[31] *Ibid.*

warfare. The Conservatives could work well with the Christian Socialists on general political lines, especially when an attack on democratic parliamentarianism was involved. But agreement on tactics and aims was difficult and occasional. [32]

The Hergt leadership and the Christian Socialists were both anxious for positive cooperation with the government, basing their argument partly on what they perceived to be sentiment in the Party and Nationalist electorate at large. Strongest opposition to that view in the inner councils came from the Old Conservatives and Racists who were eventually able to muster enough support to put some check on the tendencies of the leadership. [33]

Even stronger hostility to the Christian Socialists was expressed by the fugitive Kappist, Gottfried Traub, who recommended the DNVP make use of rival workers' groups: "The DNVP must come into much closer contact with the [non-striking] company unions and other elements of the working class, especially with the present National Socialists, and not restrict its associations to the Christian Socialists alone. The tactics of the Christian Socialists often do not differ at all from the campaigning of the Social Democrats. . . ." [34] Though Traub was, of course, a discredited man and had no influence in the inner circles of the Party any more, his opinion was shared by many who were closely connected with the countless patriotic and militarist societies, small and large, that were unofficial arms of the DNVP. Out of that milieu were founded new Nationalist labor organizations that rejected the idea of the strike, and that challenged the right of the Christian Socialists to represent Nationalist labor. [35] They also were against political com-

[32] W MS, pp. 267-8; WP: Westarp to Graf Seidlitz, June 29, 1920.

[33] WP: Brauer to Heydebrand, Jan. 16, 1922.

[34] WP: Traub to Westarp, Dec. 23, 1920.

[35] E.g., Fritz Geisler's *Nationalverband deutscher Berufsverbände;* *Kzztg.,* Nov. 1, 1920 (P.M.).

promises designed to prepare the way for entering government, and carried on a running debate with the older labor groups. The feuds occasionally burst into verbal fireworks that ruffled feelings and left a poor public impression. [36] The leadership imposed a truce on the hostilities as far as it could, with indifferent success. But the new so-called patriotic unions were too small a group to be a serious challenge to the Christian Socialists. More significant than their numbers was the encouragement they received among the various groups in the DNVP that were opposed to the Christian Socialist outlook. [37]

Probably more disturbing to the Christian Socialists than their pip-squeak rivals were the developments that had permitted Westarp to gain more influence and prominence in the Party. They had done their worst against the Conservatives without being able to check them. In the Racist controversy they felt with the leadership, on the other hand, that they had achieved a victory. The real issue had not been anti-Semitism but rather whether the Party would follow a radical opposition policy that might go to the extreme of violence. [38] While the majority opposed such a solution, the Conservatives remained ambiguous.

The ambiguous nature of Conservatives on the subject of positive cooperation in the republican state was due to the character of their political organization after the Revolution. As Conservatives, many felt their first duty was to face reality rather than to hedge excessively on principles. Those landowners who were allied to the Farmers' League, for example, felt their social and economic well-being de-

[36] Cf., Wolf and Anhäuser, Reich Debates, Dec. 11, 1926, vol. 391, p. 8469.

[37] The Pomeranian *Landbund,* for example, supported Wolf's *Reichslandarbeiterbund* in preference to similar Christian Social unions of farmhands; WP: v. Oertzen to *Reichstagsfraktion,* March 4, 1925.

[38] Annelise Schulz, p. 66.

pended on their ability to function in government. Like other economic interest groups they knew what they wanted, and wanted to achieve their ends quickly. But the administration of the skeleton Conservative organization, the DKP, was not of this type. It was a small, cautious, tightly knit group of men of the old generation who never lost sight of their Prussian-Conservative mission in German public life, who never forgot that the DNVP represented no more than a desperate expedient, at best a gamble for survival. The men of the DKP after 1918 were the rump reactionary Old Conservatives who thought of themselves as the personification of monarchism and the imperial values of Prussia-Germany. As such they hoped to achieve power in the new state in order to restore the old. Although a successful *coup d'état* was an acceptable means to this end, they were not entirely incapable of contemplating temporary cooperation with the Republic. But such cooperation had its decided limits. Permanent long-term aims could not be sacrificed for easy short-term gains. This meant to Conservatives that their effort could not be tainted in any way by collaboration with the Marxist-revolutionary Social Democrats, for such collaboration could occur only at the cost of their self-respect, and would in their eyes be an advertisement of moral bankruptcy.

After the June, 1920, election there was a period of suspense for the Conservatives. Would the DNVP enter government, and if so under what conditions? The character of the Party would have been basically affected if, at this point, the leadership had again seriously pursued its earlier *Ordnungsprogramm,* and had offered to accept support from the left (assuming that such support was forthcoming). Westarp did what he could to prevent the possibility, though his remarks indicated it was not easy to overcome the collaborative tendency of the Hergt wing. The fact was, in any case, that no other party really was interested in cooperating with the Nationalists, certainly not in government. Westarp wrote: "The question of participating in government did not come up at all because we were cut dead on all sides. Even Heinze's declarations [from the DVP] in favor of forming a bourgeois coalition with us were only platonic. Nevertheless wide circles in the [Nationalist] *Fraktion* were thoroughly convinced that they had learned one lesson from the election, namely that the electors expected positive cooperation from us under any condition, and not barren opposition. It required very definite intervention [from the oppositionists in the Party] to prevent us from supporting, in spite of all, a vote of confidence, and from issuing academic statements about our readiness to collaborate even with the Social Democrats." [39]

In spite of Westarp's intervention, Heydebrand objected to his lieutenant's increasingly close identification with the DNVP. He was perplexed by Westarp's growing influence in Nationalist councils, and feared the DKP might become tainted through Westarp's dual association. For that reason also he objected for a time to Westarp's appointment as editor-in-chief of the *Kreuzzeitung*, the principal Conservative organ. When Westarp did take over the political direction of the paper at the end of 1919, he did so only after agreeing to the following explicit policy: "The *Kreuzzeitung* is called on by its entire history and tradition to be, and to remain in every way, an independent Conservative organ, outspokenly Christian in its basis, and monarchist, authoritarian, and aristocratic in character." [40]

Heydebrand hated the present political reality with the unbending bitterness of an old and isolated man, almost to the extent of denying the necessity of coming to terms with everyday life. Not all Conservatives were happy to find themselves growing weaker while the Nationalists

[39] WP: Westarp to Traub, July 3, 1920.
[40] W MS, pp. 177-9; statement of Sept. 17, 1919.

steadily increased their strength. Their weakness acted in many ways to encourage even more stubborn adherence to their own special point of view. As the possibility of bringing decisive influence to bear on the DNVP scarcely existed, the strictest Conservatives did not want to commit themselves finally and irrevocably to the new Party. They would retain the Conservative *Hauptverein* and prepare some day to re-emerge from their obscurity to lead Germany back to its true heritage. On the other hand, it was Westarp's intention to work in the DNVP, to do his best to direct the new Party into Conservative channels, but always holding himself ready to meet changing conditions. "I also recognized," he wrote, ". . . an obligation to make practical concessions to other points of view, insofar as such concessions were at all tolerable and appeared essential to the best interests of Nationalist unity. . . . I defended a policy of uncompromising firmness against the external enemy and against the ruling representatives of the [republican] system. But within the DNVP, I struggled to iron out differences, and did so down to the bitter end of my own departure from the Party in 1930." [41]

Westarp exerted himself to the utmost to bridge the differences between the Racists and the Nationalist leadership. All Conservatives were behind him in the effort because the Racists were their closest supporters in the DNVP. The Racists were also bitterly opposed to the democratic Republic, although not always enthusiasts for a Hohenzollern restoration. Then, too, the dream still persisted of the Anti-Semites as a potential rank-and-file for a DKP with leaders and few followers. Naturally, Conservatives fought their hardest to prevent the events at Görlitz and their sequel in 1922. When they lost their attempt, it was plain to all that the Conservatives, despite their rump organization, were, and would for a long time remain, a broken reed.

[41] W MS, pp. 398-9.

The key to Conservative influence in the DNVP in the beginning had been the fact that the Conservatives provided much of the money and physical facilities to see the new Party through its first elections. It took a long while after that, actually, for the DNVP to get on its feet financially, and it can be doubted that it ever was on a truly sound basis. Financial difficulties facing the Executive after the 1920 election, for example, caused great concern with no easy solution in sight. [42] Nevertheless, within the year the DNVP made a wide canvass for a "Hergt Fund" with enough success to leave gloomy feelings in the circles of orthodox Conservatives. But regardless, as early as the spring of 1919, the DNVP had ceased to depend on Conservative funds, although contributions were always welcome. It is questionable whether by 1922 there were any significant financial resources still left to the DKP. In January of that year headquarters felt that financial prospects for the DKP were very poor: "In the political field the DNVP is now drawing all that is humanly possible from sources on the right for its Hergt Fund (*Hergt-Spende*) ." [43]

If the DKP was a negligible financial asset for the DNVP, its good will was still a valuable commodity. However discredited the Conservative name may have been in the country at large, it still represented a respected tradition in many middle- and upper-class circles. This was a political potential that the DNVP could not afford to alienate, especially with its constant loss of members who were Liberals, Free Conservatives, and Racists. After the 1920 election, Conservatives sensed a much friendlier reception in the Nationalist Executive than had previously been the case. Representatives from East Prussia and Pomerania even went so far as to urge that more prominence be given

[42] WP: Schroeter to Heydebrand (n.d., but probably after July 1, 1920) .

[43] WP: Brauer to Heydebrand, Jan. 16, May 3, 1922.

to Conservative views in the DNVP. [44] It was true nevertheless that Conservatives were still accepted in the inner circle
on good behavior only. Westarp, recognizing this, was
anxious to avoid upsetting the balance by giving the Nationalists any hint of continued separate Conservative
activity. [45]

Despite Westarp, the inner core of the DKP had definite
ideas for the continued separate identification of their organization and, if necessary, of its revival as an active
force. [46] However, there was good reason to feel that by
1922 the Conservatives had as much, or even more, need
of the DNVP than it did of them. Heydebrand himself
was well aware that the Conservatives had not the proper
resources for independent action, and that anyway the
climate of opinion was unfavorable for such an attempt.
Though Conservatives had complaints enough concerning
Nationalist leadership, their differences were far from in-
superable. [47] After the experience of the Racist controversy,
Conservatives had to reassess their position. They had failed
to keep the Racists in the DNVP, and many Anti-Semites
of the DKP would have shifted their support to the splinter
party. But the extremism of the Racist leaders antagonized
the cautious Conservative leaders. Westarp was not willing
to abandon new-found security in the DNVP for a place
in the unstable Racist camp. In the long run there was no
common ground for the right radicals and most aristocrats.

A few words should be added on the group in the DNVP
who most strongly opposed the thought of assuming responsibility in the state, or in any way cooperating with the

[44] WP: Schroeter to Heydebrand, July 1, 1920.
[45] WP: Brauer to Heydebrand, Oct. 7, 1921.
[46] *Ibid.*
[47] WP: Brauer, May 5, 1922, report of session of *Engerer Vorstand*
of the DKP, May 3, 1922, with the participation of Heydebrand,
Westarp, Graf Seidlitz, Kreth, Graf Behr, v. Brockhausen, v. Dallwitz,
Wiegand, Brauer.

Republic. It was composed of individuals mostly of a National Liberal and West German background, mostly Pan-Germans, no particular friends of the East Elbian aristocracy. [48] These were in spirit the same kind of people who were Kappists, even though they might have doubted the wisdom of that particular adventure. By 1922, Pan-Germans who had not gone along too closely with the Kappists and Racists were the most recognizable representatives in the DNVP of the policy of active, uncompromising opposition. They never tired of admonishing Nationalists and their leadership on their laxity in the application of their anti-parliamentarian principles. It was a contradiction in terms for Nationalists to offer their services to the governmental operations of a democratic parliamentarian state. Indeed, even participation in the Reichstag was not strictly compatible with the Party's inner nature, as the oppositionists understood it. As Alfred Hugenberg asserted in the course of a Party dispute, "A Nationalist who has innerly become a parliamentarian is nothing but a German Democrat." [49] In 1928 he became head of the Nationalist Party in a dramatic turn of events that foreshadowed the collapse of the Republic. Until then he had to watch his colleagues move toward closer relations with government, and eventually join two cabinet coalitions.

When coalition negotiations fell through for the DNVP after the 1920 election, there seemed nothing left of the possibility of participating in government until a cabinet crisis or new election. The Party set about mending its fences and struggling with its internal problems, which were serious enough. Helfferich's influence in the Party

---

[48] Freytagh-Loringhoven, p. 9. This right wing was early identified with names in the Constituent Assembly and Reichstag of persons like Hugenberg, Schirmacher, Graef-Thüringen, v. Graefe-Goldebee, Oberfohren, and Traub.

[49] Hugenberg to Westarp, in 1927, quoted by Kriegk, p. 80.

was considerable from the time of his election to Parliament—more than was generally realized. As Westarp observed, "The position of Helfferich in the Nationalist *Fraktion* and in the Party Executive was hardly apparent in its full extent to the public. At sessions of these bodies during the Reichstag period when he was with us, very few important political and legal questions were discussed where his advice was not prominent and influential." [50] In the Racist controversy Helfferich emerged plainly as one of the chief prosecutors for the leadership. Then, on the national level, the influence was greatly increased by the unexpected shift in the political scene that installed the government of his friend Wilhelm Cuno in November, 1922.

The Cuno government lasted only nine months in office. It was in theory, a non-party government; at least, its head and some of his cabinet were experts with no political affiliations. It had to solve the economic and political impasse both in foreign and domestic policy that had made it impossible for the Wirth government to continue, and depended on the support of the middle-class parties for its continued existence. For the Nationalist Party this situation was to provide it suddenly with the much-desired possibility of influencing the policies of national government, [51] although the potential was not realized to its fullest degree. Nationalists, as could be expected, were divided on the extent to which they should support Cuno. As Westarp reported publicly later, "I am a witness to the fact that Helfferich struggled heatedly but vainly with us in many a case to get a different approach toward the Cuno government. Our criticism and opposition then were not simply made-to-order for the purpose of strengthening the position

[50] Westarp, introduction, *Helfferichs Reichstagsreden 1922-24*, p. 23.
[51] HvSP, item 153: Prof. Martin Spahn (DNVP) to Seeckt, Dec. 21, 1923 (20 pp.), p. 2.

of the government, but most often were meant very seriously." Westarp concluded that the Cuno government was dominated neither by the DNVP nor Helfferich. [52]

However, informal relations of the Cuno government and the DNVP were close. Because of personal ties and sympathies many individual Nationalists and cabinet members freely exchanged views. [53] The Hergt-Helfferich leadership found itself suddenly with more influence than ever before in certain high places. With the change their appetite for further, real power was of course whetted, but apart from such considerations friendly collaboration appeared all the more necessary because of the Ruhr emergency after the Franco-Belgian occupation. The Cuno régime benefited from the maximum patriotic appeal of the situation. On another important score the DNVP found its status enhanced: Karl Helfferich was a key adviser during those months of disastrous inflation.

Most important perhaps for the DNVP was the close contact it had now with the formulation of foreign policy, the area on which Nationalist sentiment was nearest to united. The Party solidly backed the strong resistance the government proposed to take in face of Allied demands and threats. French force was to be resisted at all costs. Nationalists perhaps hoped to consolidate their own Party and to improve relations with other parties by leading a hate campaign against the enemy. In this they were less than successful as French force proved more than a match for the verbal attacks of German parties. Racists, among others, were outspoken opponents of Cuno who seemed to have remarkably few friends in the country. [54] The Nationalist leadership watched gloomily as the Cuno govern-

[52] Westarp, introduction, *Helfferichs Reichstagsreden 1922-24*, p. 29.
[53] WP: Brauer to Heydebrand, Dec. 6 and 23, 1922,
[54] WP: Westarp, "Der Ruhrkampf. Regierung Cuno. Regierung Stresemann." Unpublished MS, fragment, pp. 1, 2, 10, 27. Also *Kzztg.*, Jan. 7, 1923.

ment failed to master a rapidly deteriorating political situation. It supported him for fear of a successor who was worse, but had little reason to believe he could last.

Clearly, Cuno's decision to abandon his struggle in deteriorating circumstances in August, 1923—the decision that brought Gustav Stresemann to the chancellorship—came as a bitter disappointment to the ambitious Nationalists. For more than two years they had had to bear Stresemann's pointed criticism in innumerable speeches and articles. One of the country's most indefatigable publicists and political organizers, he continued to denounce their right-wing and monarchist opposition. Because of their former high regard for him in the days when he was also an ardent monarchist and patriot in their sense, most Nationalists could now only regard Stresemann as a turncoat. Besides, they were insulted by his decision to include Socialists in his first cabinet, and *eo ipso* keep the Nationalists in opposition. The difficulties Stresemann was to experience with the Socialists were naturally applauded as just deserts by the government's right-wing detractors. When, despite Socialist wishes, Stresemann moved to remove what he felt were insupportable left revolutionary elements from the governments of Saxony and Thuringia, the right found it hard to give the chancellor full credit for the strength of his decision. The right was in the mood for the even more drastic measure of military dictatorship for all of Germany. The left, of course, was correct in its criticism of Stresemann for failing to act with equal stringency against the recalcitrant but right-wing government of Bavaria. Stresemann hesitated while the Bavarian military garrison verged on mutiny in its obligations to the Berlin command.

German diplomatic missions abroad were informed that the second Stresemann Cabinet was a non-Socialist variant of the Weimar coalition. Center and DDP had nullified the idea, circulated by the DNVP during the crisis, of a broader bourgeois coalition. Then Stresemann's attempts to bring in the Nationalists got nowhere with their spokesmen. The greater part of the German People's party, added the official informant, joined with the coalition parties. [55] The message described more of a bid than Nationalist circles admitted. Clearly inferred also was the fact of definite pressure within the DVP for more consideration of the Nationalist position, and if possible closer relation with them in government. It was indeed Scholz who urged in this connection, "Ties must be found [with them], no matter how hard that may be." [56]

How maddeningly difficult the attempt might be to establish such relations with the DNVP could be seen in the way the Party judged identical measures proposed first by Cuno's government, and now again by Stresemann's. It seemed that the DNVP attacked the financial measures of the new government even before it had had a chance to develop any. Stresemann's Cabinet was carrying on with taxes established by the Cuno régime and at the time strongly supported by Helfferich and the entire DNVP. [57] Such turnabouts were not unusual tactics.

With the currency and, it seemed to many, the economy on the verge of collapse, and the country near civil war, the enemies of the Republic took heart. Racists and Pan-Germans pressed their separate plans for counter-revolution, while General von Seeckt seriously considered assuming the role of German dictator. Some Nationalists were sympathetic to these schemes—Westarp, for example, was reported to be on the Seeckt bandwagon—but the majority

[55] Germany. Auswärtiges Amt. Records of the Weimar Republic, National Archives, Washington, D.C., microfilm roll 2281, serial 4525, frame 136699 (hereafter cited as: GFO.W: 2281/4525/136699), Maltzan to (30) German missions abroad, Berlin, Oct. 6, 1923 (copy).

[56] SP: 3159/7394/171304-11, Dr. Scholz at DVP Fraktionssitzung, Sept. 12, 1923.

[57] SP: 3159/7394/171302-3, Stresemann's secretary to DVP Halle, Sept. 10, 1923.

of moderate Nationalists continued to work for a compromise solution that would give them an entry into government. The slight taste of influence that they had obtained from Cuno sharpened their appetite and their ambition. They pursued the game of parliamentary politics and negotiation through a long and disappointing stretch.

General von Seeckt, the "lonely poplar" as many called him, was perhaps for once not displeased to find himself besieged with visitors urging such plans on him that he might someday be inclined to take. "My time in the next few days is already booked by [prospective] visitors," he wrote his wife, "and just who all don't intend to come! Today [for example] Hergt and Westarp. There is enormous excitement in the air and, as a result, uncertainty—to my mind more than can be justified, but to be sure the situation is coming to a head." [58] But within weeks a point of no return was reached in Bavaria.

Seeckt tried to reach an amicable understanding with the ranking Bavarian civil authority, Special Commissioner Gustav von Kahr. What Seeckt wrote him on November 5 may also be regarded as representative of majority feeling in right-wing circles like the DNVP:

The last time I had the honor to talk to you the Wirth Cabinet was in office which, because of its Socialist tinge, you believed had to be opposed. I anticipated its collapse and thought it preferable to wait until that time. After the [governmental] change, when the Cuno Cabinet had been formed without Socialist participation, I detected better understanding between federal and Bavarian policy. With considerable sympathy for the chancellor, a long-standing and good acquaintance, I sought to intrude myself—not without success—into his domestic leadership, [but] only so far as necessary to assure his support in all questions relating to the armed forces and rearmament. More was done in this area in this time than I can [here] explain. I personally regretted the end of the Cuno Cabinet; it fell of its own weakness.

[58] HvSP, roll 28, p. 251, Berlin, Sept. 23, 1923.

Vis-à-vis Chancellor Stresemann I have sought to represent the necessities of military policy, and [especially] argued against a pause in rearmament. Although I found understanding and support, the Stresemann Cabinet with its Socialist members was unable, any more than the Cuno Cabinet without them, to do anything about the anti-military efforts of the Prussian government. I have always considered the almost entirely Socialist-dominated Prussian government as a greater danger to the political development of the Reich than the Reich government itself. I have moreover from the beginning considered it my task to make the Reichswehr a support of the authority of the Reich, not of a particular government. I see my task in that light today still. For that reason also I hold to constitutional forms and procedures. . . .

On the other hand [the Reichswehr] can not allow a change [of régime] to be undertaken by some irresponsible and unauthorized force. . . .[59]

For the Nationalists, as for Seeckt, the dilemma of the Bavarian situation lay in the fact that the authority of Berlin was challenged, and with it the integrity of the military command. On the other hand, they had to recognize their sympathy with the rightist régime of Bavaria, and their hostility to the entrenched Socialist government of Prussia. Yet, emotionally, most Nationalists were deeply Prussian, and for that reason strong believers in the rights of the federal states.

As for the National Socialists—the Nazis, this group got no more sympathy from the Nationalists than had the Racists who were thrown out of the Party at Görlitz in the autumn of 1922. The same Racists indeed were still a thorn in the Party's flesh. Many of them, aligned for the time being with Hitler's party, took part in the Nazi revolutionary plans. Graefe and others were present during the short-lived November Beer Hall putsch in Munich. A member of the *Mittelpartei* in the Landtag, former Bavarian Justice

[59] HvSP, roll 22, Stück 154, Seeckt to Kahr, Berlin, Nov. 5, 1923.

Minister C. Roth, ran into trouble with his Nationalist colleagues because of his too warm espousal of Hitler's cause. [60]

Ludendorff also found the Nationalist attitude negative regarding cooperation with the *völkisch* movement. The possibility of cooperation was slight, he noted, as long as the Nationalists put the Racists in the same category as Communists, that is, as radicals of only a somewhat different color. "As long as the present Nationalist leadership is in office," he wrote, "there is no hope. Time after time they have stabbed me in the back." In his lonely fight for Germany's honor and rights, as he saw it, only the Racists supported him. "Even old comrades have turned away." The allusion clearly included the Nationalists. [61] But more important than their relations with the Racists were, for the members of the German National People's Party, their relations with Stresemann and the German People's party.

The German People's party, as we have noticed earlier, had originally been close to the DNVP in its views and attitudes, despite the general antagonism of their components in the empire. In the first months after their formation, as we have also seen, there were men in both parties who hoped for a permanent close working alliance or even complete fusion. Hergt found a sympathetic and cooperative counterpart in the head of the DVP *Fraktion* in the National Assembly, Karl Rudolf Heinze. Consequent relations of their *Fraktionen* in the National Assembly and the Prussian House were very good through 1919, while the parties avoided quarrels elsewhere as much as possible. At

[60] United States. Department of State. Records, National Archives, Washington, D.C., document no. 862.00/1341 (hereafter cited as: DS: 862.00/1341), R. D. Murphy, U.S. Vice-Consul in charge, Munich, Confidential Political Report, Political Movements in Bavaria, Oct. 17, 1923.

[61] Bundesarchiv Koblenz. Ludendorff Miscellany. Handwritten letter of Ludendorff to (unidentified) "Hochverehrte Excellenz," April 17 (no year). His comments are *à propos* regardless of the year he wrote them.

the turn of the year 1919-1920, however, relations deteriorated as each party sought to assert its distinctive character. As the Nationalists began to feel their strength after the Kapp putsch, they became more vocally monarchist, more sharply anti-Semitic, more uncompromisingly bourgeois and anti-Socialist. By late 1920 and in following years they consequently became less *koalitionsfähig* and more rigid in their attitude than they had appeared during the first months of the Hergt-Free-Conservative leadership.

Gustav Stresemann, for his part, resisted tendencies to draw the DVP into any political extreme. He stressed the strategic middle position of the DVP and expected to pick up numerous defectors not only from the DNVP, but from the less vigorous German Democratic party. The DVP, Stresemann argued, could grow as a National Liberal party but would lose its distinctive attraction to the middle class if it were too closely allied with the Conservative DNVP. [62] Stresemann, like most Nationalists, was alarmed at the tide of resentment that set in against them following the Kapp putsch. Stresemann was particularly unhappy to find himself compromised in the public eye by his attempted role of honest broker during the putsch, and resented the odium of being labeled a reactionary leader of the right. [63] Consequently, while most Nationalists after the putsch were repudiating the Kappists, Stresemann moved as sharply from the Nationalists. He made it clear that the DVP would work loyally *with* government and, given the opportunity, *in* government on the basis of the Weimar Constitution. The DVP sought responsibility in the state in coalition with all the positive elements of society—a grand coalition

[62] Stresemann to Reinhard Liebe, June 12, 1919, SP: 3079/6920/137557.

[63] For examples of criticism, see Chancellor Müller, Reich Debates, March 29, 1920, vol. 332, p. 4935ff.; Erich Koch-Weser's Diary, note on Cabinet meeting of March 16, and entry for March 18, 1920, KWP: folder 25 (provisional).

that would eventually extend through the political spectrum. Though such a grand coalition might not be possible at the moment, the DVP under Stresemann's direction was now willing to work even with the Socialists. Stresemann's bold position was not won without tension and debate within his own party, but his attitude was decisive. [64]

Count Westarp, who did not want the DNVP to ally itself with the liberal DVP, welcomed Stresemann's honesty. Those Nationalists who were disappointed by Stresemann did what they could to undermine his position in his own party, and to impune his patriotism under one pretext or another. The Racist Graefe particularly resented Stresemann's claim that the Nationalist right would sooner or later have to face realities by working with the left, although that view was also expressed by the Hergt-Free-Conservative Nationalists. Stresemann's letter to Graefe on the subject is worth repeating:

You see, as the source of estrangement of both parties, our apparent intention of joining after the election with the present majority and under circumstances of forming a front against the so-called extreme right. It is also your contention that the voters expected of us an election slogan calling for a national front against the government of revolution, and that they wanted the parties that had been in opposition until now to join in government only in a situation where they could have the decisive role. In my opinion, you go too far in your optimism if you think that we have come so far in Germany that our parties can form the principal part of the new government. The task of political policy seems rather to consist at the moment of trying

[64] *Deutsche Stimmen,* Sept. 26, 1920; Stresemann to Louis Ravené, Sept. 16, 1920, SP: 3089/6926/138524-5; Stresemann to Rudolf Heinze, Dec. 23, 1920, SP: 3090/6931/139429; Stresemann to Brune, Feb. 4, 1921, SP: 3095/7004/142730; DVP Executive Committee, March 8, 1921, SP: 3094/7003/142550-65; Stresemann to W. O. Rose, Oct. 22, 1921, SP: 3093/6992/140593-4; Rost to Stresemann, Oct. 28, 1921, SP: 3093/6992/140595-8; Stresemann to A. H. Tillmanns, Sept. 17, 1921, SP: 3109/6997/141454-5.

to cut down the superior influence the SPD has today, and to restrict it to a smaller area. It seems to me that a government without the Social Democrats would not be possible at all for the next two or three years, because without them we should be staggering from one general strike to another. [65]

Certainly this attitude on the part of Stresemann indicated a realistic open-mindedness far broader than that expressed by Hergt, even in his *Ordnungsprogramm*. In fact the generous attitude in the DVP was tending to grow and to win out over other views while, on the other hand, in the DNVP the *Ordnungsprogramm* withered on the vine. Consequently, through the spring of 1920, there were many quarrels between DVP and DNVP over the question of responsibility in government, and particularly over the matter of cooperation with the left.

The parties found temporary solidarity again only when the Kapp putsch caught both of them unawares. Both joined in ambiguous watchfulness during the crisis, and then tried to play the parts of honest brokers during the dénouement. Some of that comradeship lasted through the elections of June, 1920. When the right-wing parties practically doubled their size at that time, Nationalist leaders were encouraged and excited. They informed the DVP they were ready to form a middle-class government. [66] But Nationalist hopes were ill founded. The DVP under Stresemann's influence was well on the way to becoming a governmental, even republican, party to an extent impossible for the DNVP. Knowing that irreconcilable elements in the DNVP would never collaborate with the SPD, the DVP was unwilling to wreck its chances of entering government merely to satisfy the requirements of Nationalist propriety. But when the SPD refused to join a government that included the right-wing People's party, the DNVP did expect

[65] Stresemann to v. Graefe, Jan. 23, 1920, in Stresemann, *Vermächtnis*, I, 17.

[66] *Kzztg.*, June 16, 1920 (A.M.).

an invitation from the latter to help them form a cabinet. No invitation or other encouragement came. The DNVP found it had few friends among other parties. As a monarchist anti-Semitic organization it remained highly suspect to the prospective partners in a coalition. Consequently the DNVP was left out of the first bourgeois government that was formed in the Republic, the Fehrenbach Cabinet— a bitter experience for the Hergt leadership, and a disappointment for the Nationalist groups that counted on political gains through direct influence on government.

Stresemann in a conciliatory gesture called on the DNVP to continue to perform in opposition the service of neutralizing Socialist influence in politics, the same function the DVP was trying to fulfill in government. He described the situation as a division of labor in which the DNVP had by far the easier role; Nationalists could follow their natural inclinations, while Populists were called on to make many sacrifices for the sake of the coalition. [67] That role was perfectly acceptable to those in the DNVP who thought of themselves as primarily Conservatives, Pan-Germans, or Racists. It was accepted only reluctantly by the many others of the Hergt, Christian Socialist, Free Conservative, and agrarian groups.

In the following months it seemed to some observers that the DNVP was becoming even more rightist than it had been, as opposition elements gained prominence in the Party and as the famous *Ordnungsprogramm* disappeared completely. Noticeable, too, were the increasingly distant relations of the DNVP and DVP. [68] This deterioration in relations was due not only to reaction following the snub in July, and the disparity of party situations after the formation of the Fehrenbach government. It was to some extent forced on the Nationalist leadership that was struggling

[67] "Δ" (Stresemann), "Politische Umschau," in *Deutsche Stimmen,* Sept. 26, 1920, p. 650.

[68] *Berliner Tageblatt,* Jan. 25, 1921 (P.M.).

against the Racist faction and defending itself from charges of being soft and revisionist. The leadership could not afford to lose face by appearing to defer excessively to Populist desires. Indeed, one of the precipitants of the Racist crisis in the DNVP was the *Fraktion's* attempt to silence Graefe's criticism at a parliamentary session of December 18, 1920. In his bill of complaint against the leadership, Graefe condemned its attempts to suppress the Party's sharp opposition wing. In his opinion the DNVP had to make clear the fact that it could not enter government unless a fundamental change in the constitutional system had occurred, or was in prospect. That principle had to be recognized and accepted as the basis for any negotiations that might be contemplated with the DVP, the Center, or any other political party.[69] Since such views were being militantly expressed and could prove popular with the rank and file, the leadership clearly had to be careful and watch its step in any subsequent dealings with the DVP.

DNVP-DVP relations remained cool and correct even when the DVP took the initiative early in 1921 to inquire under what conditions the Nationalists would enter government. Since July, 1920, a notable stiffening had occurred in the Nationalist attitude, largely under the influence of the Party rank and file. Racist and Pan-German propaganda had been most effective in the local branches of the Party where men thought in blunt terms. They tended to credit the alarmist reports circulated by the extremists, and feared a possible sellout by the leadership to get into government. To placate these people Hergt had to leave the impression that he was perfectly capable of keeping the DVP in its place, and had no intention of betraying Nationalist principles. His announced formula was no coalition except in a national emergency. [70] Stresemann was aware of the situa-

---

[69] WP: v. Graefe, "Vorschläge für Beschlüsse der Fraktion in der zum 20.1.21. anberaumten Sitzung."

[70] *Berliner Tageblatt*, Feb. 17, 1921 (A.M.).

tion in the DNVP. The attitude of the Nationalist *Fraktion* remained friendly, though understandably cautious. At least the door to agreement was not permanently closed, [71] and there was room to maneuver in case of a real emergency.

Actually nothing came of the February, 1921, talks except bad feeling. In the field, recriminations grew during the year, even though in May the DVP left the government and rejoined the opposition camp. Hergt expressed his regrets, no doubt sincerely, to Stresemann over the prevalence of name-calling and mudslinging which he called harmful and undesirable. He asked for a truce, but with little result. [72] The Party was asserting itself from the grass roots in a way that the leadership could hardly check. The possibility of close DNVP-DVP relations was, for the time being, remote.

Some improvement was seen when the DVP joined the government of Wilhelm Cuno, which the DNVP also supported. This ended abruptly when the Cuno government was replaced by Stresemann's first Cabinet of August, 1923, that included Socialists. When the Socialists resigned two months later the technical, though slight, possibility of Nationalist participation existed. The DNVP was unwilling to give the first Stresemann Cabinet even a vote of confidence, and denounced the pressure from "street Communists" that they held responsible for the fall of Cuno. Their attitude to the second Stresemann Cabinet was more difficult to decide.

Nationalist opposition was still far from being the united front it appeared to be. Forces were still at work within the DNVP that favored sensible compromise and participation in government, though their influence was undefined and vague. Among them were some industrialists and leaders of the Ruhr resistance who wanted to alleviate the serious economic condition of the Rhine and Ruhr quickly. More-

[71] "Δ" (Stresemann), *Deutsche Stimmen*, Feb. 20, 1921, p. 115.

[72] Hergt to Stresemann, July 5, 1921, in *Berliner Tageblatt*, Aug. 10, 1921 (A.M.) .

over, the uncontrolled inflation and consequent economic dislocation everywhere did much to convince Nationalists, like others, that passive resistance could not be kept up indefinitely. [73] In a similar category was Heydebrand's surprising, though privately expressed, opinion that the DNVP ought not necessarily deny itself the chance to gain power in the Stresemann régime, even with the presence of Socialists. [74] Apparently he felt the domestic and international situation of Germany was too serious for Nationalists to stand aloof. His opinion was not shared by the Conservative voice in the DNVP, Count Westarp.

Westarp was pleased to observe that the DVP actually never invited the DNVP to join the second Stresemann Cabinet, but confined itself only to asking about the position the DNVP proposed to take in the vote of confidence and enabling legislation. Westarp was against any Nationalist participation, in any case, until Stresemann had given assurance that he would avoid cooperating with the Socialist government of Prussia, and was well aware that no such assurance was likely. The Nationalist *Fraktion,* which, for the most part, was willing to enter any middle-class cabinet, showed less and less liking for Stresemann, who was acquiring the reputation of being not only liberal in domestic affairs, but insufficiently tough toward the Allies in foreign affairs. After some days of unsuccessful bickering Hergt, who by himself would have been able to come to terms with Stresemann, had to admit that he was unable to control the Party at this point. [75] The situation was complicated by the appointment of Count Kanitz as food minister. [76] National-

[73] Westarp in *Kzztg.,* Sept. 30, 1923 (A.M.); WP: "Ruhrkampf" fragment, p. 18.

[74] WP: reference to Heydebrand's card of Sept. 26, 1923, in Brauer to Heydebrand, Oct. 10, 1923.

[75] Stresemann, *Vermächtnis,* I, 195-200. Suggested replacement for Stresemann was Otto Wiedfeldt.

[76] Oct. 22. Kanitz had supported Kardorff in 1920.

ists were angry because Kanitz, a member of their Prussian *Fraktion,* had accepted without Party authority. It was particularly irritating that he took over a ministry of vital importance to agrarians. [77]

Stresemann, for his part, did not want his second Cabinet to be considered a right-wing cabinet, and stressed the new formation rather as a broad, middle-class creation. British Ambassador Lord D'Abernon, for one among foreign representatives, fully appreciated the situation. [78]

Meanwhile, pressures both for and against participation in government plagued the Nationalist Party leadership to prevent a clear line. Moreover, when the Stresemann government fell in November, the president of the Republic failed to give the DNVP a chance to form the new cabinet. Though the Nationalist leadership wanted the job, it had failed to sweeten its approach to President Friedrich Ebert and the other middle-class parties. The Party had considered itself essential beyond reality, and had priced itself out of the market.

The fact is that President Ebert, who by natural inclination disliked the political views of his last two chancellors, was encouraged by many to look elsewhere, including among others General Wilhelm Groener. Groener, for one, blamed Cuno for having made dangerous concessions to Bavaria from the national point of view. Stresemann's government, to his mind, had also failed to solve the urgent problems of the day despite vigorous activity. He called on Ebert to find a way to save the country. [79]

Indeed President Ebert took matters more firmly in his

[77] WP: "Ruhrkampf" fragment, p. 47. Cf., Thomsen, Reich Debates, March 7, 1924, vol. 361, p. 12692; Kanitz, *ibid.,* p. 12693.

[78] GFO.W: 2281/4525/136673-4, M(altzan) to Staatssek. (Carl v. Schubert), "Aufzeichnung," Berlin, Nov. 2, 1923.

[79] Bundesarchiv Koblenz. Kurt von Schleicher, Papers, folder 17/I, document pages 12-7 (hereafter cited as: KvSP: 17/I/12-7), Groener to Ebert, Berlin, Nov. 1, 1923 (copy).

hands when he refused Stresemann power to dissolve the Reichstag. But many sensed the growing power of the army behind the scenes. As American Ambassador Alanson B. Houghton reported in a telegram dispatch to his government: "In reality von Seeckt now dominates the situation. [80] The ambassador's report was correct, not only because of the extraordinary powers given Seeckt in the emergency of actual and threatened disobedience, both civil and military, but also in the growing pretensions of the army. The army assured itself in all deliberateness of the friendliness of the new government of Wilhelm Marx.

The situation was apparent at the *Vortrag* in the *Truppenamt* on December 7. On the subject of "armament" ("Wehrhaftmachung") Major Kurt von Schleicher commented: "On this question the position of the Reichswehr vis-à-vis any government depends. Where a government does not accept this necessity, it is an impossible government given the present state of affairs. The present [Marx] government will surely cooperate with us, but not all of its subordinate agencies. . . ." [81] The *Truppenamt* a few days later distributed confidential summaries of the *Vortrag,* referring to consultation between Marx and the army before he took office. The report expressed satisfaction with the new strengthened Enabling Act. It was to be expected that the Reichstag would be sent home for the time being—a measure, incidentally, that the DNVP opposed. The army and the DNVP seemed to have lost *rapport* on this question. But naturally the DNVP did not want to be put out of action at this key juncture unless by a full-fledged military dictatorship. The DNVP wanted at least a parliamentary committee to function in Berlin. And, in case of an outright dissolution, they wanted an election. General Otto

[80] DS: 862.00/1351, telegram 206, Houghton, Berlin, Nov. 16, 1923.

[81] KvSP: 17/I/24-6 Truppenamts-Vortrag, Dec. 7, 1923. Present were, among others, Lt.-Col. v. Stülpnagel, Gen. Hasse, Maj. v. Schleicher. Quotation is from Schleicher report.

Hasse, who could not know much about the complications within the DNVP, wrote bemusedly: "Here we see opponents of parliament who are at the same time its vigorous advocates—[thus we see the contradiction of] theory and practice. It is hard to refrain from writing satire. Very quickly the tactics of the right concerning the new formation of a cabinet have proved themselves to be mistaken." [82]

General Hasse's observation was not *mal à propos*. In 1923 the Nationalist Party was very much at cross purposes, and serious signs were evident that the leadership was losing hold. Hergt was unable to carry the Party with him on the question of parliamentary tactics and coalition politics. This was true particularly as local organizations effectively mustered pressure on headquarters in Berlin. The sharp opposition group had some reason for satisfaction as they blocked the appeasers, yet they had not really won the day. In Bavaria and Württemberg, southern Nationalists already had entered bourgeois coalitions. [83] And in Berlin most members of the *Fraktionen* were as determined as ever to find a place for the DNVP in the cabinets of the Reich and Prussia. The question—and it was a tantalizingly difficult one—was on what conditions. As Westarp said on behalf of the Party which more than ever had become his own, "The will to power is not only a right under the parliamentary system, it is also the duty of a large party and leaders conscious of their ability." [84]

[82] KvSP: 17/I/27-31, Reichswehrministerium (Heer), Truppenamt, no. 106/23. Berlin, Dec. 11, 1923. (Gen.) Hasse to (listed) departments, transmitting report of Vortrag in Truppenamt of Dec. 7, 1923; the contents to be kept confidential, and the document to be destroyed once contents noted.

[83] WP: Leopold v. Schrenck to Westarp, Nov. 27, 1923.

[84] Westarp, Reich Debates, June 5, 1924, vol. 381, pp. 111-2, 117.

VII
The Dawes Plan Crisis

It was not easy for German statesmen to face the question of reparations due to the Allies under the peace terms of 1919. Besides the obvious economic sacrifice and political difficulties involved, the payment of reparations was fraught with emotional complications. To help Germany out of the impasse on reparations, the Allies in April, 1924, presented the Dawes Plan that to many Germans appeared a reasonable and honorable solution. That school of thought, which coincided with major business interests, expected substantial economic recovery would follow the flow of fresh investment funds and the international regulation of Germany's postwar obligations. Though the optimism was justified, there were many persons who regarded the plan, and the policy of fulfillment on which it was based, as anathema. The fight between the two views within the DNVP hurt the Party more seriously than any previous argument. As Hergt remarked, "Until 1924 the unity of the Nationalist approach was disturbed only by struggles over the extent and methods of our Racist policy, and even then was kept mainly in the Party circle. Then the vote on the Dawes Plan severely shocked the Party over a considerable period of time, and in public. [Since then] the Party has been unable to recover its tranquillity." [1]

In the Dawes Plan crisis, time finally caught up with the DNVP, which now paid the penalty of its internal diversity. Surprisingly, the test issue was not on a purely domestic

[1] Oskar Hergt, "Geleitwort zu Walther Graef (Anklam), 'Der Werdegang der Deutschnationalen Volkspartei 1918-1928,'" in Weiss, ed., *Der Nationale Wille,* p. 12.

question, but in the realm of foreign affairs where Nationalists were usually united. However, as Otto Hoetzsch explained, the significance of the Dawes Plan was that it
"shifted the reparations problem out of the sphere of politics into that of economics and finance." [2] Economic interest
was the Achilles heel in the tough Nationalist exterior, and,
particularly in 1924, economic pressures proved insurmount-
able.

If, in its very being, the DNVP represented a corporate
protest against the November Republic that to Nationalists
symbolized the Reich's defeat and shame, it also was pledged
to oppose the Versailles Treaty that symbolized national
humiliation and betrayal. Indeed, the Nationalist program
of 1920 officially established the primacy of foreign policy
in the party consciousness, acknowledging sentiment constantly affirmed by members. [3] In the Nationalist Party it
was almost axiomatic that Allied demands were to be resisted with firmness and even force, and there was universal
agreement that any effort to appease the enemy by attempted
fulfillment of impossible reparations requirements would
lead to ruin. [4]

The postwar atmosphere provided the Nationalist Party
with excellent material for propaganda. Even the most conservative of Nationalists did not hestitate to use Marxist
analogies to drive home a point. Westarp, for example, frequently told meetings that for Germans the "fight against
the Versailles *Diktat* is the class war of an entire nation reduced to proletarian status [in the struggle] against its ex-
ploiters." [5] He thought the picture of Germany as a proletarian people exploited by the power of foreign capitalism

[2] Hoetzsch, p. 63.

[3] Traub, Reich Debates, Feb. 20, 1919, vol. 326, pp. 202-10; Westarp,
"Ein Jahr Aussenpolitik," in Lambach, ed., *Politische Praxis 1926*, p.
46.

[4] Westarp, *loc. cit.*, p. 29.

[5] W MS, p. 279; *Kzztg.*, Dec. 28, 1919.

had a particular appeal to the working class. He encouraged the Christian Socialists to use the argument as often as possible, since he supposed it was more effective coming from their wing of the Party than from his. [6] The Christian Socialists did anyway often speak in such terms, as for example, Walther Lambach in the Reichstag: "We have become a working-class people among the peoples of the world. From that fact develops the necessity for us, and for me as a Nationalist worker in particular, to take the same stand as a nation in the economic struggle against the capitalist peoples of the Entente that we workers do in our struggle with the whole class of German employers. That is, we must keep a solid front in our fight against the capitalists and resolve all differences among ourselves."[7] Such talk might be supposed to lead in the direction of the curious ideological hybrid called National Bolshevism—the idea that extreme right and extreme left would find salvation by uniting to overwhelm the respectable and cowardly middle class. But no time need be spent on pursuing this subject. It leads nowhere. National Bolshevism remained an insignificant lunatic fringe of political opinion.

Within the DNVP indeed even the idea of an Eastern orientation in foreign policy, once a Conservative favorite, was by no means automatically accepted. The Treaty of Rapallo with Soviet Russia was only reluctantly and gradually accepted. Nationalist dislike of the treaty was most apparent in the Nationalist press and at local meetings, but even in the *Fraktion* hostile voices were heard, especially from Racists. [8] The leadership remained neutral on the merits of the treaty, but defended the right of Chancellor

---

[6] W MS, p. 281.

[7] Lambach, Reich Debates, Aug. 5, 1920, vol. 345, p. 710.

[8] Freytagh-Loringhoven, Reich Debates, Dec. 12, 1925, vol. 388, p. 4823 (at that date, he pointed out, the entire Party favored Rapallo); WP: Brauer to Heydebrand, July 8, 1922.

Wirth's government to negotiate without Allied approval. [9] Conservatives, including Heydebrand, Hoetzsch, and Westarp, were much more positive in their support; although they did not underestimate the danger of Bolshevism, they welcomed Rapallo as a gesture of German defiance. [10] Most convinced was Otto Hoetzsch, Russian expert and historian of the University of Berlin, who was urging the government to force favorable revision of reparations and the Eastern frontier, and also elimination of the rankling war-guilt clause. At the Görlitz Congress, Hoetzsch argued that, in the spirit of the Rapallo action, Germany should undertake an aggressive foreign policy to recover status and self-respect. [11]

The leadership welcomed arguments for a vigorous foreign policy and did not hesitate to insist on sharp opposition to the government where it saw deference to the Allies. [12] Helfferich particularly pursued the theme of resistance with oratorical brilliance, declaiming on a typical occasion in the Reichstag: "The only possibility we see for saving Germany is revision of the Versailles Treaty and of the London ultimatum. . . . We expect . . . the national government . . . to find a final solution by saying: 'We will go just so far and no more!' " [13]

Helfferich became the Party's chief spokesman against the fulfillment policy of German governments because of

[9] WP: Brauer to Heydebrand, April 24, 1922. Bracketed with the resolution in this report by Brauer were the names: Hergt, Westarp, Lindeiner.

[10] WP: Heydebrand at session of *Engerer Vorstand* of DKP, May 3, 1922; Orientation Report for Heydebrand, apparently corrected by Westarp, Berlin, June 2, 1922. Also Freytagh-Loringhoven, Reich Debates, Dec. 12, 1925, vol. 388, p. 4823.

[11] Hoetzsch at Party Congress, Görlitz, Oct. 27, 1922, reported in *Berliner Lokal-Anzeiger*, Oct. 28, 1922 (A.M.).

[12] Cf., Hergt, Reich Debates, July 8, 1920, vol. 344, p. 345; May 10, 1921, vol. 349, p. 3637.

[13] Helfferich, Reich Debates, March 16, 1922, vol. 353, p. 6319.

his oratory, his expertise in economics and public finance, and his personal dedication to the cause. He dated the beginning of the policy of fulfillment with the acceptance by Chancellor Wirth of the London ultimatum of May 5, 1921. This was a policy he held responsible for the greatest social and economic evils of postwar Germany: the inflation, the collapse of the currency, and ruin of the middle class. [14] As an expert Helfferich had a considerable following, especially on matters involving reparations. [15] With his assistance the position of the DNVP on foreign affairs remained negative.

Were it not for the negative attitude of the Nationalist Party, middle-class unity might well have been a political reality in the Republic. That at least was the feeling of Gustav Stresemann in January, 1924. He thought, too, that a united front needed the Nationalists if it were to succeed. The course of national politics would largely be determined by the decision the DNVP might take, either to remain in opposition, or to work with the Reich on the basis of the Constitution. [16] A good many Nationalists, on the other hand, had vague mostly unfounded hopes that some extra-constitutional action like a dictatorship of General von Seeckt might yet be possible. They continued to harass Stresemann's foreign policy at every turn, and managed to bring into their fold a secessionist group called the National Liberal Union (*Nationalliberale Vereinigung*) that had left the DVP.

Opposition to the fulfillment policy and to Stresemann

[14] Helfferich, *Die Politik der Erfüllung* (Munich, Berlin, Leipzig, 1922), p. iii; cf. also, Helfferich, Reich Debates, June 23, 1922, vol. 355, p. 7992; and speech at meeting of *Parteivertretung*, Berlin, Sept. 14-5, 1922, reported in *Berliner Lokal-Anzeiger*, Sept. 16, 1922 (P.M.).

[15] W MS, pp. 236-7, 363: WP: "Ruhrkampf" fragment, p. 23. Even Westarp, who differed with Helfferich on other matters, depended on him in technical financial questions. They also worked well together to oppose fulfillment policies.

[16] Stresemann, *Vermächtnis*, I, 287.

was played up in the election campaign of May, 1924. [17] But, for its positive contribution, the Party chose to stand on the *Rentenmark*, the miracle of sound new currency that it credited to the invention of Helfferich. Helfferich had, of course, contributed many valuable ideas during 1923 on how the inflation might be ended and sound currency re-introduced, but his ideas were pooled by the government with many others. That did not prevent the DNVP for claiming sole credit in exaggerated terms. [18] The Party Congress in Hamburg acclaimed their man as the hero of the economic battle with flags and cries of "Heil Helf-ferich!" [19] And leaflets to the German housewife read: "Helfferich's money put your household planning back on a sound basis. Helfferich's Party can also give your people a strong, reliable national leadership." [20]

But Helfferich assumed an even more important role in the campaign as the chief opponent of the Dawes Plan. Within days of the announcement of the plan, he attacked it in an article called "The Second Versailles" which was the keynote of the opposition. He claimed the plan would nullify the country's economic sovereignty, and leave the threat of further sanctions still hanging over their head. [21] Ironically, this was Helfferich's last public action. He was

---

[17] Westarp, *Kzztg.*, April 5, 1924 (P.M.). Westarp liked Hergt's speech.

[18] Cf., article "Rentenmark," in Weiss, ed., *Pol. Handwörterbuch*, p. 667: "One can say without the slightest exaggeration that Dr. Helfferich contributed through his work more than any other deputy, or than all the parties of the so-called 'great' or 'Weimar' coalition, to save the entire German people at the time of its greatest distress and danger, as well as to rescue the unity of the German Reich created by Bismarck."

[19] Weiss, in Weiss, ed., *Der Nationale Wille*, p. 376; Westarp, introduction, *Helfferichs Reichstagsreden 1922-1924*, p. 33.

[20] Stuttgart Collection: Leaflet no. 232, published by DNVP, Berlin.

[21] Stresemann, *Vermächtnis*, I, 254; *Kzztg.*, April 18, 1924 (A.M.); article "Reparationspolitik," in Weiss, ed., *Pol. Handwörterbuch*, p. 679; Hilpert, p. 1391.

killed soon after in a railway accident that was a major disaster for the DNVP. The Nationalists lost in Helfferich the strong, authoritative voice of a talented expert at a particularly bad time, just as problems of domestic and international finance dominated the scene. [22] Observers outside of the Party did not hesitate to say that in Helfferich the DNVP had lost its only talent. [23]

Despite this personal loss, the DNVP did very well at the polls. The May election gave the extremist parties considerable gains at the expense of the moderate Socialists, Populists, and Democrats. Communists obtained 62 seats where they had previously held 17; Racists rose to 32 from 3; Nationalists took 96 compared to their earlier 65 to become the strongest single party in the Reichstag. There were, in addition, 10 seats obtained by the *Landbund* on its own which could be considered close to the DNVP. The combined *Fraktion* had six more members than the Socialist party. [24] In round numbers the DNVP received 5,696,000 votes, or 19.5 per cent of the total, and the *Landbund* 574,-000, or 2 per cent. [25] The unexpected strength was also repeated locally in Württemberg where Nationalists returned 28 members to the Landtag to make up 25 per cent of the House. [26]

Although its plurality was less than 22 per cent, the DNVP was now confident that it had a mandate from the country, and immediately made a bid to form the new government. Hergt announced on May 7, "We have now become the strongest party in the new Reichstag, and with quiet confidence we anticipate proper recognition by the

[22] Quaatz, pp. 244, 247.

[23] *Berliner Tageblatt,* April 24, 1924 (P.M.).

[24] Horkenbach, pp. 193, 419.

[25] *Ibid.,* table opposite p. 400; also, Meinrad Hagmann, *Der Weg ins Verhängnis* (Munich, 1946), p. 14.

[26] Marquardt, p. 23.

responsible authorities." [27] He did not reject the Dawes Plan outright, but pointed out his Party still maintained grave reservations concerning certain aspects of it. In face of that ambiguous attitude the Reich government of Chancellor Marx declared itself in duty bound to remain in office to conduct vital negotiations in progress with Allied experts, and to remain in office at least until the new Reichstag met. The government's position was backed up by the parties. [28]

But Stresemann had not yet given up hope for the DNVP or for his foreign policy. He was sure that the election results would bring their own corrective. "Growth brings responsibility." [29] He was so confident of the soundness of his own judgment that he could hardly conceive of the Nationalists acting in a way much different from his once they grasped the realities of the situation. Yet, while he and others of his party were willing to bring the DNVP into government, they doubted this could be done. Stresemann was well aware of the DNVP's inner uncertainty on major issues. He wrote, "[Those] persons who are reasonable enough to understand that we must now proceed on the basis of the experts' report [Dawes Plan] do not know whether they are still a majority within the [Nationalist] *Fraktion*. But naturally unity on the subject of foreign policy is a prerequisite for any cabinet." Participation of Nationalists in government depended on their attitude to the crucial Dawes Plan. Even so, they could not expect to lead any cabinet after the *Fraktion* of the Center party (65 seats) unanimously voted against such a government. It might still be possible for the Nationalists to be part of a cabinet led by the Center. But Stresemann also cautioned,

[27] *Kzztg.*, May 7, 1924 (P.M.) .

[28] Horkenbach, p. 193.

[29] Stresemann to Dr. Jarres, May 9, 1924, in Stresemann, *Vermächtnis*, I, 405.

"We are still pretty much in the dark on the attitude of the Nationalists in decisive questions." [30]

Nationalist spokesmen did nothing to improve the situation [31] except to invite representatives of the Center party, DVP, and Bavarian *Volkspartei* to parley. Discussions were complicated by a decision of the government parties that the Dawes Plan had to be accepted or rejected in its entirety, removing it from the field of negotiation with the DNVP. [32] In view of their attitude, the most positive Nationalist suggestion was the person of Grand Admiral von Tirpitz for the office of chancellor. It was perhaps supposed he would be welcomed as an elder statesman who transcended the usual narrow party limits. [33] The talks brought no results as long as the DNVP failed to give an answer on the key issue of its attitude to the Dawes Plan,[34] and Chancellor Marx reformed his government on the basis of the previous one. [35] The DNVP was bitterly disappointed at the rebuff, and prepared to make the maximum difficulties for the Marx-Stresemann cabinet. [36] Ironically, in the test, the crisis was to come not in the government but in the ranks of the Nationalist Party.

In the history of the DNVP, August 29, 1924, was Black Friday. The tense occasion was the third reading in the Reichstag of the most crucial of the legislation needed to implement the Dawes Plan. It was the Railway Law, the only one—because it had the character of a constitutional amendment—that needed a two-thirds, rather than a simple, majority. Since there seemed little chance that the vital bill

[30] Stresemann to Otto Hembeck, May 13, 1924, in Stresemann, *Vermächtnis*, I, 408.

[31] Otto Hoetzsch, *Kzztg.*, May 14, 1924 (P.M.).

[32] Stresemann, *Vermächtnis*, I, 408-9; Horkenbach, p. 193.

[33] *Kzztg.*, May 22, 1924 (A.M.).

[34] Stresemann, *Vermächtnis*, I, 411.

[35] Horkenbach, p. 194. The government was re-formed on June 3, 1924.

[36] WP: Brauer to Heydebrand, June 20, 1924.

would pass, the President was expected to dissolve the House and appeal again to the country. The DNVP had finally, despite some momentary reluctance, come out against the Dawes Plan as a whole. It had opposed the plan doggedly through the summer, and in the Reichstag showed no sign of relenting until, on the crucial vote, the *Fraktion* split down the middle. Forty-eight Nationalist ayes assured the passage of the Railway Law, removing the last major hindrance to the Dawes Plan. The unexpected development caused turmoil in and out of the Party, and has been the subject of controversy since.

I would question the explanation in a recent study that, "[w]ithin the [DNVP], political fanaticism struggled against the lure of foreign loans. On August 23rd, the *Reichsverband of German Industry*, which was [to be] the main beneficiary of the loans—had spoken in favor of the Dawes plan in an almost unanimously carried resolution. As this industrial organization was one of the principal financial supporters of the DNVP, this measure could not be ignored by the party." [37] It was, of course, true that many financial arrangements (not least, the foreign credit) that the Dawes Plan provided were attractive to German industry, especially in the West. The Dawes Plan meant, too, an end of foreign occupation and restoration as far as possible of normal economic conditions. As a Nationalist observer commented, "Industry thinks in West German terms. In substance that means it thinks along economic and not political lines. Many of their best men do think along Nationalist lines. But again that does not mean that they are also able to ally that thought with Nationalist politics." [38] It is also true that pressure from the West was strong enough to sway many Nationalist *Fraktion* members in late August. [39] It was not true that the DNVP took orders from, or

[37] Kaufmann, p. 132.
[38] HvSP, item 153; Spahn to Seeckt, Dec. 21, 1923.
[39] Graef, p. 44; Quaatz, p. 254; Freytagh-Loringhoven, p. 25.

depended on, the *Reichsverband der Deutschen Industrie* (RDI).

Certainly the Nationalist Party received substantial sums from industry, mostly channeled through the person of Alfred Hugenberg. But there were already signs that money was no longer flowing as it once had [40]—witness the dearth of funds in the May campaign. Moreover the opinions of industry were well known on the Dawes Plan from the beginning, and did not come as a surprise in August. On the other hand, many industrialists who were convinced adherents of the DNVP were also outspoken critics of the Dawes Plan. On May 19, for example, some five hundred members of the *Deutsche Industriellen-Vereinigung*, influenced by Pan-German attitudes, met in Berlin to protest the views of the RDI on the Dawes Plan and fulfillment policies. [41] Hugenberg, the principal industrialist spokesman in the DNVP, was no more disposed to accept the judgment of the majority of industrialists. As head of the Party's Committee of German Industrialists, Hugenberg flatly disputed the stand of the RDI. [42] His influence was perhaps not what it might have been because he was a sick man in this period, and had been little seen in public life of late. His contacts even with the right wing of the *Fraktion* had perforce declined.[43] Still, from his sickbed he sent a strong letter to the Party leader on the eve of the vote summing up his complete antipathy to the Dawes Plan. [44] The letter was to be a valuable weapon in his armory in later years when he became chief contender for the position of party head.

---

[40] *Berliner Tageblatt,* Jan. 13, 1926, from DVP agency, "Deutscher Zeitungsdienst."

[41] *Kzztg.,* May 20, 1924 (A.M.).

[42] *Ibid.,* May 3, 1924 (P.M.).

[43] Freytagh-Loringhoven, pp. 26, 51.

[44] Hugenberg to Hergt, Aug. 26, 1924, in Alfred Hugenberg, *Streiflichter aus Vergangenheit und Gegenwart* (Berlin, 1927), p. 97.

Helfferich was no less determined in his opposition than Hugenberg, and, in addition, had the health and energy to pursue the campaign in public view. With his tragic death the spirit of the campaign collapsed. He was the one man in the DNVP who had the strength, the singleness of purpose, and who commanded sufficient respect to hold the Party to a consistent line of opposition. [45] With Helfferich dead, the Party kept a generally negative, but far from clear, attitude that exacerbated its relations with other parties and spoiled its chances of joining a government coalition. It was as though the leadership was either uncertain of itself, or was unwilling to reveal its tactical hand prematurely. If, on the other hand, the leadership knew its position, it failed miserably in convincing members of the Party on the correctness of its decision. Discipline in the *Fraktion* and Party at large temporarily collapsed.

The DNVP issued its first official "no" to the Dawes Plan in July—"no," that is, to the plan in its present form. [46] Helfferich personally had seemed rather opposed to any form. At the same time Otto Hoetzsch made no secret of his belief that to reject the Dawes Plan entirely, even with its present imperfections, would be an unwise, even an unfortunate procedure. He feared rejection would bring a disastrous repetition of the inflation. Moreover, the Dawes Plan, by bringing the United States into the picture, would diminish French influence and promise more objective treatment of Germany. On the whole, the Dawes Plan represented to Hoetzsch an improvement in Germany's international status and offered prospects of even more favorable revision of her obligations. [47] Hoetzsch's point of view had support in the Party, including Wilhelm Bazille, head of

[45] My interview with Hergt, Aug. 14, 1952; Weiss, ed., *Pol. Handwörterbuch,* p. 675; Marquardt, p. 46, Hilpert, pp. 1407-8; WP: Westarp to Heydebrand, April 28, 1924.

[46] Weiss, ed., *Pol. Handwörterbuch,* p. 682.

[47] Hoetzsch, in Weiss, ed., *Der Nationale Wille,* p. 98.

the Württemberg Nationalists and head of the state government. He too saw salvation only with the foreign credits of the Dawes Plan. [48] Racist enemies charged Hoetzsch and the DNVP of treachery and of subservience to industry, of turning Helfferich's "second Versailles" into Hoetzsch's "first Canossa." [49] As usual, their judgment was wide of the mark.

There is no evidence that the DNVP was succumbing to the organized pressure of big business. There were many other pressures involved, and despite them the chief spokesmen of the Party, including representatives of industry, remained opposed to the Dawes Plan consistently to the end. Other positions taken by individuals in the *Fraktion* were no doubt based largely on economic reasons, but were individual decisions nonetheless. The result was an unwelcome shock to the leadership.

One major cause of what happened was the decision of the *Reichslandbund* (RLB), the principal agrarian group, to reverse its position at the last moment. It is not clear exactly what considerations weighed heaviest, but the group in the last hours pressed actively for acceptance of the plan. [50] It is likely that not so much the Dawes Plan as the promise of a *quid pro quo* from the government was the chief attraction. The RLB was, above all else, a governmental pressure group in the DNVP.

A less obvious, but nonetheless real, pressure group was the German army under General von Seeckt who saw no possibility of success in a resistance policy, and who feared a swing to the left in case of new elections. Seeckt was interested in acceptance of the Dawes Plan less for any merits of its own, than for the unfortunate consequences he expected of rejection. [51] Anxious to see the Rhineland soon

[48] Marquardt, p. 50.
[49] v. Graefe, quoted in *Berliner Tageblatt,* Aug. 3, 1924 (A.M.).
[50] Hilpert, p. 1390.
[51] HvSP, roll 28: Seeckt to wife, Aug. 29, 1924; Seeckt, ed. Rabenau,

evacuated, he also felt that economic concessions by Germany could replace military ones. He therefore turned to the DNVP, the Party that controlled the outcome and that presumably was sensitive to the army's wishes. One may doubt the judgment of Seeckt's biographer, Friedrich von Rabenau, who wrote, "The Nationalists were in fact originally united against the idea of accepting. Seeckt's influence acted almost instantaneously, although he did not win over every vote. Of course, the fear of dissolution of the Reichstag also played a part in determining the action of the parties on the right." [52] Seeckt himself was not so confident, as he wrote his wife two days before the vote, "Politically things are looking worse today. . . . As I was coming from riding I spoke to Professor Hoetzsch on the street. He was completely of my opinion, but he had little confidence in his Party." [53]

The Party leadership was of course aware of the military, as well as economic and regional pressures on the question. It was not disposed to accept the well-known industrial point of view, nor did it react to the others. Agrarian and military pressure was built up late in the summer, even at the last minute after President Ebert's dissolution threat on August 25, and after the DVP on August 28 offered to take the Nationalists into government as a *quid pro quo*. Hergt tried to establish a definite negative position for the Party independent of special considerations. But, more cautious than Helfferich, he hesitated to commit the Party officially one way or the other when the Allied plan was first announced. Not until the London Conference in July was flat opposition made clear.

Hergt, of course, knew that he had not pleased everyone

---

p. 405.

[52] Seeckt, ed. Rabenau, pp. 404-5.

[53] Seeckt to wife, Aug. 27, 1924, quoted in Seeckt, ed. Rabenau, p. 405.

in the Party by his negative decision. Technically, at least on some points of honor, Germany had obtained slight satisfaction in London—Germany was accepted as an equal, her economic and fiscal unity was to be restored, procedure on sanctions was to be more cautiously regulated. [54] Hergt, in a long letter justifying his actions after the event, noted: "Pressure from economic groups, particularly from industry and agriculture, in favor of an agreement on the Dawes report made itself felt in a constantly increasing degree, and came from the occupied areas as well as from all Germany. In addition there was the general, and all too understandable, pressure of the Party for a change . . . by [our] entry into the governments of the Reich and of Prussia, there to make our influence felt in future foreign and domestic policy." [55] In order to hold his own against such sentiments, Hergt realized he could not entirely rule out the possibility of compromise on the Dawes Plan. He felt he could not close the door completely to agreement, but had to justify his negative attitude beyond reasonable doubt. When the government ignored Nationalist demands for new negotiations with the Allies and changes in the enabling legislation, Hergt attacked the Dawes agreements in vigorous terms. He personally had no reason to feel the *Fraktion* did not support him despite disagreement with Hoetzsch. [56] But there was in fact little to justify his optimism; he had badly misjudged the situation in his Party.

Since Hergt saw no way to agreement with the government before the formal signing of the treaty in London, he prepared to block the enabling legislation. He mistakenly thought the government had no intention of dissolving the Reichstag and calling new elections in case it failed.

[54] Horkenbach, p. 196.

[55] WP: Hergt to *Landesverband Ostpreussen,* Sept. 9, 1924 ("streng vertraulich").

[56] *Ibid.*; also Hergt, Reich Debates, Aug. 25, 1924, vol. 381, p. 807.

The misconception was cleared up when chancellor and president on August 25 threatened dissolution in case two-thirds were not obtained. Hergt described the reaction in the *Fraktion*: "The announcements did not fail to leave their impression on the *Fraktion*. Even without that development, there had already been strong doubts on the part of some persons in the group that there would be any possibility for negotiations abroad along the lines we wanted should the Dawes legislation be rejected. On the other hand the opinion was gaining more and more ground that the government would in fact act in accordance with its pronouncements and dissolve the Reichstag in case it failed to get the needed two-thirds majority, and would anyway sign in London on August 30. Moreover, the *Fraktion* appraised our chances in an election very pessimistically for the most part. And there was only one opinion on the significance of a defeat in the election: the DNVP would be excluded from any participation in government in the Reich and Prussia for a long time to come."[57]

August 25, the day Hergt spoke in the Reichstag, was a Monday. Hergt learned that week that a few isolated deputies were wavering and inclined to accept the Dawes legislation. He ascribed no importance to them. He continued to work along established lines to force new diplomatic negotiations, to prepare for a dissolution if necessary, and he was optimistic about the Party's chances in an election. But, while he pursued this policy in agreement with Count Westarp, a growing part of the *Fraktion* was taking another approach. Hergt later claimed to have had no knowledge at all of the fact that a large number of members met privately to determine means of passing the bills in question. Rather, that fact came to his surprised attention for the first time on the morning of Wednesday, August 27, the day on which a conference had been called of the heads of the

[57] See fn. 55; cf. also, Freytagh-Loringhoven, p. 25.

provincial branches of the Party (*Landesverbandsvorsitzende*). That morning a deputation of part of the *Fraktion* informed him that about thirty colleagues, among them every one from the occupied areas, were prepared to accept the Dawes report. Nevertheless it was still Hergt's impression that the group would not act separately unless it were sure that enough others in the *Fraktion* were available to assure the two-thirds majority. [58] Apparently Hergt did not believe any others would be found.

To meet the new situation in the *Fraktion*, however, Hergt appeared before the local Party heads that day with what he called a middle-of-the-road proposal. He revived the half-forgotten suggestion that the DNVP introduce an amendment to the Dawes legislation containing the Party's principal conditions of agreement. The Party would demand prior guarantees for the early evacuation of the Ruhr, for determination of definite reparations obligations, and for recall of the war-guilt lie. Then, if that amendment were turned down by the House, the Party could vote solidly against the legislation with a clear conscience. As Hergt reported the reception of his proposal, the support he received was "almost unanimous." [59] Other sources confirm him: of the 42 present, 39 voted with him. The 3 negative votes were West and South Germans. [60] With this mandate from the Party at large, Hergt returned to the *Fraktion* on the same day, August 27, to obtain similar approval from the deputies. The talks within the parliamentary group were long and painful, and for Hergt less satisfactory than with the local Party heads. Although he felt he had a considerable majority with him even in the group, he decided not to force individuals who felt strongly the other way. Though no permission was given for individual

[58] See fn. 55.
[59] *Ibid.*
[60] *Berliner Tageblatt,* Aug. 27 (P.M.), 28 (A.M.), 1924; Hilpert, p. 1408.

action, it was not decided to impose Party discipline on
the vote. The bitter discussion in the *Fraktion* ended in a
draw. As Hoetzsch described the situation to Seeckt, "They
had a very tough fight in the House today." [61]

Then, on August 28, the *Fraktion* of the DVP in a
masterly stroke suddenly offered to bring the DNVP into
government in return for their support of the Dawes legislation. [62] A similar offer followed, though unauthorized,
from the Executive of the Center *Fraktion*. [63] This strategy
hit the Nationalist leadership in its most vulnerable spot,
since such an offer could not simply be ignored. As Hergt
explained, "Given the tremendous difficulty of the general
situation and the various attitudes of the Party, it would
have been an impossibility to turn down flat offers like
that. The economic interests, industry as well as agriculture, were meanwhile applying pressure for an agreement
with increasing strength, while from the Reichswehr also
came urgent insistance that we come to terms." [64] Although
Hergt doubted that this was the proper time for the DNVP
to enter government, he did consult with the DVP and
Center parliamentary groups. Hergt pointed out that the
DNVP could not be bought by a few cheap portfolios. [65]
The Nationalists' arrogant demand for the chancellorship
promptly ended the talks. [66]

More promising appeared to be a separate discussion
with Stresemann. In return for Nationalist help Stresemann
seemed willing to repudiate the war-guilt clause of the
Versailles Treaty, and to accept publicly some basic Nationalist principles in foreign policy. The government

[61] Seeckt to wife, Aug. 27, 1924, in Seeckt, ed. Rabenau, p. 405.
[62] *Kzztg.*, Aug. 30, 1924 (A.M.).
[63] Horkenbach, p. 199.
[64] See fn. 55.
[65] My interview with Hergt, Aug. 14, 1952.
[66] WP: Westarp's report to *Engerer Vorstand* of DKP, Oct. 11, 1924,
quoted by Brauer to Heydebrand, Oct. 14, 1924.

actually did issue a declaration the same day denying sole German responsibility for the war. The Nationalist *Fraktion* was immediately inspired to declare that a significant change in the situation had occurred. But the government statement was really not as complete as the Nationalists had expected, or as they thought Stresemann had promised. [67] Hergt was gravely displeased.

Now that the leadership felt assured of its strength in the crisis and of the fact that the Nationalists were indispensable to the government, Hergt could only characterize as absurd a suggestion from the cabinet that both Social Democrats and Nationalists enter a coalition. That was a far cry from the onetime *Ordnungsprogramm* of the same Hergt who now was closer than ever to Count Westarp in his point of view. Hergt was unwilling to give up his insistence that the DNVP enter government on its own terms. He wrote, "In my opinion Nationalist leadership was the indispensable symbol for our Party of the fact that from now on there would be no more of the weak policy we have had so far, particularly as concerned implementation of the Dawes report. It was my opinion that change in Prussia could be effected more quickly and with less friction if there existed a Nationalist chancellor to exercise influence from his vantage point in the Reich." [68]

In that statement Hergt was, of course, justifying himself in face of critics who accused him of weakness and betrayal of principles. This he denied in pointing out the nature of final negotiations before the fateful vote. On the morning of August 29, the day of the vote, he talked again with the chancellor. For the last time he asked if the government was prepared to give the DNVP a directing influence on foreign policy in line with the Party's strength. When the chancellor declined, Hergt made clear that the

[67] Horkenbach, p. 199.
[68] See fn. 55.

Nationalist *Fraktion* would then defeat the Dawes Plan. The *Fraktion* was accordingly advised in caucus.

But it was too late for such an approach in the *Fraktion*. Too many hopes had been raised. Reasons for the unsatisfactory outcome now seemed too flimsy to satisfy those who believed that the country's hope lay in the Dawes agreement. The leadership had itself been ready to bargain, and had considered a *quid pro quo*. It seemed to a sizable minority not enough to let the whole issue turn on the question of a Nationalist chancellorship. As Hergt instructed the *Fraktion* firmly to oppose the Dawes legislation, the bell was already ringing for a division on the Reichstag floor.

After the chaos sorted itself out the Nationalist *Fraktion* found it had split down the middle with 48 voting for the Dawes Plan, and 52 against. [69] The Communists and Nazis in the House raised a tremendous jeer at the Nationalist "betrayal." [70] The common belief was that all the Nationalist threats of preventing the plan were a dishonest maneuver to get concessions, and that the Nationalists all along had planned this underhanded way of passing the Railway Law. The truth was that Hergt was shocked at the last minute to find a large pro-Dawes faction among the Nationalist deputies, but there was nothing more he could do. No order to split the vote was given; the split was the result of forces that got out of hand, with unfortunate results for the Party. From this time on men were to carry the permanent labels of *Ja-Sager* and *Nein-Sager*.

Of the extreme oppositionist sentiment in the Party little had to this point been heard. They were satisfied that in this issue at least their viewpoint would win out with the support of the leadership. They complacently approached the crucial vote with no thought that a substantial defec-

[69] See fns. 55 and 65.
[70] Stresemann, *Vermächtnis*, I, 524.

tion would nullify their position. Consequently their wrath knew no bounds, and they even attempted to intimidate the rest of the *Fraktion* by seeking contact with the Nazis. [71]

On the other hand, the high command of the army was jubilant at the result of vote. Though Seeckt with exaggeration claimed a personal victory, he had had his own representative, Kurt von Schleicher, in the Reichstag on the whole day of the twenty-ninth working for the army's interest. One can only speculate with what effect. Even Seeckt railed against the "stupidity and clumsiness" of Hergt which "cried to high heaven." Not so much Hergt's DNVP as Stresemann's DVP gratified the army by its general position. [72]

The wave of recriminations was not long in coming, with strong abuse of the Nationalist leadership for its middle-of-the-road course. By the government parties Westarp and Hergt were accused of dishonesty: "They themselves negotiated with us on the possibility of entering government if they accepted the report. Now on the other hand they allow themselves to be fêted as opponents of the plan (*Nein-Sager*)." [73] The criticism was not undeserved; they had considered the possibility of a deal despite their general opposition to Dawes. The leadership actually fell between two stools on August 29 when it failed both to get control of government and to keep unanimity in the *Fraktion*.

Hergt regretted afterward that he omitted one move that might have saved the day: he had not called together the Executive before instructing the deputies on the vote. [74]

[71] Hilpert, p. 1409.

[72] HvSP, roll 28: Seeckt to wife, Aug. 29, 1924; Rabenau in his transcription of the same letter, p. 405, deleted the reference to Hergt, with no indication of the omission.

[73] Stresemann to Dr. v. Campe, Sept. 8, 1924, in Stresemann, *Vermächtnis*, I, 559.

[74] See fn. 65.

But even the weight of the *Vorstand* might have been insufficient. Hergt had not even threatened to resign, later pleading the futility of such an action. "As mentioned, the leadership of the *Fraktion* was taken completely by surprise by the developments as they occurred in the parliamentary group because it had been informed for the first time on Wednesday morning of what had been taking place in the interval. Under these circumstances the leadership could not have forced any other outcome in the matter even by direct intervention of its personal influence such as bringing on a leadership crisis." [75] When in the coming weeks the leadership crisis did come, it was the result of Hergt's weakness, not his own strong action.

For the public naturally some explanation had to be found for the split, and this was a denial that there was a split. The Party, it was stated, remained opposed to the London agreement; the Nationalists who voted for it did so not out of conviction of its merits, but to relieve the pressure from the Allies. The government's repudiation of the war-guilt clause of the Versailles Treaty made technical acceptance of the agreement honorable, and the Nationalist Party could morally contemplate participation in such a cabinet. [76] The Nationalist campaign had been designed, after all, to oppose the Dawes Plan without exposing the country to arbitrary action by the enemy.

The differences in the Party however could not be so easily explained to its own membership. The Bavarian section criticized the *Ja-Sager* for breaking the discipline of the *Fraktion*. For the sake of the Party a solid vote in either direction would have been better than a split. [77] Hoetzsch, who had been prominent in the camp of Dawes supporters, was able to say that "inwardly and outwardly

[75] See fn. 55.

[76] *Kzztg.*, Aug. 30, 1924 (A.M.); Weiss, ed., *Pol. Handwörterbuch*, p. 685; Hilpert, p. 1434.

[77] Hilpert, pp. 1389, 1425-39.

Party and *Fraktion* have withstood this severe and onerous test." [78] That judgment is open to question.

While the Dawes Plan still was in the planning and negotiating stage, the focus of power and responsibility lay in the leadership, Executive, and Reichstag *Fraktion* of the DNVP. The Party at large was still called in on occasion for consultation through representatives of the regional branches, but the role of these conferences was formal and advisory. The same might be said of the annual congresses despite the heated debates that occasionally flared there. The Party at large was used to being directed on matters of policy—despite inadequacies of organization—and this seemed proper in a party of order and authority. Regional groups made their opinions known to the leadership; it was up to the leadership to interpret, reconcile, and finally to direct. But it was in the course of the Dawes crisis that the informal relationship of leadership, *Fraktion,* and Party—agreement by discussion—broke down. Not discussion, but action thereafter dominated the scene as self-willed elements went their own way. Among the many Nationalists who felt that the Party had betrayed its principles there was a feeling of dismay and a growing demand for retribution. Animosity was directed against the men in Parliament for being either weak-willed or selfish compromisers, and above all against the leadership that had bungled the situation beyond description. This attitude, as might be guessed, was most vocal among Pan-Germans and among the Old Conservatives, and with the Prussian Junkerdom among agrarians rather than the small landowners of the RLB.

Of positive support for Hergt there was little evidence. As Seeckt observed, the only point of agreement in the DNVP after August 29 seemed to be the conviction that the leader would have to go. [79] Even Hoetzsch was reported

[78] Hoetzsch, in Weiss, ed., *Der Nationale Wille,* p. 101.
[79] HvSP, roll 28: Seeckt to wife, Sept. 4, 1924.

to have expressed this opinion, while in his electoral district the local organization was calling for his own resignation from the Reichstag. [80] The leadership question was brought to a crisis level without delay by the *Landesverband* in East Prussia. On September 5 it sent Hergt a resolution of the Provincial Executive, backed by the heads of the *Kreisvereine*, expressing loss of confidence in his leadership and asking for his resignation and that of his first assistant in the Party apparatus, Lindeiner-Wildau. Censure came from countless other units of the Party at all levels, and from the DKP. The Conservatives were particularly sharp in a resolution that read, "The Inner Executive (*Engerer Vorstand*) has learned with indignation of the result of the vote on the London agreement, and of the attitude of the DNVP that was revealed at that time. The Executive expects an immediate and clear explanation of this behavior which directly contradicts all earlier pronouncements of the Party." [81] A committee was also set up by individuals of various right-wing organizations, but mainly Pan-Germans and Conservatives, to demand a change of Nationalist leadership and to press for a firm opposition policy.

Hergt felt the extreme oppositionists were making him a scapegoat and was unwilling to comply with their wishes. He scornfully termed their activity as bustle *ut aliquid fiat,* really *ut aliquid fieri videatur.* He was presented a resolution of eighteen local party heads calling for an immediate change of leadership with minimum publicity. A further provision of their resolution, termed by Hergt "the maddest of all," was for the head of the Party not to take part personally in any future negotiations for the formation of a government. On the other hand the oppositionists, or at least the local organizations of the Party, were to have representatives constantly present at such negotiations. The

[80] WP: Brauer to Heydebrand, Sept. 10, 1924.
[81] *Kzztg.,* Sept. 6, 1924 (P.M.).

suggested successor as head of the Party and *Fraktion* was Count Westarp! Hergt wrote of these developments to Westarp who had disappeared from the scene soon after the culmination of the Dawes affair, staying aloof in a South German village. [82]

Hergt clearly was not anxious to give up his position. It was folly, he said, to raise the issue of leadership at a time when the Party needed to save its strength for the general political arena. He particularly deplored a change in orientation further to the right that would only result in serious internal dissension, and give an excuse to other parties to renege on their promises to the DNVP. Hergt's solution to the present unrest and disunity was to participate in government. That wider responsibility and field of action would more than compensate for the temporary failure of tactics on the Dawes Plan. [83]

Westarp did nothing to encourage Hergt's enemies, but also did not share the leader's optimism over the possibilities for the DNVP in government. He would not interfere with talks that had already begun, but expected no positive results. He saw no reason for the Party after the Dawes vote to get the satisfaction from the other parties that it had been unable to get before. With the trump card gone, there was precious little to negotiate with. Westarp did not want a change in leadership, but, if it had to come, the current discussions on possible participation in government should, he thought, be first completed. Westarp, who early in 1924 had succeeded Heydebrand as head of the DKP, promised to use his influence with the Conservative party and *Kreuzzeitung* in the leadership question. He particularly asked the editor of the *Kreuzzeitung* to correct the impression that Westarp was in favor of the removal of Hergt. [84]

[82] WP: Hergt to Westarp, Sept. 15, 1924.
[83] *Ibid.*
[84] WP: Westarp to Hergt, Sept. 18, 1924.

The case presented by Hergt at preliminary meetings of Party representatives on September 18 was the same as in his communication to Westarp. Hergt, backed by Lindeiner-Wildau, repeated his belief that the unity of the Party would best be preserved by an active policy, preferably in the federal government. The DNVP would be satisfied if it had adequate influence in a cabinet where it held four portfolios: vice-chancellery, interior, finance, and commerce. In his opinion a change of leadership should take place only if negotiations with the other parties failed, in which case the DNVP would enter a campaign of sharpest opposition. Reaction to his presentation was favorable, though the decision remained with the full meeting of Party representatives at the end of the month. Meanwhile Lindeiner privately urged Westarp to assume a leading role in the leadership, and promised him the ministry of the interior if the talks with the coalition were successful. On the other hand the Party's prospects were dismal if the talks failed: "I am convinced that our Party with its present composition cannot be held together indefinitely any more in a position of unqualified opposition. If we wish to maintain it, and strengthen it further as an influential and powerful movement of the right, then we must now take over power in the state." [85] With that preparation, Hergt threatened the government, the other parties, and the public with the consequences of a refusal to take the DNVP into the coalition. He threatened by obstruction to block the work of Parliament, in that way to bring on a major political crisis. The only persons who approved were the extremists in the Party, and they still were anxious to get rid of Hergt. [86]

What actually occurred at the end of September was a compromise in the leadership crisis, in which Hergt saved

[85] WP: Lindeiner-Wildau to Westarp, Sept. 22, 1924; cf., *Berliner Tageblatt*, Sept. 19, 1924 (P.M.); *Kzztg.*, Sept. 20, 1924 (P.M.).

[86] Georg Foertsch, *Kzztg.*, Sept. 20, 1924 (P.M.).

face while the oppositionists got much of what they wanted. Hergt voluntarily withdrew without forcing the issue. It was clear, despite his vigorous defense, that his usefulness as leader was over when he failed to reconcile dissension after the Dawes vote. He told Party representatives that he intended to give up his offices in the Party and *Fraktion* at the end of negotiations for the formation of a new government regardless of their outcome. Since Hergt's decision was final, no personal unpleasantness developed. In a reasonable compromise Hergt was offered the post of vice-chancellor should the DNVP enter government. [87] As graciously as was possible under the circumstances, the unpleasantness of an extended public leadership crisis was avoided.

News of the forthcoming resignation was suppressed until the negotiations ended. Meanwhile the Party representatives published a significant communiqué to advertise the good feeling in their midst: "The Party representatives and the chairmen of the regional organizations are unanimous in their determination to preserve the unity of the Party. Now that the Reichstag has passed bills to implement the London agreement, and now that these are binding laws which must be carried out, it is the duty of the Party to assure itself influence in the interpretation, operation, and improvement of these laws. The Party representatives therefore approve the action of the *Fraktion* in not refusing the negotiations proposed by Chancellor Marx on the subject of Nationalist participation in the government." [88] The delegates, in backing the strong desire of the *Fraktion* to seek a place in government, also, in this important statement, acknowledged the fact of the Dawes Plan and the obligation of working within its framework now that it

[87] WP: Westarp to *Engerer Vorstand* of DKP, Oct. 11, 1924, reported by Brauer to Heydebrand, Oct. 14, 1924; Westarp to v. Dommes, Oct. 10, 1924.

[88] *Kzztg.*, Sept. 30 (A.M.), Oct. 1 (A.M.), 1924.

was the law of the land. This appeared the Party's first step on the road to a fulfillment policy, Stresemann-style.

One can picture the new dilemma that faced Nationalists of the opposition school. They abhorred acceptance of the Dawes Plan in any form. Yet the very presence of the Party in any government from this time would have involved technical acceptance of the plan, even though the Party might have been working to revise or subvert it. Moreover, it must be understood that the September compromise on the leadership satisfied the anti-Hergt, but not the anti-governmentalist, feeling in the Party. These were attitudes that frequently, but not always, coincided.

Count Westarp was anti-governmental, but not necessarily opposed to Hergt. Still, he had prolonged his stay in Württemberg not just for a rest, but out of political prudence. He did not approve of the agitation against Hergt, yet was also no enthusiast of Hergt's solution of rushing into government. [89] When he was back on the political scene in Berlin after the important meetings were over, he avoided giving encouragement to either movement. Privately he warned the Prussian and Reich *Fraktionen* against their governmental enthusiasm, though with little effect. Westarp, of course, accepted the majority decision on procedure but tried to prevent the Party from making what would to him be intolerable sacrifices for the sake of a Nationalist cabinet. Assurances on foreign policy were prominent prerequisites in his mind for any Nationalist participation. No one in the Party this time suggested, it might be noted, that a coalition with the SPD was possible; this was a limit that could not be crossed as far as Westarp and probably most Nationalists were concerned. [90]

In all this one might very well wonder what the feeling of the government parties was. The leadership and *Fraktion* of the DNVP apparently took it for granted that the

[89] WP: Westarp to Hergt, Sept. 18, 1924.
[90] WP: Westarp to v. Dommes, Oct. 10, 1924.

Nationalists had a place in the cabinet for the asking, that somehow it was their due as a result of pledges made in the dying days of August when the Dawes Plan still hung in the balance. But actually the DVP was the only party which had made any sort of commitment. And presumably there were serious doubts in many minds as to what agreements had supposedly been made then with the Nationalists. After all, Hergt had himself broken off the talks after prolonging them to the last minute, and had stalked off with the avowed intention of defeating the Dawes Plan. Acceptance was due only to the courage and determination of rebellious individuals in the Nationalist *Fraktion* and not the decision of the leadership or the DNVP at large. Nevertheless, after the Dawes fight a number of persons in the DVP pressed for inclusion of the DNVP in the Reich cabinet in accordance with the promise made by them in August. [91]

It was apparent to Stresemann however that the promise could not easily be honored unless the *Ja-Sager* were able to maintain themselves in the DNVP. "It seems to me hardly possible to pursue successfully with the Center and the Democrats the idea of bringing the Nationalists into the coalition while one regional organization of the DNVP after another puts itself on the side of those who voted against the Dawes Plan, or even demands the expulsion of those who voted for it. For that reason I believe that we must wait awhile to see what developments take place within the Nationalist Party itself before the subject of their participation can be pursued any further." [92] A resolution of the DVP Reichstag *Fraktion* reaffirmed their desire to broaden the coalition with the Nationalists, and the attitude of the DNVP by the end of September seemed to show that the forces of reason had prevailed. Negotiations began, but their failure was assured when Chancellor Marx in-

[91] Graef, p. 45.
[92] See fn. 73.

sisted on the idea of extending the cabinet left to the SPD as well as right to the DNVP. Both of those groups made difficulties, and the talks ended without results. [93]

Westarp blamed the stalemate on the Center party leadership; two-thirds to three-quarters of the membership would have approved collaboration with the DNVP, he estimated, had not Wirth threatened to leave the Center and found a separate Christian Democratic party if that occurred. [94] On the other hand, the DVP was threatening to break up the government unless the Center party and the Democrats accepted the Nationalists. But the Democrats still refused to extend the coalition to the right, and made a bid to keep the present alignment intact. A further attempt of Chancellor Marx to enlarge the cabinet with three Nationalist ministers, and with Otto Gessler of the DDP as army minister, was turned down by both Democrats and Nationalists. To break the impasse the cabinet appealed to the nation. The Reichstag was dissolved, and an election called for December 7. [95] With dissolution further work on the coalition was out of the question. Hergt, as he promised, resigned and was temporarily replaced by Friedrich Winckler, head of the Prussian *Fraktion,* a moderate Conservative and prominent Protestant layman. [96]

For weeks it had been rumored that Westarp would be Hergt's successor, and if he had really pressed for it the position might well have been his. But Westarp hesitated to appear as Hergt's rival, nor did he want to be remiss in any way in his duties to the Old Conservative organization. Soon after Helfferich's death, even, there had been

[93] Horkenbach, p. 201.

[94] Westarp, Oct. 11, 1924; see fn. 87.

[95] Horkenbach, pp. 201-2.

[96] He was president of the Senate of the Old Prussian Church, according to W. Kähler, "Deutschnationale Kulturpolitik," in Weiss, ed., *Der Nationale Wille,* p. 194. News of the resignation and succession, *Berliner Tageblatt,* Oct. 24, 1924 (A.M.); *Kzztg.,* Oct. 24, 1924 (A.M.).

some speculation in the DKP that Westarp might someday become head of the Nationalist *Fraktion,* or even of the whole DNVP. Seidlitz of the Silesian Conservatives let it be known that he would gladly accept chairmanship of the DKP in Westarp's place should he assume office in the DNVP. [97] In the course of the summer, Brauer had occasion to note the influence Westarp was apparently obtaining in the *Fraktion*: "The leadership of the Nationalist parliamentary group now lies largely in Count Westarp's hands. However, it seems to me that he needs to have nerves of steel in order to endure the constant interference of Hergt. . . ." [98] Brauer was only approximately correct; Westarp's influence was still personal, based on whatever respect he could command as an individual. Ever since 1919, as the main representative of Prussian values in the Party, he had had to fight for his existence. Not until the 1922 Racist crisis had he established himself firmly as a potential leader in the DNVP, though he had always been a man to reckon with. Even so he had not even yet won over all the Conservatives in the *Fraktion* to his side. Among some extreme Old Conservatives, also, he seemed too closely identified with purely Nationalist interests. [99] Westarp saw the possibility of taking over leadership of the DNVP without hurting Hergt as a result of the latter's own decision to resign, but he would not do so without the approval of his Old Conservative associates.

The remnant Conservative organization was far from enthusiastic over the prospect of Westarp's promotion in the DNVP. [100] Westarp, of course, realized this when he sounded out the Inner Executive of the DKP at its meeting

[97] WP: Brauer lamented the fact to Heydebrand, since he did not feel Seidlitz was suited for the position (n.d., but the transcript appeared between entries for April 28, and June 20, 1924).

[98] WP: Brauer to Heydebrand, July 5, 1924.

[99] *Ibid.* Kreth suggested the latter motivation for Steiniger.

[100] WP: Brauer to Heydebrand, Sept. 10, 1924.

on October 11. He mentioned then the possibility of his becoming chairman of either the Nationalist *Fraktion* or Party, and asked whether it would be possible for him to remain chairman of the DKP at the same time. He warned the Conservatives against any thought of independent political activity at that time. He specifically condemned the rumored plan of the Pan-Germans to set up a new party in secession from the DNVP. Come what may, he said, Conservatives must seek to preserve their values in and through the DNVP. The meeting backed him up on the general subject of Conservative-Nationalist relationships, but made clear that the Executive did not want its chairman saddled with responsibility for the leadership of another party lest the DKP completely lose its freedom of action. There was little enough left for it to do as it was. While they definitely did not want Westarp to become Nationalist leader, they had fewer objections to his becoming head of the *Fraktion,* or eventually something like the Prussian interior ministry. [101] Thus it was mainly the negative attitude of the DKP that prevented Westarp from becoming Hergt's successor in the fall of 1924. The position was almost his for the asking, and came his way finally a year later—a remarkable career for one who in 1918 was virtually an outcast.

The Dawes crisis did not hurt the Nationalist Party at the polls, surprisingly. In the December election the DNVP in fact made some slight gains, but hardly impressive when compared to the substantial increase of the SPD. Hergt certainly was satisfied by the result, in which he saw somehow a vindication of his policy and some compensation for his defeat of August 29 in the *Fraktion.* Hergt was able to boast that under his leadership the DNVP had continually grown in strength and prestige. [102] The truth was the Dawes crisis had caused more damage to the Party within than

[101] WP: Brauer to Heydebrand, Oct. 14, 1924.
[102] See fn. 65.

without. Yet, despite talk of secession by extreme opposi-
tionists in Conservative and Pan-German circles, no serious
action in that direction started. Still, there was no way for
Hergt to rescue his position as leader. He was replaced in
October as head of the Party by Friedrich Winckler, a
political nonentity, and in December as chairman of the
Fraktion by the agrarian, Martin Schiele. [103] Significantly,
neither new man could be labeled by an August 29 vote:
Winckler, because he was not a member of the Reichstag;
Schiele, because he had been absent that day.

After his resignation Hergt remained largely in the
background either by choice or necessity. His period of
leadership had not been distinguished. Still, as an individual he had been pliable and with him the Party certainly had grown. Though at first Hergt had relied heavily
on the Free Conservative group, after their departure he
came to depend much more on the forces of business, agriculture, Christian Socialists, and especially the talents of
Helfferich. They were the ones that helped him weather
the Racist storm in 1922, and to keep an upper hand over
the Conservatives and Pan-Germans. Two years later the
situation was much different. In the Dawes test he lost
control precisely of those forces—business, agriculture, and
Christian labor—that had been his mainstay although he
himself had remained, as leader, independent. He lost their
good will while alienating further the sharp opposition.
Helfferich was no longer around to help him out of the
dilemma. Westarp, to whom he turned by default, was at
best a cautious, somewhat reluctant, and finally ineffectual
guide in a situation not of his making or choosing.

When Hergt stood aside as leader, it seemed that the
day of the independent Nationalist that he tried to represent also passed, and that of agrarians and Conservatives
arrived. In the wings meanwhile Pan-Germans and like-

---

[103] *Berliner Tageblatt*, Dec. 18, 1924 (A.M.).

minded Nationalists prepared for their entrance on the scene. Internally the situation in the fall of 1924 was still very bad, and much tension and bad feeling poisoned the atmosphere. Hoetzsch broke his long association with the *Kreuzzeitung*; local Party organizations maligned and demanded the recall of their representatives who were *Ja-Sager*; regional organizations feuded with *Fraktionen* in Reich and state; Christian Socialists disputed with Pan-Germans, Conservatives, and especially the *Vereinigte Vaterländische Verbände* that supported their archenemies, the so-called yellow unions; South and West Germany were at odds with the Center and East. It was a period of tremendous uncertainty for Nationalists, yet they were still able to get together to fight a successful electoral campaign.

That was because there were still certain basic instincts that were Nationalist beyond the wide differences on tactics. All Nationalists shared an incomparable jingoist attitude toward the Republic, the functions of government, and relations with foreign countries. And this had its counterpart in the German people. There is no doubt also that the regional appeals used by various elements of the DNVP in each electoral district had their powerful effect. But from these local interests was derived the tremendous urge, the will to power that was both the Party's strength in the campaigns and weakness in its own inner councils. Differences in tactics had made the Dawes situation a severe crisis for the DNVP. It was neither the first nor last such crisis. The crises were to persist, finally to destroy that Nationalist coalition that had come together in the November, 1918, emergency. Electorally the DNVP was able to achieve impressive results through the years. But the substantial structure that had been raised by 1924 was built on shifting sands. Disintegration potentially could be quick and disastrous. That was the lesson and portent of Dawes.

Three men succeeded Hergt as leader of the DNVP

before the Party was extinguished, with all parties but one, in 1933. Friedrich Winckler's régime was merely a brief interregnum of a few months. But under the modified Conservative leadership of Westarp in the three following years (1925-1928), the Party took the bold step of participating in two government coalitions with rather unfortunate results. Westarp however lost not only the friendship and support of Pan-Germans and industry, but also won the enmity of many of his Old Conservative, monarchist colleagues. Alfred Hugenberg, representing the forces of militant anti-Weimar Pan-Germanism got a firm grip on the Party in 1928 and proceeded to attack its internal divisions by drastic rationalization; opponents of his policy and methods were driven from the Party.

The difficulties of the Party's early years were portents of worse struggles to come. Though Hergt blamed his failure on lack of support in the ranks, the situation really was a mirror of the rifts in the conscience of the political right that frequently confronted the most moderate Nationalist with a dilemma. None caused more anguish than the question of responsibility in opposition. From the record the opposition of the DNVP was far from loyal, as was finally clear to all during the Kapp putsch. The Party was in its essence anti-republican and anti-democratic. It could work with the state only on behalf of a different constitutional system, an authoritarian philosophy, and the special economic interests of its members. From the point of view of the government parties and supporters of the Weimar Republic the DNVP represented a negative, corrosive, subversive force in the nation—in short, nothing less than a dangerous and reckless opposition that damaged rather than enhanced political life. Gerhart Hauptmann spoke for many when he wrote, "The so-called German Nationalists would contribute much to the inner tranquillity of the country if they finally stopped insulting the vast majority of their patriotic countrymen by their very use of the term 'German National.' Since they consider themselves alone to be patriots they naturally arouse the strongest resentment of the German people. And this perhaps hinders whatever good might lie in their Party." [104]

[104] Gerhart Hauptmann to Mayor Hesse of Dessau (a member of the Democratic party), Nov. 12, 1924, in *Berliner Tageblatt*, Nov. 15, 1924 (A.M.).

Bibliographical Note

For reasons of economy I do not attempt to list here all the items I may have examined in the course of my research. Instead I offer this note together with a list of authors and titles. The reader interested in pursuing the subject of Weimar politics should examine the extensive topical compilation of current writing in issues of the *Vierteljahreshefte für Zeitgeschichte*. He will find lists of older material in *From Weimar to Hitler*, The Wiener Library, Catalogue Series, 2 (London, 1951), soon to be reissued in a revised, extended form. Valuable bibliography is included in the second edition of Karl Dietrich Bracher, *Die Auflösung der Weimarer Republik* (Stuttgart, Düsseldorf, 1957). Helpful guides to the relevant literature in the field are also Bruno Gebhardt, *Handbuch der Deutschen Geschichte*, vol. 4 (Stuttgart, 1959), and Albert Schwarz, *Die Weimarer Republik* (Constance, 1958).

The best introduction to the history of the Weimar Republic are Erich Eyck's two volumes. [1] However, they do not quite supersede the earlier studies of Arthur Rosenberg, [2] Friedrich Stampfer, [3] Ferdinand Friedensburg, [4] and S. William Halperin. [5]

On party history in general, mention should be made of Ludwig Bergsträsser, *Geschichte der politischen Parteien in Deutschland*, 7th ed. (Munich, 1952), and Sigmund Neumann, ed., *Modern Political Parties* (Chicago, 1956). Werner Liebe, *Die*

---

[1] *Geschichte der Weimarer Republik.* 2 vols. (Erlenbach-Zurich, Stuttgart, 1954-6). Volume 1 of the translation as *A History of the Weimar Republic* was published in 1962 by the Harvard University Press.

[2] *Entstehung und Geschichte der Weimarer Republik.* 2 vols. in 1. (Frankfurt/M., 1955).

[3] *Die vierzehn Jahre der ersten deutschen Republik* (Hamburg, 1947).

[4] *Die Weimarer Republik* (Hanover, Frankfurt/M., 1957).

[5] *Germany Tried Democracy* (New York, 1946).

Deutschnationale Volkspartei 1918-1924 (Düsseldorf, 1956), based on important material, should be read in conjunction with my work. [6] Important special studies on other political groups are those of Hans Booms on the German Conservative party, [7] Karl Bachem on the Center party, [8] Karl Wortmann on the German Fatherland party, [9] and three authors on the Pan-German League: Mildred Wertheimer, [10] Lothar Werner, [11] then, most recently, Alfred Kruck. [12] On the German People's party now available are Roland Thimme, *Stresemann und die Deutsche Volkspartei 1923-1925* (Lübeck, Hamburg, 1961), and Wolfgang Hartenstein, *Die Anfänge der Deutschen Volkspartei, 1918-1920* (Düsseldorf, 1962). I was unfortunately not able to take these last two titles into account in this book. Sarah R. Tirrell has examined the formation of the Farmers' League, [13] while Alexander Gerschenkron presents an economist's analysis of Germany's agrarian problems. [14]

Newspapers, periodicals, pamphlets, campaign and other propaganda material are rich sources that must be searched out and carefully sifted, although several lives would be inadequate to complete the task. One should not underestimate the value of the insight, the basic information, and the feel for local color that come from tackling mountains of newsprint. I made heavy use of the Conservative *Neue Preussische (Kreuz-) Zeitung,* the Hugenberg-controlled *Berliner Lokal-Anzeiger,* the Democratic *Berliner Tageblatt,* and Stresemann's *Deutsche Stimmen.* The *Bibliothek für Zeitgeschichte,* Stuttgart, has a particularly extensive collection of pamphlets and propaganda material. The

[6] See review by Andreas Dorpalen in *Journal of Modern History* XXX, 1 (March, 1958).

[7] *Die Deutschkonservative Partei* (Düsseldorf, 1954).

[8] *Vorgeschichte, Geschichte und Politik der Deutschen Zentrumspartei.* 9 vols. (Cologne, 1931-2).

[9] *Geschichte der Deutschen Vaterlands-Partei 1917-1918* (Halle, 1926).

[10] *The Pan-German League 1890-1914* (New York, 1924).

[11] *Der Alldeutsche Verband 1890-1918* (Berlin, 1935).

[12] *Geschichte des Alldeutschen Verbandes 1890-1939* (Wiesbaden, 1954).

[13] *German Agrarian Politics after Bismarck's Fall* (New York, 1951).

[14] *Bread and Democracy in Germany* (Berkeley, Los Angeles, 1943).

Deutschnationale Schriftenvertriebsstelle in Berlin must have published thousands of pamphlets in the course of its existence. Some items are cited in the text, and included in the list of authors and titles. Most valuable of official Party publications were the yearbooks issued from time to time as guides to the history, aims, and recent experience of the DNVP. They also served as reference books on the Party line in election campaigns. In this category are the two volumes of *Politische Praxis* edited by Walther Lambach in 1926 and 1927, [15] and the *Politisches Handwörterbuch (Führer-ABC)* edited by Max Weiss in 1928. [16] Max Weiss in the same year also published a valuable collection of essays on the history of the Party. [17]

Indispensable among government publications are the stenographic reports of debates in the National Constituent Assembly [18] and the Reichstag. [19] They can profitably be supple-

[15] *Politische Praxis 1926* (Hamburg, Berlin, 1926) contains the following articles of special interest: Emil Hartwig, "Aus der Geschichte der deutschnationalen Arbeiterbewegung," pp. 289-94; Arno Kriegsheim, "Die politische Bedeutung des Reichs-Landbundes," pp. 295-303; Kuno Graf v. Westarp, "Ein Jahr Aussenpolitik," pp. 26-47. *Politische Praxis. Jahrgang 1927* (Hamburg, Berlin, 1927).

[16] Berlin, 1928.

[17] *Der Nationale Wille.* Werden und Wirken der Deutschnationalen Volkspartei 1918-1928 (Essen, 1928) contains the following articles of special interest: Walther Graef, "Der Werdegang der Deutschnationalen Volkspartei 1918-1928," pp. 15-53; Emil Hartwig, "Deutschnationale Arbeiterbewegung," pp. 215-24; Oskar Hergt, "Geleitwort zu Walther Graef (Anklam), 'Der Werdegang der Deutschnationalen Volkspartei 1918-1928,'" pp. 10-14; Otto Hoetzsch, "Die Aussenpolitik der Deutschnationalen Volkspartei," pp. 83-117; W. Kähler, "Deutschnationale Kulturpolitik," pp. 178-203; Reinhold Georg Quaatz, "Zur Geschichte der Wirtschaftspolitik der Deutschnationalen Volkspartei," pp. 244-59; Max Weiss, "Organisation," pp. 362-90.

[18] Germany. Verfassunggebende Deutsche Nationalversammlung. *Verhandlungen der verfassunggebenden Deutschen Nationalversammlung. Stenographische Berichte,* vols. 326-33 (Berlin, 1919-20). The sessional papers were published as: *Anlagen,* vols. 335-43 (Berlin, 1919-20).

[19] Germany. Reichstag. *Verhandlungen des Reichstages. Stenographische Berichte,* vols. 344ff. (Berlin, 1920ff.).

mented by reference to debates in the various state legislatures. Oskar Hergt, it will be recalled, was a member of the Prussian Constituent Assembly [20] rather than of the national body at Weimar. Cuno Horkenbach has compiled from official sources a basic reference work for Weimar Germany in *Das Deutsche Reich von 1918 bis heute* (Berlin, 1930) and its two companion volumes for 1931 and 1932. Wladimir Woytinski summarizes much statistical information in *Zehn Jahre neues Deutschland* (Berlin, 1929); Meinrad Hagmann [21] and Wilhelm Dittmann [22] analyze election results, the latter with excellent maps and diagrams. Of course, to avoid the occasional errors of secondary accounts, final election figures should be taken from the reports of the *Statistisches Reichsamt*. [23]

Basic as they are, the printed papers, memoirs, and books of political contemporaries must be used with as much caution as their unpublished *Nachlässe*. Essential references in this category are the volumes of Gustav Stresemann, [24] Hans von Seeckt, [25] Otto Gessler, [26] and Hans Luther. [27] Among other works by *engagés* I would cite the studies of the German Conservative party by Ernst von Heydebrand [28] and Count Westarp, [29] Karl Helfferich's

[20] *Sitzungsberichte der verfassunggebenden Preussischen Landesversammlung. Tagung 1919/21*, vol. 1ff. (Berlin, 1919-21).

[21] *Der Weg ins Verhängnis*. Reichstagswahlergebnisse 1919 bis 1933 besonders in Bayern (Munich, 1946).

[22] *Das politische Deutschland vor Hitler* (Zurich, New York, 1945).

[23] In particular, *Vierteljahreshefte zur Statistik des Deutschen Reiches*. For Prussia see the *Statistisches Jahrbuch für den Preussischen Staat* published by the *Preussisches Statistisches Landesamt*.

[24] *Vermächtnis*, ed., Henry Bernhard, 3 vols. (Berlin, 1932-33).

[25] *Seeckt. Aus seinem Leben 1918-1936*, ed., Friedrich v. Rabenau (Leipzig, 1940).

[26] *Reichswehrpolitik in der Weimarer Zeit* (Stuttgart, 1958).

[27] *Politiker ohne Partei* (Stuttgart, 1960).

[28] "Beiträge zu einer Geschichte der Konservativen Partei in den letzten 30 Jahren (1888 bis 1919)," in *Konservative Monatsschrift* LXXVII, 16-19 (Berlin, 1920), pp. 497-504, 539-45, 569-75, 605-11, 638-44.

[29] *Konservative Politik im letzten Jahrzehnt des Kaiserreiches*. 2 vols. (Berlin, 1935); *Die Regierung des Prinzen Max von Baden und die Konservative Partei 1918* (Berlin, 1928); *Am Grabe der Parteiherrschaft* (Berlin, 1932).

speeches, [30] Alfred Hugenberg's articles, [31] Heinrich Class' memoirs, [32] Otto Hoetzsch's lectures, [33] and the study of the DNVP by Axel Freiherr von Freytagh-Loringhoven. [34]

A large part of my interest in the subject of this book derives from the fresh material I found in the literary estate of Kuno Graf von Westarp, a major source for the political history of the first decade of the Weimar Republic. In 1952 I was among the first scholars granted permission to examine it and to be impressed by the quantity and quality of the papers collected by Count Westarp through a long political career, although not all survived the hazards of war. Count Westarp, conscious of the needs of historians, himself made good use of the materials in his own writing on the development of Conservative policy in the empire and Republic. He began, but did not complete, the work intended to cover the period of the Republic. However, he left a massive draft, well over a thousand pages, of the first volume entitled: "Konservative Politik in der Republik 1918-1932. Erstes Buch: Neue Aufgaben und Ziele. Bis zum 6.6.1920." A small section was edited by Werner Conze under the title of *Das Ende der Monarchie am 9. November 1918,* published in Berlin in 1952. The manuscript, written in the years 1933-42, but mainly during 1935-37, is a virtual collection of documents in quotation or summary. The original materials, deposited in the *Reichsarchiv* after completion of the manuscript, are presumed lost, and only fragments of chapters exist for the second book. From 1920 the Westarp Papers contain the infinite variety of official and private correspondence, special studies, and memoranda that I have abundantly cited in my footnotes. When I used them the Westarp Papers were in no permanent order. However, an edition is to appear in the series of source materials published by the *Kommission für Geschichte des Parlamentarismus und der politischen Parteien* in Bonn.

[30] *Reichstagsreden, 1920-1922* (Berlin, 1922); *Helfferichs Reichstagsreden 1922-1924* (Berlin, 1925).

[31] *Streiflichter aus Vergangenheit und Gegenwart* (Berlin, 1927).

[32] *Wider den Strom.* Vom Werden und Wachsen der nationalen Opposition im alten Reich (Leipzig, 1932).

[33] *Germany's Domestic and Foreign Policies* (New Haven, 1929).

[34] *Deutschnationale Volkspartei* (Berlin, 1931).

I was able to glean many items of interest from unpublished manuscripts of Hans Hilpert and Ernst Marquardt, and a privately circulated memoir of Gottfried Traub: Hilpert on Bavaria,[35] Marquardt on Württemberg,[36] and Traub on the *Deutsche Vaterlandspartei* and Kapp putsch.[37] I greatly benefited in the preparation of my book from information and insight gained from examination of the papers of Gustav Stresemann, Erich Koch-Weser, Wilhelm Groener, Hans von Seeckt, Eugen Schiffer, Kurt von Schleicher, and of numerous other political figures, papers now mainly collected in the holdings of the *Bundesarchiv* in Coblenz. A notable lack in my documentation is the large collection of party materials to be found in the *Deutsches Zentralarchiv* at Potsdam, and described in *Übersicht über die Bestände des Deutschen Zentralarchivs Potsdam* (Berlin, 1957). My requests for permission to visit this archive were, on more than one occasion, refused by the East German authorities.

[35] "Meinungen und Kämpfe. Meine politischen Erinnerungen." Unpublished manuscript, undated, private possession, Munich.

[36] "Kaempfer fuer Deutschlands Zukunft und Ehre. Umrisszeichnungen aus der Geschichte der deutschnationalen Volkspartei Württembergs." Unpublished manuscript, dated Stuttgart, 1934. *Württemberger Landesbibliothek.*

[37] "Erinnerungen" (parts 3-5), (Munich, mimeographed, n.d.). Parts 1-2, covering the pre-1918 period, were privately printed in Munich in 1949.

Principal Abbreviations
Used in Footnotes

DS	United States, Department of State. Records.
ESP	Eugen Schiffer, Papers.
GFO.W	Germany. Auswärtiges Amt. Records of the Weimar Republic.
HvSP	Hans von Seeckt, Papers.
KvSP	Kurt von Schleicher, Papers.
KWP	Erich Koch-Weser, Papers.
Kzztg.	*Neue Preussische (Kreuz-) Zeitung.*
Prussian Debates	Germany. Prussia. Verfassunggebende Preussische Landesversammlung. *Sitzungsberichte . . .*
Reich Debates	Germany. Verfassunggebende Deutsche Nationalversammlung, or Reichstag, *Verhandlungen . . .*
SP	Gustav Stresemann, Papers.
Stuttgart Collection	*Bibliothek für Zeitgeschichte.*
W MS	Kuno Graf von Westarp, "Konservative Politik in der Republik 1918-1932."
WP	Kuno Graf von Westarp, Papers.

Select List
of Authors and Titles

Aandahl, Fredrick. "The Rise of German Free Conservatism." Unpublished dissertation, Princeton, 1955.

Arnim, Hans von and Georg von Below, eds. *Deutscher Aufstieg. Bilder aus der Vergangenheit und Gegenwart der rechtsstehenden Parteien* (Berlin, 1925).

Arendt, Otto. "Freiherr von Gamp," in Hans von Arnim and Georg von Below, eds., *Deutscher Aufstieg* (Berlin, 1925).

Bachem, Karl. *Vorgeschichte, Geschichte und Politik der Deutschen Zentrumspartei.* 9 vols. (Cologne, 1931-2).

Baumont, Maurice. *L'Essor industriel et l'impérialisme colonial 1878-1904* (Paris, 1949).

Beckmann, Ewald. "Stellung nehmen!" in *Ostpreussische Zeitung,* Dec. 10, 1918; "Unser Streben," *loc. cit.,* Dec. 5, 1918.

Bergsträsser, Ludwig. *Geschichte der politischen Parteien in Deutschland.* 7th ed. (Munich, 1952).

Berliner Lokal-Anzeiger. Berlin.

Berliner Tageblatt. Berlin.

Bibliothek für Zeitgeschichte. Stuttgart. Collection of political pamphlets. Cited in footnotes as: Stuttgart Collection.

Booms, Hans. *Die Deutschkonservative Partei* (Düsseldorf, 1954).

Bracher, Karl Dietrich. *Die Auflösung der Weimarer Republik* (Stuttgart, Düsseldorf, 1957).

Braun, Friedrich Edler von. *Wiederaufbau der deutschen Wirtschaft* (Berlin, 1921). DNVP pamphlet.

Braun, Walter. *Evangelische Parteien in historischer Darstellung und sozialwissenschaftlicher Beleuchtung* (Mannheim, 1939).

Buchheim, Karl. *Geschichte der christlichen Parteien in Deutschland* (Munich, 1953).

Burgmeister, —. "Mein Austritt aus der Deutschnationalen Volkspartei," in *Berliner Tageblatt,* May 18, 1920 (P.M.).

Calker, Fritz van. *Wesen und Sinn der politischen Parteien* (Tübingen, 1930).

Class, Heinrich. *Wider den Strom*. Vom Werden und Wachsen der nationalen Opposition im alten Reich (Leipzig, 1932).

Curtius, Julius. "Die deutschnationale Volkspartei, ihre Zusammensetzung, Grundsätze, Taktik nach dem Berliner Parteitag vom 12. und 13. Juli 1919," in *Deutsche Stimmen* 42 (Oct. 19, 1919), pp. 708-17.

Dallwitz, Hans von. "Aus dem Nachlass des ehemaligen Kaiserlichen Statthalters von Elsass-Lothringen, früheren Preussischen Ministers des Innern von Dallwitz; herausgegeben von Albert v. Mutius," parts 1 and 2, in *Preussische Jahrbücher* CCXIV, 1 (Oct., 1928), pp. 1-22, and 2 (Nov., 1928), pp. 147-66.

Deutsche Stimmen. Berlin.

Deutsches Wollen ("Mitteilungen der DNVP"). DNVP periodical.

Deutsche Zeitung. Berlin.

Deutschnationale Arbeitertagung in Hannover am Dienstag, den 26. Oktober 1920 (n.p., n.d.). DNVP pamphlet.

Dittmann, Wilhelm. *Das politische Deutschland vor Hitler* (Zurich, New York, 1945).

Epstein, Klaus. *Matthias Erzberger and the Dilemma of German Democracy* (Princeton, 1959).

Evangelisch-soziale Stimmen. Bethel.

Eyck, Erich. *Geschichte der Weimarer Republik*. 2 vols. (Erlenbach-Zurich, Stuttgart, 1954-6), trans. *A History of the Weimar Republic*. 2 vols. (Cambridge, Mass., 1962-).

Feiling, Keith. "British Parties: Some Reflections on Their History," in *University of Toronto Quarterly* XIX (1950), pp. 213-8.

Freiheit. Berlin.

Freytagh-Loringhoven, Axel Freiherr von. *Deutschnationale Volkspartei* (Berlin, 1931).

Friedensburg, Ferdinand. *Die Weimarer Republik* (Hanover, Frankfurt/M., 1957).

Gebhardt, Bruno. *Handbuch der Deutschen Geschichte*, vol. 4 (Stuttgart, 1959).

Gengler, Ludwig Franz. *Die deutschen Monarchisten 1919 bis 1925* (Kulmbach, 1932).

Germany. Auswärtiges Amt. Records of the Weimar Republic.

Microfilm, National Archives, Washington, D.C. Cited in foot-notes as: GFO.W.

Germany. Reichstag. *Verhandlungen des Reichstages. Steno-graphische Berichte,* vols. 344ff. (Berlin, 1920-1930). Cited in footnotes as: Reich Debates.

Germany. Statistisches Reichsamt. *Statistisches Jahrbuch für das Deutsche Reich.* Annual.

Germany. Statistisches Reichsamt. *Vierteljahreshefte zur Statistik des Deutschen Reiches.*

Germany. Verfassunggebende Deutsche Nationalversammlung. *Verhandlungen der verfassunggebenden Deutschen National-versammlung. Stenographische Berichte,* vols. 326-33. Cited in footnotes as: Reich Debates. *Anlagen,* vols. 335-43 (Berlin, 1919-20).

Germany. German Democratic Republic. Deutsches Zentral-archiv. *Übersicht über die Bestände des Deutschen Zentral-archivs Potsdam* (Berlin, 1957).

Germany. Prussia. Verfassunggebende Preussische Landesver-sammlung. *Sitzungsberichte der verfassunggebenden Preus-sischen Landesversammlung. Tagung 1919-21,* vol. 1ff. (Berlin, 1919-21). Cited in footnotes as: Prussian Debates.

Germany. Prussia. Preussisches Statistisches Landesamt. *Statis-tisches Jahrbuch für den Preussischen Staat.* Annual.

Gerschenkron, Alexander. *Bread and Democracy in Germany* (Berkeley, Los Angeles, 1943).

Gessler, Otto. *Reichswehrpolitik in der Weimarer Zeit* (Stuttgart, 1958).

Getrennt marschieren, vereint geschlagen werden! Ein Wort an den werktätigen Mittelstand (Berlin, 1920). DNVP Berlin pamphlet.

Gordon, Harold J., Jr. *The Reichswehr and the German Re-public* (Princeton, 1957).

Graef, Walther. "Der Werdegang der Deutschnationalen Volks-partei 1918-1928," in Max Weiss, ed., *Der Nationale Wille* (Essen, 1928), pp. 15-53.

Graefe, Albrecht von. *Damals in Weimar 1919.* Ein Blick hinter die Kulissen. Der Verrat am Deutschen Volk (Berlin, 1929).

———. "Partei und Judenfrage." Unpublished manuscript, dated Goldebee, February 5, 1920. WP.

Grundsätze der Deutschnationalen Volkspartei (Berlin, n.d.).
DNVP pamphlet.

Hagmann, Meinrad. *Der Weg ins Verhängnis*. Reichstagswahler-gebnisse 1919 bis 1933 besonders in Bayern (Munich, 1946).

Halperin, S. William. *Germany Tried Democracy* (New York, 1946).

Hartenstein, Wolfgang. *Die Anfänge der Deutschen Volkspartei, 1918-1920* (Düsseldorf, 1962).

Hartwig, Emil. "Aus der Geschichte der deutschnationalen Arbeiterbewegung," in Walther Lambach, ed., *Politische Praxis 1926* (Hamburg, Berlin, 1926), pp. 289-94.

————. "Deutschnationale Arbeiterbewegung," in Max Weiss, ed., *Der Nationale Wille* (Essen, 1928), pp. 215-24.

Helfferich, Karl. *Fort mit Erzberger!* (Berlin, 1919). Pamphlet of *Der Tag*.

————. *Der Friede von Versailles* (Berlin, 1919). DNVP pamphlet.

————. *Helfferichs Reichstagsreden 1922-1924* (Berlin, 1925).

————. *Die Politik der Erfüllung* (Munich, Berlin, Leipzig, 1922).

————. *Reichstagsreden, 1920-1922* (Berlin, 1922).

———— and Jakob Wilhelm Reichert. *Das zweite Versailles*. Das Reparationsgutachten der alliierten Experten (Berlin, 1924).

Hergt, Oskar. *Gegenwart und Zukunft der Deutschnationalen Volkspartei* (Berlin, 1919). DNVP pamphlet.

————. "Geleitwort zu Walther Graef (Anklam), 'Der Werdegang der Deutschnationalen Volkspartei 1918-1928,'" in Max Weiss, ed., *Der Nationale Wille* (Essen, 1928), pp. 10-14.

Herre, Paul. *Kronprinz Wilhelm* (Munich, 1954).

Hertzman, Lewis. "The Founding of the German National People's Party (DNVP), November 1918-January 1919," in *Journal of Modern History* XXX, 1 (March, 1958), 24-36.

————. "The German National People's Party (DNVP), 1918-1924." Dissertation, Harvard, 1955.

Hesnard, O. *Les partis politiques en Allemagne* (Paris, 1923).

Heydebrand und der Lasa, Ernst von. "Beiträge zu einer Geschichte der Konservativen Partei in den letzten 30 Jahren (1888 bis 1919)," in *Konservative Monatsschrift* LXXVIII,

16-9 (Berlin, 1920), pp. 497-504, 539-45, 569-75, 605-11, 638-44.

Hieb und Stich (Berlin, 1932). DNVP pamphlet.

Hiller von Gaertringen, Friedrich Freiherr. "Die Deutschnationale Volkspartei," in Erich Matthias und Rudolf Morsey, eds., *Das Ende der Parteien 1933* (Düsseldorf, 1960).

—————. *Fürst Bülows Denkwürdigkeiten.* Untersuchungen zu ihrer Entstehungsgeschichte und ihrer Kritik. (Tübingen, 1956).

Hilpert, Hans. "Meinungen und Kämpfe. Meine politischen Erinnerungen." Unpublished manuscript, undated, private possession, Munich.

Hoetzsch, Otto. "Die Aussenpolitik der Deutschnationalen Volkspartei," in Max Weiss, ed., *Der Nationale Wille* (Essen, 1928), pp. 83-117.

—————. *Germany's Domestic and Foreign Policies* (New Haven, 1929).

Horkenbach, Cuno. *Das Deutsche Reich von 1918 bis heute* (Berlin, 1930). Plus supplements for 1931 and 1932.

Hugenberg, Alfred. *Streiflichter aus Vergangenheit und Gegenwart* (Berlin, 1927).

Jahrbuch der Deutschnationalen Volkspartei 1920 (Berlin, 1920).

Jahrbuch der Deutschnationalen Volkspartei 1921 (Berlin, 1921).

Junius Alter (Franz Sontag). *Nationalisten.* Deutschlands nationales Führertum der Nachkriegszeit (Leipzig, 1930).

Kähler, W. "Deutschnationale Kulturpolitik," in Max Weiss, ed., *Der Nationale Wille* (Essen, 1928), pp. 178-203.

Kaufmann, Walter H. *Monarchism in the Weimar Republic* (New York, 1953).

Koch-Weser, Erich. Papers. *Bundesarchiv,* Coblenz. Cited in footnotes as: KWP.

Korrespondenz der Deutschnationalen Volkspartei. Berlin.

Kriegk, Otto. *Hugenberg* (Leipzig, 1932).

Kriegsheim, Arno. "Die politische Bedeutung des Reichs-Landbundes," in W. Lambach, ed., *Politische Praxis 1926* (Hamburg, Berlin, 1926), pp. 295-303.

Kroschel A. W. *Das Deutschnationale Gewissen* (Berlin, 1920).

Kroschels Gewissen (Berlin, 1920). DNVP pamphlet.

Kruck, Alfred. *Geschichte des Alldeutschen Verbandes 1890-1939* (Wiesbaden, 1954).

Lambach, Walther. *Die breitere Front im politischen Kampf* (Berlin, 1922). DNVP pamphlet.

————, ed. *Politische Praxis 1926* (Hamburg, Berlin, 1926).

————, ed. *Politische Praxis. Jahrgang 1927* (Hamburg, Berlin, 1927).

————. "Um die Führung im Reiche," in W. Lambach, ed., *Politische Praxis. Jahrgang 1927* (Hamburg, Berlin, 1927), pp. 49-62.

Liebe, Werner. *Die Deutschnationale Volkspartei 1918-1924* (Düsseldorf, 1956). See review by Andreas Dorpalen in *Journal of Modern History* XXX, 1 (March, 1958), pp. 72-3.

Lindeiner-Wildau, Hans-Erdmann von. *Wir und die Deutsche Volkspartei* (Berlin, 1921). DNVP pamphlet.

Ludendorff, Erich. Ludendorff Miscellany. *Bundesarchiv*, Coblenz.

Luther, Hans. *Politiker ohne Partei* (Stuttgart, 1960).

Marquardt, Ernst. "Kaempfer fuer Deutschlands Zukunft und Ehre. Umrisszeichnungen aus der Geschichte der deutschnationalen Volkspartei Württembergs." Unpublished manuscript, dated Stuttgart, 1934. *Württemberger Landesbibliothek.*

Müller, Karl von. *Das betörte deutsche Volk.* Mahnworte für die Wahlen zur Nationalversammlung (Berlin, 1919). DNVP pamphlet.

Mumm, Reinhard. *Christlich-sozial und Deutschnational.* Ein Wort gegen die Zersplitterungssucht (Berlin, n.d.). DNVP pamphlet.

————. *Der christlich-soziale Gedanke* (Berlin, 1933).

Nationalliberale Correspondenz. Berlin.

Naumann, Friedrich. *Die politischen Parteien* (Berlin, 1910).

Neue Preussische (Kreuz-) Zeitung. Berlin. Cited in footnotes as: *Kzztg.*

Neumann, Sigmund, ed. *Modern Political Parties* (Chicago, 1956).

Nichols, J. Alden. *Germany after Bismarck.* The Caprivi Era 1890-1894 (Cambridge, Mass., 1958).

Nipperdey, Thomas. *Die Organisation der deutschen Parteien vor 1918* (Düsseldorf, 1961).

Ostpreussische Zeitung. Königsberg.

Pachter, Henry M. "Freedom and Democracy in Germany," review article in *World Politics* XI, 2 (Jan., 1959), pp. 300-1.

Phelps, Reginald H. "Aus den Seeckt-Dokumenten," in *Deutsche Rundschau* LXXVIII, 9 (Sept., 1952), pp. 881-92, and 10 (Oct., 1952), pp. 1013-23.

Philipp, Albrecht. *Bilanz und Aufgaben deutschnationaler Arbeit 1928* (Dresden, 1928). DNVP Saxony pamphlet.

Pollock, James K., and Homer Thomas. *Germany in Power and Eclipse* (Toronto, New York, London, 1952).

Quaatz, Reinhold Georg. "Zur Geschichte der Wirtschaftspolitik der Deutschnationalen Volkspartei," in Max Weiss, ed., *Der Nationale Wille* (Essen, 1928), pp. 244-59.

Röder, Adam. *Der deutsche Konservatismus und die Revolution* (Gotha, 1920).

Roland von Bremen. *Die neue Heilsbotschaft* 卐 (Berlin, 1924).

Rosenberg, Arthur. *Entstehung und Geschichte der Weimarer Republik.* 2 vols. in 1 (Frankfurt/M., 1955).

Rüffer, Paul. *Die deutsche Gewerkschaftsbewegung in der Gegenwart* (Berlin, 1927). DNVP pamphlet.

Schiffer, Eugen. Papers. *Hauptarchiv,* Berlin-Dahlem. Cited in footnotes as: ESP.

Schleicher, Kurt von. Papers. *Bundesarchiv,* Coblenz. Cited in footnotes as: KvSP, followed by folder and document numbers.

Schulz, Annelise. *Die Stellungnahme der deutschnationalen Volkspartei zu den Problemen der Sozialpolitik* (Rostock, 1927).

Schuon, Hermann. *Der Deutschnationale Handlungsgehilfen-Verband zu Hamburg* (Jena, 1913).

Schwäbischer Merkur. Stuttgart.

Schwarz, Albert. *Die Weimarer Republik* (Constance, 1958).

Seeckt, Hans von. Papers. Microfilm, National Archives, Washington, D.C. Cited in footnotes as: HvSP.

————. *Seeckt. Aus seinem Leben 1918-1936.* ed. Friedrich von Rabenau (Leipzig, 1940).

Spahn, Martin. *Der Weg zur deutschen Rechten.* Rede . . . auf dem dritten Parteitage der Deutschnationalen Volkspartei in München am 2. September 1921 (Berlin, 1921). DNVP pamphlet.

Spohr, Elizabeth. *Deutschnationale Vertretung der Frauenin-
teressen in der Preussischen Landesversammlung* (Berlin, n.d.).
DNVP pamphlet.

Stahlhelm, Der. Erinnerungen und Bilder (Berlin, 1932).

Stampfer, Friedrich. *Die vierzehn Jahre der ersten deutschen Republik.* 3rd ed. (Hamburg, 1947).

Stoltenberg, Gerhard. *Der Deutsche Reichstag 1871-1873* (Düsseldorf, 1955).   ,

Stresemann, Gustav. Papers. Microfilm, National Archives, Washington, D.C. Cited in footnotes as: SP, with references in turn
to microfilm roll number, serial number of document collection, and individual frame number(s). E.g., SP: 3163/7409/
174367-9 (footnote 4 of chapter one).

————. *Vermächtnis.* ed., Henry Bernhard. 3 vols. (Berlin,
1932-3).

Taube, Max. *Das wahre Gesicht der Parteien.* Ein Führer durch
das Parteiwesen (Berlin, 1919). DNVP pamphlet.

Thimme, Roland. *Stresemann und die Deutsche Volkspartei
1923-1925* (Lübeck, Hamburg, 1961).

Tirrell, Sarah Rebecca. *German Agrarian Politics after Bismarck's
Fall.* The Formation of the Farmers' League (New York, 1951).

Traub, Gottfried, "Erinnerungen," parts 3, 4, and 5 (Munich,
mimeographed, n.d.). Traub papers are now in the *Bundesarchiv,* Coblenz.

Troeltsch, Ernst. *Spektator-Briefe.* Aufsätze über die deutsche
Revolution und die Weltpolitik, 1918-22 (Tübingen, 1924).

United States. Department of State. Records, National Archives,
Washington, D.C. Cited in footnotes as: DS, followed by document number.

Valentin, Veit. *1848. Chapters of German History* (London,
1940).

Vierteljahreshefte für Zeitgeschichte. Munich.

*Vorwürfe gegen die Deutschnationale Volkspartei und ihre
Widerlegung* (Berlin, 1920). DNVP pamphlet.

Waite, Robert G. L. *Vanguard of Nazism* (Cambridge, Mass.,
1952).

Weiss, Max, ed. *Der Nationale Wille.* Werden und Wirken der
Deutschnationalen Volkspartei 1918-1928 (Essen, 1928).

————. "Organisation," in Max Weiss, ed., *Der Nationale Wille*

(Essen, 1928), pp. 362-90.

————, ed. *Politisches Handwörterbuch (Führer-ABC)*, (Berlin, 1928).

Werner, Lothar. *Der Alldeutsche Verband 1890-1918* (Berlin, 1935).

Wertheimer, Mildred S. *The Pan-German League 1890-1914* (New York, 1924).

Westarp, Kuno Graf von. "Ein Jahr Aussenpolitik," in W. Lambach, ed., *Politische Praxis 1926* (Hamburg, Berlin, 1926), pp. 26-47.

————. *Das Ende der Monarchie am 9. November 1918* (Berlin, 1952).

————. *Am Grabe der Parteiherrschaft* (Berlin, 1932).

————. *Konservative Politik im letzten Jahrzehnt des Kaiserreiches.* 2 vols. (Berlin, 1935).

————. "Konservative Politik in der Republik 1918-1932." Manuscript among the Westarp Papers, written 1933-42. Cited in footnotes as: W MS.

————. Papers. Private possession. Gärtringen, Württemberg. Cited in footnotes as: WP.

————. *Die Regierung des Prinzen Max von Baden und die Konservative Partei 1918* (Berlin, 1928).

Wheeler-Bennett, John. *The Nemesis of Power.* The German Army in Politics, 1918-1945. (London, 1954).

Wiener Library. London. *From Weimar to Hitler.* Catalogue Series, 2 (London, 1951).

Winnig, August. *Das Reich als Republik 1918-1928* (Berlin, 1929).

Wortmann, Karl. *Geschichte der Deutschen Vaterlands-Partei 1917-1918* (Halle, 1926).

Woytinski, Wladimir. *Zehn Jahre neues Deutschland* (Berlin, 1929).

Württemberger Bauern- und Weingärtnerbund—Bund der Landwirte in Württemberg. *Wahlhandbuch für das Wahljahr 1928* (Stuttgart, 1928).

Ziele der Deutschnationalen Volkspartei (Berlin, n.d.). DNVP pamphlet.

Zmarzlik, Hans Günter. *Bethmann Hollweg als Reichskanzler 1909-1914* (Düsseldorf, 1957).

Index